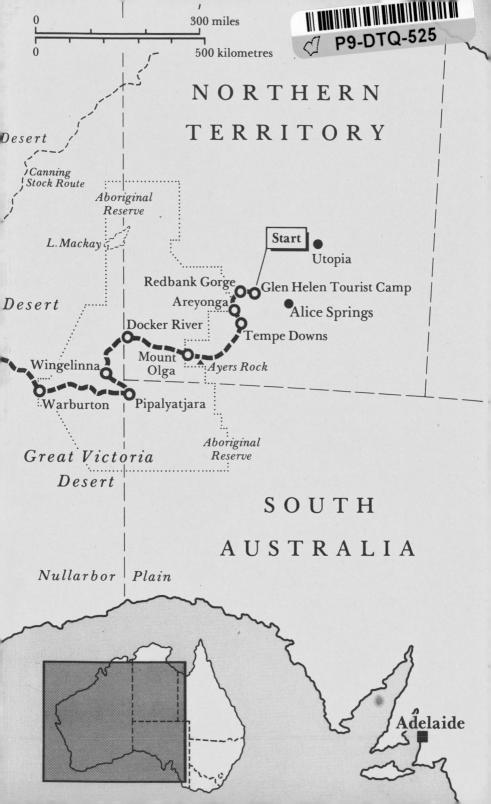

TRACKS

Robyn Davidson

TRACKS

BOOK CLUB ASSOCIATES
LONDON

Printed in Great Britain by
Butler & Tanner Ltd, Frome and London

For Nancy and the Blue Wrens

Anna knew she had to cross the desert. Over it, on the far side, were mountains – purple and orange and grey. The colours of the dream were extraordinarily beautiful and vivid … The dream marked a change in Anna, in her knowledge of herself. In the desert she was alone, and there was no water, and she was a long way from the springs. She woke knowing that if she was to cross the desert she must shed burdens.

Doris Lessing, *The Golden Notebook*

Contents

Illustrations

Acknowledgments

I should like to thank Rick Smolan for permission to use in the book fourteen of his photographs: nos 2, 13–23, 30 and 31. He also took the colour photograph reproduced on the front of the jacket by courtesy of Contact from Colorific. Toly Sawenko and Jenny Green generously let me have their pictures which appear as nos 1, 3–11, 28 and 29. The spectacular photograph of the Macdonnell Ranges (no. 12) was provided by Colour Library International, and the Sydney *Daily Mirror*, whose reporter was among those who found me on the road to Wiluna, kindly sent me nos 26 and 27. The others are from the few I took myself.

The endpaper map was drawn by Ray Martin of Art Services.

TRACKS

Part One

Alice Sprung

1

I ARRIVED in the Alice at five a.m. with a dog, six dollars
and a small suitcase full of inappropriate clothes. 'Bring a
cardigan for the evenings,' the brochure said. A freezing
wind whipped grit down the platform and I stood shivering,
holding warm dog flesh, and wondering what foolishness had
brought me to this eerie, empty train-station in the centre
of nowhere. I turned against the wind, and saw the line of
mountains at the edge of town.

There are some moments in life that are like pivots around
which your existence turns – small intuitive flashes, when you
know you have done something correct for a change, when
you think you are on the right track. I watched a pale dawn
streak the cliffs with Day-glo and realized this was one of
them. It was a moment of pure, uncomplicated confidence
– and lasted about ten seconds.

Diggity wriggled out of my arms and looked at me, head
cocked, piglet ears flying. I experienced that sinking feeling
you get when you know you have conned yourself into
doing something difficult and there's no going back. It's all
very well, to set off on a train with no money telling yourself
that you're really quite a brave and adventurous person, and
you'll deal capably with things as they happen, but when you
actually arrive at the other end with no one to meet and
nowhere to go and nothing to sustain you but a lunatic idea
that even you have no real faith in, it suddenly appears much
more attractive to be at home on the kindly Queensland
coast, discussing plans and sipping gins on the verandah with
friends, and making unending lists of lists which get thrown
away, and reading books about camels.

The lunatic idea was, basically, to get myself the requisite number of wild camels from the bush and train them to carry my gear, then walk into and about the central desert area. I knew that there were feral camels aplenty in this country. They had been imported in the 1850s along with their Afghani and North Indian owners, to open up the inaccessible areas, to transport food, and to help build the telegraph system and railways that would eventually cause their economic demise. When this happened, those Afghans had let their camels go, heartbroken, and tried to find other work. They were specialists and it wasn't easy. They didn't have much luck with government support either. Their camels, however, had found easy street – it was perfect country for them and they grew and prospered, so that now there are approximately ten thousand roaming the free country and making a nuisance of themselves on cattle properties, getting shot at, and, according to some ecologists, endangering some plant species for which they have a particular fancy. Their only natural enemy is man, they are virtually free of disease, and Australian camels are now rated as some of the best in the world.

The train had been half empty, the journey long. Five hundred miles and two days from Adelaide to Alice Springs. The modern arterial roads around Port Augusta had almost immediately petered out into crinkled, wretched, endless pink tracks leading to the shimmering horizon, and then there was nothing but the dry red parchment of the dead heart, god's majestic hidy-hole, where men are men and women are an afterthought. Snippets of railway car conversation still buzzed around in my head.

'G'day, mind if I sit 'ere?'

(Sighing and looking pointedly out the window or at book.) 'No.'

(Dropping of the eyes to chest level.) 'Where's yer old man?'

'I don't have an old man.'

(Faint gleam in bleary, blood-shot eye, still fixed at chest

20

level.) 'Jesus Christ, mate, you're not goin' to the Alice alone are ya? Listen 'ere, lady, you're fuckin' done for. Them coons'll rape youze for sure. Fuckin' niggers run wild up there ya know. You'll need someone to keep an eye on ya. Tell youze what, I'll shout youze a beer, then we'll go back to your cabin and get acquainted eh? Whaddya reckon?'

I waited until the station had thinned its few bustling arrivals, standing in the vacuum of early morning silence, fighting back my unease, then set off with Diggity towards town.

My first impression as we strolled down the deserted street was of the architectural ugliness of the place, a discomforting contrast to the magnificence of the country which surrounded it. Dust covered everything from the large, dominant corner pub to the tacky, unimaginative shop fronts that lined the main street. Hordes of dead insects clustered in the arcing street lights, and four-wheel-drive vehicles spattered in red dirt, with only two spots swept clean by the windscreen wipers, rattled intermittently through the cement and bitumen town. This grey, cream and hospital-green shopping area gradually gave way to sprawling suburbia until it was stopped short by the great perpendicular red face of the Macdonnell Ranges which borders the southern side of town, and runs unbroken, but for a few spectacular gorges, east and west for several hundred miles. The Todd River, a dry white sandy bed lined with tall columns of silver eucalypts, winds through the town, then cuts into a narrow gap in the mountains. The range, looming menacingly like some petrified prehistoric monster, has, I was to discover, a profound psychological effect on the puny folk below. It sends them troppo. It reminds them of incomprehensible dimensions of time which they almost successfully block out with brick veneer houses and wilted English-style gardens.

I had planned to camp in the creek with the Aborigines until I could find a job and a place to stay, but the harbingers of doom on the train had told me it was suicide to do such a thing. Everyone, from the chronic drunks to the stony men and women with brown wrinkled faces and burnt-out expressions, to the waiters in tuxedos who served and consumed enormous amounts of alcohol, all of them warned me against it. The blacks were unequivocally the enemy. Dirty, lazy, dangerous animals. Stories of young white lasses who innocently strayed down the Todd at night, there to meet their fate worse than death, were told with suspect fervour. It was the only subject anyone had got fired up about. I had heard other stories back home too – of how a young black man was found in an Alice gutter one morning, painted white. Even back in the city where the man in the street was unlikely ever to have seen an Aborigine, let alone spoken to one, that same man could talk at length, with an extraordinary contempt, about what they were like, how lazy and unintelligent they were. This was because of the press, where clichéd images of dirty, stone-age drunks on the dole were about the only coverage Aborigines got, and because everyone had been taught at school that they were not much better than specialized apes, with no culture, no government and no right to existence in a vastly superior white world; aimless wanderers who were backward, primitive and stupid.

It is difficult to sort out fact from fiction, fear from paranoia and goodies from baddies when you are new in a town but something was definitely queer about this one. The place seemed soulless, rootless, but perhaps it was just that which encouraged, in certain circumstances, the extraordinary. Had everyone been trying to put the fear of god into me just because I was an urbanite in the bush? Had I suddenly landed in Ku Klux Klan country? I had spent time before with Aboriginal people – in fact, had had one of the best holidays of my entire life with them. Certainly there had been some heavy drinking and the occasional fight, but that was part of the white Australian tradition too, and could be found in most pubs or parties in the country. If the blacks here were like the blacks there, how could a group of whites be so consumed with fear and hatred? And if they were different here, what had happened to make them that way? Tread carefully, my instincts said. I could sense already a camouflaged violence in this town, and I had to find a safe place to stay. Rabbits, too, have their survival mechanisms.

They say paranoia attracts paranoia: certainly no one else I met ever had such a negative view of Alice Springs. But then I was to get to know it from the gutters up, which may have given me a distorted perspective. It is said that anyone who sees the Todd River flow three times falls in love with the Alice. By the end of the second year, after seeing it freakishly flood more often than that, I had a passionate hatred yet an inexplicable and consuming addiction for it.

There are fourteen thousand people living there of whom one thousand are Aboriginal. The whites consist mainly of government workers, miscellaneous misfits and adventurers, retired cattle or sheep station owners, itinerant station workers, truck drivers and small business operators whose primary function in life is to rip off the tourists, who come by the bus-load from America, Japan and urban Australia, expecting high adventure in this last romantic outpost, and to see the extraordinary desert which surrounds it. There are three major pubs, a few motels, a couple of zed-grade restaurants, and various shops that sell 'I've climbed Ayers Rock' T-shirts, boomerangs made in Taiwan, books on Australiana, and tea towels with noble savages holding spears silhouetted against setting suns. It is a frontier town, characterized by an aggressive masculine ethic and severe racial tensions.

I ate breakfast at a cheap café, then stepped out into the glaring street where things were beginning to move, and squinted at my new home. I asked someone where the cheapest accommodation was and they directed me to a caravan park three miles north of town.

It was a hot and dusty walk but interesting. The road followed a tributary of the Todd. Still, straight columns of blue

23

smoke chimneying up through the gum leaves marked Aboriginal camps. On the left were the garages and workshops of industrial Alice – galvanized iron sheds behind which spread the trim lawns and trees of suburbia. When I arrived, the proprietor informed me that it was only three dollars if I had my own tent, otherwise it was eight.

My smile faded. I eyed the cold drinks longingly and went outside for some tepid tap water. I didn't ask if that were free, just in case. Over in the corner of the park some young folk with long hair and patched jeans were pitching a large tent. They looked approachable, so I asked if I could stay with them. They were pleased to offer me shelter and friendliness.

That night, they took me out on the town in their beat-up panel-van equipped with all the trappings one associates with free-wheeling urban youth – a five million decibel car stereo and even surf-boards . . . they were heading north. We drove into the dusty lights of the town and stopped by the pub to pick up some booze. The girl, who was shy and very young, suddenly turned to me.

'Oo, look at them, aren't they disgusting. God, they're like apes.'

'Who?'

'The boongs.'

Her boyfriend was leaning up against the bottle-shop, waiting.

'Hurry up, Bill, and let's get out of here. Ugly brutes.' She folded her arms as if she were cold and shivered with repulsion.

I put my head on my arms, bit my tongue, and knew the night was going to be a long one.

The next day I got a job at the pub, starting in two days. Yes, I could stay in a back room of the pub, the payment for which would be deducted from my first week's wages. Meals were provided. Perfect. That gave me time to suss out camel business. I sat in the bar for a while and chatted with the regulars. I discovered there were three camel-men in town – two involved with tourist businesses, and the other an old Afghan who was bringing in camels from the wild to sell to Arabia as meat herds. I met a young geologist who offered to drive me out to meet this man.

The minute I saw Sallay Mahomet it was apparent to me that he knew exactly what he was doing. He exuded the bandy-legged, rope-handling confidence of a man long accustomed to dealing with animals. He was fixing some odd-looking saddles near a dusty yard filled with these strange beasts.

'Yes, what can I do for you?'

'Good morning, Mr Mahomet,' I said confidently. 'My name's Robyn Davidson and um, I've been planning this trip you see, into the central desert and I wanted to get three wild camels and train them for it, and I was wondering if you might be able to help me.'

'Hrrrmppph.'

Sallay glared at me from under bushy white eyebrows. There was a dry grumpiness about him that put me instantly in my place and made me feel like a complete idiot.

'And I suppose you think you'll make it too?'

I looked at the ground, shuffled my feet and mumbled something defensive.

'What do you know about camels then?'

'Ah well, nothing really, I mean these are the first ones I've seen as a matter of fact, but ah ...'

'Hrrmmph. And what do you know about deserts?'

It was painfully obvious from my silence that I knew very little about anything.

Sallay said he was sorry, he didn't think he could help me, and turned about his business. My cockiness faded. This was going to be harder than I thought, but then it was only the first day.

Next we drove to the tourist place south of town. I met the owner and his wife, a friendly woman who offered me cakes and tea. They looked at one another in silence when I told them of my plan. 'Well, come out here any time you like,' said the man jovially, 'and get to know the animals a bit.' He could barely control the smirk on the other side of his face. My intuition in any case told me to stay away. I didn't like him and I was sure the feeling was mutual. Besides, when I saw how his animals roared and fought, I figured he was probably not the right person to learn from.

The last of the three, the Posel place, was three miles north, and was owned, according to some of the people in the bar, by a maniac.

My geologist friend dropped me off at the pub, and from there I walked north up the Charles River bed. It was a delightful walk, under cool and shady trees. The silence was often broken by packs of camp dogs who raced out with their hackles up to tell me and Diggity to get out of their territory, only to have bottles, cans and curses flung at them by their Aboriginal owners, who none the less smiled and nodded at us.

I arrived at the door of a perfect white cottage set among trees and lawns. It was an Austrian chalet in miniature, beautiful, but crazy out there among red boulders and dust devils. The yards were all hand-hewn timber and twisted ropes – the work of a master-craftsman. The stables had arches and geraniums. Not a thing was out of place. Gladdy Posel met me at the door – a small, bird-like woman, middle-aged, with a face that spoke of hardship and worry and unbending will. But there was a suspiciousness in it also. However, she was the first person so far who had not greeted my idea with patronizing disbelief. Or perhaps she just hid it better. Kurt, her husband, was not there so I arranged to come and see him the next day.

'What do you think of the town so far?' she asked.

'I think it stinks,' I replied and instantly regretted it. The last thing I wanted to do was to set her against me.

She smiled for the first time. 'Well, you might get on all

26

right then. Just remember, they're mostly mad around here and you have to watch out for yourself.'

'What about the blacks?' I asked.

The suspiciousness returned. 'There's nothing damnwell wrong with the blacks except what the whites do to them.'

It was my turn to smile. Gladdy, it appeared, was a rebel.

The next day, Kurt came out to greet me with as much enthusiasm as his Germanic nature would allow. He was dressed in an immaculate white outfit, with an equally crisp white turban. But for his ice-blue eyes, he looked like a bearded, wiry Moor. Standing near him was like being close to a fallen power line – all dangerous, crackling energy. He was dark brown, stringy, with hands calloused and outsized from work and he was certainly the most extraordinary individual I had ever laid eyes on. I had barely got out my name before he had led me to the verandah and begun to tell me exactly how life was to be for the next eight months, grinning, gap-toothed, all the while.

'Now, you vill come to verk for me here for eight months und zen you vill buy vone off my camelts, und I vill teach you to train zem and you vill get two vild vones und dat vill be dat. I haf just de animal for you. He hass only vone eye but, ha, dat does not matter – he is stronk and reliable enough for you, ya.'

'Yes, but ...' I stammered.

'Yes, but vott?' he shouted incredulously.

'How much will he cost?'

'Ah, ya, how much vill he cost. Ya. Let me see. I give him to you for a thousand dollars. A bargain.'

A blind camel for a thousand bucks, I thought to myself. I could buy a bloody elephant for that.

'That's very nice of you but you see, Kurt, I have no money.'

His grin disappeared like greasy water down a plug-hole.

'But I can work at the pub of course, so ...'

'Ya. Dat's right,' he said. 'Ya, you vill vork at de pub and

27

you vill stay here as my apprentice for food and rent beginning tonight and ve vill see vot you are made off, and so it
is all settled. You are a very lucky girl dat I do dis for you.'

I half understood, through my dazed incredulity, that I was
being shanghaied. He led me to my immaculate quarters in
the stable and went inside to fetch my new camel-handler's
outfit. I climbed into the great swaddling white drapes and
perched the ridiculous turban over my pale hair and eyes.
I looked like a schizophrenic baker. I laughed helplessly at
the mirror.

'Vot's da matter, you too good for it or sometink?'

'No, no,' I assured him. 'I just never saw myself as an
Afghan, that's all.'

He led me out to the camels for my first lesson.

'Now, you must start from de bottom and verk up,' he
said, handing me a dustpan and broom.

Camels shit like rabbits. Neat round little pebbles in
copious amounts. Some of it was sitting in the direction of
Kurt's pointed finger. It was only then that I realized that
on the whole five acres I had not seen a scrap of the stuff,
not a particle, and considering Kurt had eight beasts, it was,
to say the least, surprising. Hoping to impress my new boss
with my diligence, I bent down and carefully scraped every
bit into the pan and stood up waiting for inspection.

Something seemed to be wrong with Kurt. He seemed to
be having trouble with his lips, and his eyebrows were working up and down his face like lifts. His skin was turning red
under the brown. He exploded then like a volcano, blasting
me with his spit like hot lava.

'VOTT ISSS DATTTT?'

Confused, I glanced down but could see nothing. I got on
my knees but could still see nothing. Kurt threw himself on
his knees beside me and there hidden under a blade of clipped
couch grass was the most minuscule ancient morsel of camel
shit you could image. 'Clean it up!' he screamed. 'You tink
dis iss a bloody holiday or sometink?' I couldn't believe this

was happening to me; shaking, I picked up the microscopic flake. It had almost turned to dust over the years. But Kurt was appeased and we continued the rounds of the ranch.

I might have thought twice about staying there after this outburst, but it became apparent very quickly that my new demon friend was a wizard with camels. I will now, once and for all, destroy some myths concerning these animals. They are the most intelligent creatures I know except for dogs and I would give them an I.Q. rating roughly equivalent to eight-year-old children. They are affectionate, cheeky, playful, witty, yes witty, self-possessed, patient, hard-working and endlessly interesting and charming. They are also very difficult to train, being of an essentially un-domestic turn of mind as well as extremely bright and perceptive. This is why they have such a bad reputation. If handled badly, they can be quite dangerous and definitely recalcitrant. Kurt's were neither. They were like great curious puppies. Nor do they smell, except when they regurgitate slimy green cud all over you in a fit of pique or fear. I would also say that they are highly sensitive animals, easily frightened by bad handlers, and easily ruined. They are haughty, ethnocentric, clearly believing that they are god's chosen race. But they are also cowards and their aristo-cratic demeanour hides delicate hearts. I was hooked.

Kurt proceeded to outline my duties. Shit seemed to be the major problem. I was to follow the animals around all day and pick up the offending stuff. He then told me how he had once had the bright idea of shoving the inflatable rub-ber inner bladders of footballs up their anuses, but that during the day they had passed them out with a groan. I looked side-ways at Kurt. He wasn't joking.

I was also to catch the animals at four in the morning, un-hobble them (they were hobbled by straps and a foot of chain around their front legs to prevent them going too far, too fast) and lead them home in a long line, nose to tail, ready for saddling. Two or three would be used for the day's work, leading tourists around the oval for a dollar a go, while the rest would be kept in the yards. I was to tie the selected three to their feed bins, groom them with a broom, ask them to 'whoosh' (an old Afghan word meaning, presumably, sit), then saddle them with the gaudy mock-Arabian saddles of Kurt's design. This was to be the best part of my existence for the next eight months. Kurt threw me right into the thick of things which was excellent. It did not give me time to be frightened of the animals. Most of the rest of the day was spent keeping his sterile domain scrupulously clean, tidy and free of weeds. Not a blade of grass dared grow out of place.

That night, the boy who had been good enough to drive me around town came out to see how I was doing. I informed Kurt that I had a visitor, then took him back to the stables. We sat chatting, watching the iridescent blue and orange glow of late evening. I was exhausted after the day's routine. Kurt had kept me trotting at a brisk scurry from feed shed to camel to yard and back again. I had weeded a garden, trimmed a mile of couch-infested curbing with a pair of scissors, had led countless objectionable tourists around the oval on camel-back and had cleaned, mopped, scraped and lifted until I thought I would collapse. The pace had not slackened for a minute and all the while Kurt had been scrutinizing me and my work, alternately muttering that I might turn out all right and screaming abuse at me, in front of bewildered and embarrassed tourists. While I was working I was too preoccupied to think whether I would be able to stand such treatment for eight months, but as I talked to my young friend all the anger that I felt towards the man was bubbling away deep down inside. Arrogant prick, I thought. Miserable, lousy, tight, obsessional, whingeing little creep. I hated myself for my infernal cowardice in dealing with people. It is such a female syndrome, so much the weakness of animals who have always been prey. I had not been aggressive enough or stood up to him enough. And now this impotent, internal, angry stuttering. Suddenly, Kurt appeared around the corner – an apparition in white taking giant strides. I could feel his fury before he reached us and stood up to face him. He pointed a shaking finger at my friend and hissed through clenched teeth:

'You, you get out off here. I don't know who de hell you are. No vone iss allowed here after dark. You've probably been sent here by Fullarton to spy out my camel saddle designs.'

Then he glared at me. 'I heared from my own sources dat you've already been over dere. If you verk for me you don't go near da place – EVER. Do you understand?'

And then I burst. Hell had no fury by comparison. My poor young friend had disappeared, eyes bulging, into the dark and I lashed out at Kurt, calling him every name under the sun and screaming that he had a snowflake's chance in hell of ever getting me to do his dirty work again. I'd die first. I stormed into the room in a passionate rage, ferociously slammed his precious barn-door, the one that had to be handled like glass, and packed my meagre possessions.

Kurt was stupefied. He had sized me up wrongly, and pushed a sucker too far. The dollar signs faded from his eyes. He had lost a patsy and a slave. But he was too proud to apologize and the next morning, early, I moved into the pub.

2

THE PUB had four major divisions. The Saloon Bar, where I worked, catered for many of the regulars – truckies, station hands, some of them part-Aboriginal, and the occasional black ringer (station hand) who had just been paid a two-hundred-dollar cheque to be cashed at the pub, of which little would be left by the next morning. However, blacks, despite the easy pickings, were tacitly frowned upon here and didn't often cōme in. The Lounge Bar catered for tourists and some of the regulars of a slightly higher social standing although there was general flow between the two areas. The Pool Room allowed blacks in but grudgingly, and the Inner Bar, a cosy, tastelessly decorated room, was where the police, lawyers and upper-class whites drank. Here blacks were forbidden. This was not legal or stated but it was enforced none the less under the guise of, 'Patrons are requested to wear neat attire etc.' It was known by the hard cases in the saloon as the Poofters' Bar. At least this pub didn't have a dog window, as most of the others in the Northern Territory had. These were small windows around the back where booze was sold to the blacks.

I lived in a draughty cement pigeon-hole out the back, furnished with an aluminium bed covered by a stained shocking pink chenille bedspread. I wrote cheery letters home, telling everyone how I was practising animal training on giant cockroaches, how I bullwhipped them into submission but was afraid they might one day turn against me, which was why I had refrained from putting my head in their mouths. But the jokes hid a growing depression. Getting camels or even information was turning out to be infinitely harder than I had thought. By that time, word of my scheme had spread

32

1–2   Shortly before the journey. *Below*, my father (left) and I watch Sallay making a traditional pack-saddle.

3–4 *Above*, with Jenny Green (left). *Below*, Rick Smolan, who thre
times drove out into the desert to get photographs of the trip.

and it brought much derisive laughter from the patrons, and enough useless and incorrect information to stock a library of the absurd. Suddenly everyone, it seemed, knew all there was to know about camels.

One does not have to delve too deeply to discover why some of the world's angriest feminists breathed crisp blue Australian air during their formative years, before packing their kangaroo-skin bags and scurrying over to London or New York or any place where the antipodean machismo would fade gently from their battle-scarred consciousnesses like some grisly nightmare at dawn. Anyone who has worked in a men-only bar in Alice Springs will know what I mean.

Some of the men would be hanging around the doors at opening time and, after a full twelve hours of saturation, leave reluctantly, and often on all fours, at closing time. Others had their set hours and set places and set friends and swapped yarns for a while, always the same stories, always the same reactions. Others sat on their own in a corner dreaming of god knows what. Some were crazy, some were mean, and some, oh those few rare gems, were amiable, helpful and humorous. By nine p.m. some would be in tears over lost opportunities, lost women, or lost hope. And while they wept, and while I held their hands across the counter saying there there, they pissed silently and unselfconsciously up against the bar.

To really come to grips with the Australian cult of misogyny, one has to plod back through all two hundred years of white Australia's history, and land on the shore of the 'wide brown land' with a bunch of hard-done-by whingeing convicts. Actually, the place where they landed was relatively green and inviting, the wide brown stuff was to come later. One imagines life was none too easy in the colony, but the boys learnt to stick together and when they'd done their stretch, if they were still sound of limb, they ventured into the forbidding country beyond to try to scratch a pitiful

33

living. They were tough and they had absolutely nothing to lose. And they had alcohol to soften the blow. By the 1840s it began to dawn on the residents that something was missing – sheep and women. The former they imported from Spain, a stroke of genius that was to set Australia on the economic map; the latter they brought over in boats from the poor-houses and orphanages of England. Since there were never enough to go round (women, that is) one can visualize only too clearly the frenzied rush on the Sydney wharves when the girls came bravely sailing in. Such a traumatic racial memory is hard to blot out in a mere century, and the cult is sustained and revitalized in every pub in the country, especially in the outback where the stereotyped image of the Aussie male is still so sentimentally clung to. The modern-day manifestation is almost totally devoid of charm. He is biased, bigoted, boring and, above all, brutal. His enjoyments in life are limited to fighting, shooting and drinking. To him a mate includes anyone who is not a wop, wog, pom, coon, boong, nigger, rice-eye, kyke, chink, Iti, nip, frog, kraut, commie, poofter, slope, wanker, and yes, shiela, chick or bird.

One night in the pub one of the kinder regulars whispered to me, 'You ought to be more careful, girl, you know you've been nominated by some of these blokes as the next town rape case. You shouldn't be so friendly.'

I was devastated. What had I done but patted the odd shoulder or helped out the occasional paralytic or listened in silence to some heart-breaking hard luck story. I felt really frightened for the first time.

On another occasion I had taken over from someone in the Inner Bar. There were maybe half a dozen men drinking in there quietly, including two or three policemen. Suddenly an old dishevelled drunken Aboriginal woman came in and started yelling abuse and obscenities at the cops. A big burly policeman went over to her and started banging her head against the wall. 'Shuttup and get out, you old gin,' he shouted back. I was about to deparalyse my limbs, leap over the bar and stop him, when he dragged her out to the door and shoved her into the street. Not a person moved off their stools and presently everyone went back to their drinks with a few cracks about the stupidity of coons. I shed some tears behind the bar that night when no one was looking, not of self-pity but of helpless anger and disgust.

Kurt, meanwhile, had overcome his fierce pride and popped in occasionally to talk me into going back. Gladdy, whom I was much more eager to see, came in from time to time, to check on my progress and secretly to urge me to accept. After two or three months at the hotel I had saved enough to make that idea once again feasible, if not attractive. It was obvious that Kurt's was the best place to learn anything and if that meant putting up with his eccentric ways then perhaps it was the best solution. Besides, he had been charming on these visits, and had lulled me into thinking I might have made a tactical mistake.

So I began spending my spare days out there, sleeping the night, this time inside the house at Gladdy's insistence, and going back to work early in the morning. It was on one of these occasions that the pub dealt me its final blow.

I returned to my little dungeon in the wee hours of the morning to find a large, well-moulded lump of excrement snuggling almost lovingly on my pillow. As if it belonged there really. As if it had found its final resting-place at last. I had the most absurd notion that I should address it in some way – let my presence be known as if I were the trespasser. Something like, 'Excuse me, I think you have the wrong bed.' I gazed at it, mouth open, hand poised upon the door, for at least five minutes. My sense of humour, my self-confidence and my faith in humanity were all doing a perceptible fade. I handed in my notice and fled to the relative sanity of the ranch.

After that, even the rigours of Kurt's company seemed

bearable. Hard physical work out in the fresh air and hot sun, camels to be entertained by, and Gladdy, all made life look promising again. Besides, Kurt, though never exactly kind-hearted, was at least being intermittently civil. He was a wonderful teacher. He forced me to work with the animals in a way that I would have been too cowardly to attempt, but he never pushed so hard that I lost my confidence. The result was that I was fearless. There was nothing those creatures could do that scared me in the least. How I escaped serious physical damage during that time must have a lot to do with guardian angels, fairy godmothers, Kurt-cleverness and outrageous good luck. He seemed pleased with my progress with the beasts and began introducing me to the secrets of handling them.

'Remember, alvays vatch de animal, vatch him day and night and see how he tinks. Und alvays, alvays, de camelt's needs come first.'

Each of his eight animals had a distinct personality. Biddy was the matronly grande dame of cameldom and infinitely superior to anything merely human; Misch-Misch was the highly-strung, vain young aristocrat; Khartoum was the likeable nervous wreck; Ali was the sad and stoic clown; Fahani was a poor senile old lady; Aba was the backward child having trouble with puberty; and Bubby was the eternal practical joker. Dookie was the camel born to be king. I loved them all with an anthropomorphizing devotion. No matter how much I discovered about them, there was always more to learn. They continued to surprise and fascinate me until the day I left my own four on the Indian Ocean coast. I spent hours gazing at them, laughing at their antics, talking to them and touching them. They consumed all my thought and what little there was of my spare time. Instead of watching T.V. with Kurt and Gladdy of an evening, I would be out in the paddock moon-struck, listening to cud-chewing, and crooning one-sided conversations. And while this love affair was going on I didn't have to think too much about my proposed trip – it could remain a safe glow at the end of a very long tunnel.

Kurt continued to scream and berate me when I did something wrong but this I could take, even masochistically appreciate, as it kept me on my toes, combated my inherent laziness and made me learn quickly. Besides, when he actually came out with a word of praise, or a rare smile, it brought relief and pride past description. A compliment bled from the master was worth a million given freely by anyone else. There have been many happy slaves.

The ranch itself was fantastic and uncanny perched out there in the middle of the oldest rocks in the world. And it was perhaps the cold desolate lovelessness of the place that threw into sharp focus the magical and life-affirming qualities of the country around it. To enter that country is to be choked with dust, suffocated by waves of thrumming heat, and driven to distraction by the ubiquitous Australian fly; it is to be amazed by space and humbled by the most ancient, bony, awesome landscape on the face of the earth. It is to discover the continent's mythological crucible, the great outback, the never-never, that decrepit desert land of infinite blue air and limitless power. It seems ridiculous now, to talk of my growing sense of freedom given the feudal situation I was living in, but anything could be mended, anything forgotten, any doubt withstood during a walk through those timeless boulders, or down that glittering river-bed in the moonlight.

I worked sun-up to sun-down and sometimes long after, seven days a week. If we closed the ranch down for a day because of rain or because Kurt had declared a holiday, there was still mending and cleaning to be done. I began to realize that Kurt related to me exactly as he would to a camel in training. He did not, for example, allow me to wear shoes, so an extremely painful process of foot-toughening had to be suffered while my skin learnt to resist burrs shaped like maces and half an inch across. Some nights I could not sleep for the pain in my swollen, punctured and infected feet. If I objected it was taken as insubordination and, besides, my pride did not allow me to complain too often. I had created my own prison and now I had to be able to withstand anything the warder could dish out. Eventually, when my feet became blackened, tough, split and calloused, Kurt allowed me a pair of sandals. He also took a strange pleasure in watching me eat.

'Eat up, girl, that's it,' he would say as I wolfed down a gargantuan meal. 'You need your strength.' Indeed I did. He watched me like a hawk, castigated me for mistakes, and patted me and fed me when I had been good. He was moulding me like plasticine into a good placid reliable serf, who didn't kick, bite or spit.

Drawn closer by our common enemy and our alliance with the people down in the creek, Gladdy and I were developing a deep friendship. Without her, I simply could not have stayed with Kurt as long as I did. She had got a job in town primarily as a respite from her husband and because Kurt was constantly fretting and grumbling about their financial situation. The fact that the ranch was not doing as well as it should have been was due to two things; one was the long-standing feud between Kurt and Fullarton, who, according to Kurt, bribed all the tourist bus drivers into staying away; the other was Kurt's outlandish contempt for and rudeness towards the people who did come.

'Vat do you tink you are doing, you bloody idiot, on dat fence? You bloody goddam tourists, can't you bloody read? We're not open today. You tink we don't haf bloody holidays out here or sometink?'

And it was one of the few things I liked about the man. The only time Kurt and I really communicated at all, apart from camel business, was when we bitched and chuckled together about the awfulness of what he called the 'terrorists'. When Kurt was in one of his moods, he took it out on everyone, including his bread and butter. It was the only sign of

38

some innate integrity. That we developed over those months what almost amounted to a friendship I put down to the fact that I still laboured under the nice middle-class delusion that everyone was a good guy at heart if you could just get to the bottom of their problem, but he was to knock that foolishness out of me eventually. His inner workings were better left untouched. At this stage in my development, I was fatally caught in my desire to understand someone so totally outside my ken, before I came to realize that you can understand and excuse until there is nothing left to hate.

It strikes me as sad, now that I can look back on that era relatively calmly, that Kurt manufactured his own hell, because there were wonderful moments with him, long peaceful rides through the back country and learning to race camels down in the creek-bed. I galloped bareback on these occasions without a thought for the ground whizzing below those pounding legs. It was exhilaration past description. I usually rode a young bull – Dookie. He was my favourite and, I suspected, Kurt's also. One develops a special attachment to an animal in training, following the fear and concentration and difficulty to see a perfect beast gradually emerge from a frightened and unmanageable one-thousand-pounds of trouble. This was intensified by the fact that I was in training also, and Dookie and I were a team, to be put through the hoops together.

There was one flaw in Kurt's relationship to the animals: when his temper was up he could be brutally cruel. While it is true that a camel must be dealt with firmly, and bad behaviour must always be countered with severe reprimand and a few resounding clouts, Kurt almost always went overboard. The young camels especially were quite terrified of him. The first time I was witness to this fire and brimstone treatment was shortly after I arrived. Dookie had let fly a kick at Kurt who retaliated with a good fifteen minutes of beating with a chain across that leg until I thought it must surely break. I went inside to Glad and couldn't speak. I didn't speak to him for two days, not out of a desire to punish but because I just couldn't look at him. For the first and only time in our relationship Kurt was contrite. He didn't want to lose me again. But it was to happen over and over and it seemed as if everyone, including the camels, saw it as unavoidable, to be endured like everything else.

During those first months I was often overwhelmed by such despair that I thought of packing up and going home, beaten. This was countered effectively by a singularly cunning manœuvre on Kurt's part. He had given me a day off – a reward I accepted with suspicious gratitude. I could smell a rat. After complimenting me on my work, he informed me of a new financial agreement he had thought up. He would keep me working there for the eight months, then for two or three he would help me build my saddles and gear and prepare for the trip, after which he would give me three camels of my choice, free, to be returned when the trip was finished. It was, of course, too good to be true. I knew that he was playing with me, knew it, and then rejected the knowledge because I needed to believe. I looked into his eyes, through which self-interest shone like a torch, and accepted. It was a gentleman's agreement. Kurt refused to sign anything, saying that was not the way he did business, but as everyone knew, most of all me, Kurt had never been a gentleman. He had me over a barrel but there was nowhere else to go if I wanted to breathe life into my dream.

I had often told Kurt how I loved crows – they were to me the essence of wild freedom and intelligent survival. I wanted one. This is not as selfish a desire as it sounds. If you are careful, it is easy to steal a baby crow from a nest without disturbing the others or apparently distressing its parents. You can then teach it to fly and to come to you for food and affection and it need never be caged or clipped. It will, after spending an over-indulged childhood with you, begin bringing its pubescent wild friends home for afternoon teas and parties and will eventually leave you to begin a new life with its own kind out in the bush. A good system whereby everyone lives happily ever after. Kurt said he would get me a crow if it was the last thing he did. We began watching nests in the creek-bed. The parent birds were feeding several sets of squawking hungry heads forty feet up in the river gums. One hot midday, when every living thing seemed to be drowsing or sleeping, a grey crane flew into the tree opposite one of the nests and began to nod off in the heat. One of the parent crows, who had been laconically chortling to itself and who was by now obviously bored, flew across to the tree and alighted on a branch a little below the unsuspecting crane. It then hopped up on to the other's branch and, ever so quietly and nonchalantly, began sidling along it. When it was right next to the sleeping crane, it let out a raucous caw and flapped its wings. The crane shot six feet out into the air in a flurry of feathers before it realized it was the butt of a rude joke and regained its composure. After recovering from our helpless guffaws of laughter, we decided upon that nest.

The hunting of the crow was a major expedition; ropes, riding camels and lunches. Kurt assured me that he was an excellent climber and could reach the nest. However, after several attempts, although he could see the four young crows perfectly well, he could not quite reach them. He shimmied down the slippery trunk and announced plan B.

'But, Kurt, you can't do that. We don't want four crows and besides they'll be killed in the fall.'

'Nonsense. De nest is light and it vill float. Besides, da branch will cushion da fall. Anyvay, vot's it matter to you? You vanted a crow, didn't you?'

There was no dissuading him. He hoisted the rope over the branch, pulled with all his strength and down it came, branch, limb and nest with two dead birds, another which died in my hands and one with a broken leg.

I carried Akhnaton home on Dookie, wrapped in nest

feathers and inside my shirt. I rode in front so Kurt wouldn't see me crying.

Two major developments had occurred by this time that made life a shade less taxing. My sister sent me a tent which I pitched on the other side of a hill from the ranch and which gave me a certain amount of privacy. I had also begun to make friends with our neighbours. They were potters and leather craftsmen – archetypal hippies with attractive desperado overtones, who were friendly, hospitable and who talked to me in a language I had almost forgotten. They lived in the only building in Alice Springs that looked as if it belonged – a dilapidated old stone house called Basso's Farm, nestled among hills, which I loved as much as its occupants. Polly, Geoff and their small child lived at one end; Dennis, Malina and Dennis's two small boys lived at the other. Malina was a fair-skinned, red-haired Scottish lass who made superb pots but was covered in tropical ulcers, insect bites and heat rash. Unlike the rest of us, she found it hard to eulogize about the wonderfulness of deserts.

Every spare moment I had I was over there, hanging around doorways in my baker's outfit, chatting, laughing, or watching Polly stitch and fiddle with leather or change her daughter's nappies without once raising her voice or looking harassed. She was an excellent craftswoman. The bags she made were untooled, delicate, beautifully designed, fastidiously detailed and she offered to teach me how to do it. I found that I lacked her patience, dexterity and talent, but after much sweat I managed to complete two goat-skin bags that were very pretty but proved to be totally useless on the trip. The lessons, however, came in handy when I eventually began to make my own pack gear, a year later.

My social life was now centred around Basso's Farm. I would wedge in an hour or two most nights, sitting and drinking with them, waving away the flying insects that sui-cided around the pressure lamps, belly-aching about Kurt, and meeting small rare handfuls of sympathetic, friendly Alice-Springians. But by this stage I had become emotionally remote from outsiders. I was withdrawn and found it hard to relax, especially when I had to face being introduced as someone with a label – something that always instigates an identity crisis. 'I'd like you to meet Robyn Davidson, she's taking camels across Australia.' I didn't know quite how to deal with that one except to fall in with it. Another trap. It was the inauspicious beginning of the 'camel lady' image which I should have nipped in the bud right there.

It was here too, one crisp night, that I experienced my first and only vision – alcohol induced. I had put away half a bottle of tequila during the course of the evening and had stumbled outside to pee. There before me stood three ghostly camels, all saddled in beautiful Bedouin gear, staring out from the lemon trees. One of them, a white one, slowly ambled towards me. Although prophetic, it was too much for my reeling neurons at the time. I hitched my trousers with trembling fingers and fled the half mile to my tent. On the way I tripped into a ditch and lay like a felled tree, semi-conscious and blanketed in frost for the rest of the night. My headache in the morning was the size and power of a Kenworth truck which continued to change gear inside my skull for the whole of that day. During those long months I found that I was constantly projecting the images of camels on to whatever I looked at for longer than three seconds. Swaying branches became munching camel heads, dust patterns became galloping camels and drifting clouds became camels sitting down. It was a sure sign that my fragile mind was obsessed to the point of dementia and it had me vaguely worried. Whether my new friends were conscious of it or not, they helped me get through that time without too much brain damage because they formed a tenuous link with my past life, and because they made me laugh.

My tent was hardly comfortable, plonked out in the middle of the desert sun, but it was mine – my space. Akhnaton would swagger into it well before dawn, attack Diggity until she crawled protesting out of bed, and then proceed to pull the covers away from my face, peck gently at my ears and nose, and croak until I got up to feed him. He was insatiable. God knows where he put all that meat. When it was time to go to work, he would sit on my shoulder or hat until we three had climbed the hill and could see the ranch spread out below like a fake emerald, then he would gather himself for flight and soar down to the roof-top. It was the closest I have ever come to a vicarious knowledge of flight, and was well worth the rigours of his demanding nature and chronic kleptomania.

After I had made a bucket of sweet milk for the young camels, Diggity would leap six feet in the air to snap at any long neck that was trying to steal what she considered her breakfast, and the crow would dive-bomb all of them. He was an uncontrollable tease and Diggity would have dearly loved to swat him but was forbidden. She learnt eventually to accept him if not actually like him, and even tolerated taking him for rides on her back, something he enjoyed immensely, crooning and talking to himself all the while and egotistically preening his glossy blue-black feathers, and occasionally pecking her to make her hurry up. I found for the first time in my life that I really did enjoy the company of animals better than people. I was shy and confused with my own kind and did not trust them. I was sure they were all out to get me. I did not understand the change, did not realize that I had become isolated, defensive and humourless, did not know that I was lonely.

The demise of my tent was a sad affair. I was sleeping in it one night during a monumental hail-storm. The balls of ice gathered in the roof until it ripped and dumped a ton of frozen water on the occupants. It was back to Kurt's, and gradually the pressure began to build again. He complained continually that there was no money left so I decided to get a job a few nights a week at a restaurant in town. It was disgusting work but it meant I was once more relating to humans and cracking jokes in the kitchen with real people. It also meant that I was overtired at work the next day. Kurt had become increasingly truculent and lazy, leaving most of the running of the place to me which I now found I could do quite capably. It suited me because I didn't have him breathing down my neck.

One morning, however, he announced that I was to get up two hours earlier to bring in the camels. I stared at him incredulously and for the second time in my life, and the last, I fought him.

'You bastard,' I whispered. 'You incomparable bastard, how dare you ask me to do that.'

I had been with him for eight months and the day of reckoning when he would have to start helping me was looming ever closer. He had been twisting the knife harder and harder lately, in the hope that I would crack and leave of my own accord. He had performed countless little cruelties that only strengthened my resolve not to let him get at me. But now, because of my tiredness, I could hold my emotions down no longer. Kurt was shocked into stony silence, but when I returned an hour later he was deathly white and his lips had set into a hard line.

'You vill do exactly vat I tell you or you vill get out,' he hissed, as he grabbed me and shook me till my teeth rattled.

The next day I left the ranch in a daze. I was never going to get my camels or anything else. I marvelled at whatever blindness it had been that allowed me to stay as long as I did as his dupe. I moped around the neighbours' house for a few days and cried a lot and beat my chest. Then I was offered a job by that irascible old gentleman Sallay Mahomet who was to become a friend, camel-guru and saviour. He told me that anyone who could put up with Kurt for that long deserved a break, and he promptly produced a signed guarantee that if I came to work for him for a couple of months he would give me two of his wild camels. I felt like covering

45

him in grateful kisses and grovelling at his feet saying thank you thank you thank you, but that was hardly Sallay's style. We shook hands on the deal and so a whole new era began.

It was absurdly generous on Sallay's part, as he knew I would be of little assistance in the kind of work he was doing. He had heard of my plight through an acquaintance who arrived from Brisbane – a camel-man also who had crossed Central Australia twice with three of his own, the first person to do so since the early days of exploration. We both worked for Sallay during that awful summer. Perhaps it was the intolerable heat in our work-tent, perhaps it was the poisonous snakes that crawled incessantly from under the flaps across the grass floor, perhaps it was the inch-long mosquitoes who bled you during the night until you were anaemic, perhaps it was simply that all people who deal long enough with camels go slightly troppo. But whatever it was, I managed to alienate Dennis too, who earlier on had been so generously willing to help me, and our squabbles often thudded out into the soggy, broiling air. I couldn't work out this new capacity I'd acquired for creating enmity in the hearts of men.

At Kurt's place, I had learnt the finesses of camel-handling. With Sallay and Dennis I learnt the rough and tumble; the fact that these animals could and would kill if given the opportunity. With the help of Dennis's nervous 'Watch outs' and 'Be carefuls', and with Sallay's instinct to protect what he would always consider the weaker sex, I began to live in an almost permanent state of fear, not helped any by my own performance anxiety in front of these two men. While I was there, I was kicked, struck, stamped on; I fell off a bucking wild camel and had my shin crushed between the iron bar of a saddle and a tree. This was an old camel trick to get rid of unwanted people on their backs: squash them or scrape them off on a limb, or sit down and roll on top of them. I was not a good enough rider, nor did I have the physical strength to deal with this. I began to feel useless and clumsy.

The most important things Sallay taught me were how to use ropes to tie up a camel, how to carve and whittle nose-pegs from white-wood or mulga, how to splice, how to fix saddles, in fact all the myriad little bits of knowledge that would play such an important part in my survival out bush. He was an endless mine of such information. He had been with camels all his life, and although his relationship to them was anything but sentimental, and although he treated them somewhat roughly for my soft-hearted tastes, he was the best camel-man in town. He knew the animals as well as the back of his own hand, and some of that knowledge seeped into me and came out when I least expected it on my journey. I had met his wife Iris, who had an outrageous and wonderful sense of humour and who helped me to laugh at my predicament. She was a perfect contrast and complement to Sallay. They were two of the nicest people I met in that god-awful hole and I like, admire and respect them to this day. I am also eternally grateful.

One afternoon I was sleeping on my cot bathed in a pool of sweat when I woke with the eerie feeling that somebody was watching me. I thought perhaps some townsfolk had arrived and went to grab my clothes, but there was no one. I lay down again but the feeling persisted. I glanced up and saw through a two-inch hole in the roof of the tent the beady blue eye of Akhnaton, first the right, then the left, staring fixedly at my naked body. I threw a boot at him.

He was also becoming an insufferable pest with his stealing. Just when you were about to clean your teeth, he would fly into a tree with the toothbrush and not drop it until you had given up shouting and shaking your fist at him. The same thing happened with spoons the minute you sat down with the sugar bowl and a cup of tea.

I had a small ancillary sleeping tent, shaped like a cone and lashed to the jutting limb of a tree. Because of the intense heat, I slept half inside this tent and half out of it, with the

47

branch six feet above me. One morning before dawn Ark was beginning to wake me up as usual, but I had grown tired of this procedure; he was perfectly able to feed and fend for himself and should not be relying on his surrogate mother any longer. After he had unsuccessfully tried to rouse me, and after I had sworn at him to go find his own bloody breakfast, he hopped up on to that branch, walked along it, aimed deliberately, and shot a dribbling white present right into the middle of my face.

I had been in the Alice for almost a year now and I was a changed woman. It seemed I had always been there, that anything I may have been before was a dream belonging to someone else. My grip on reality was a little shaky. I wanted to see my friends again because I was beginning to realize how removed from everything but camels and madmen I had become. The time with Kurt had had a weird effect on me – I was self-protective, suspicious and defensive and I was also aggressively ready to pounce on anyone who looked like they might be going to give me a hard time. Though this may sound like a negative quality, it was essential for me to develop beyond the archetypal female creature who from birth had been trained to be sweet, pliable, forgiving, compassionate and door-mattish. I could be grateful to Kurt for that if nothing else. I also had a reinforced concrete strip down my back which successfully hid the yellow one. It wasn't so much strength I had gained, as tenacity – bulldog tenacity. I decided to fly home to Queensland, to see Nancy, my closest friend. She and I had been confidantes for years, having been through the tedium of Brisbane's post-1960s doldrums together, and come out of it with a close, tolerant, and loving friendship such as can exist only between two women who have worked hard for it. She was a yardstick against which I could measure what I had learnt and what I had felt. She was ten years older and wiser than me, and could always be depended upon to penetrate what I was thinking and help me put it into perspective. I valued that perspicacity and warmth above all else. And right now I needed a good talk over a kitchen table with her.

I flew back home in a light aircraft over the endless wastes of the Simpson Desert which had me thinking twice about the foolhardiness of my trip. Nancy and Robin lived on a fruit farm in the granite hills of southern Queensland. Oh the lush green sogginess of coastal country. It was so long since I'd been there and it now looked cramped, closed in and cluttered.

Nancy noticed immediately the changes in me and we talked into the wee hours of every morning over coffee and whisky and cigarettes. Many of my friends were there and it was indescribably good to be once again in an atmosphere of loving kindness. I entertained them with tall tales and true of the legendary West. It was like medicine to be able to laugh like that again. The afternoon before I was to leave, Nancy and I went for a walk in the bush. We didn't talk much but eventually she said, 'Rob, I really like what you're doing. I didn't understand it before, but getting off your butt and actually doing something for yourself is important for all of us. And although I can't say I won't miss you like hell, and won't worry about you often, I can say that what you're doing is great and I love you for it. It's important that we leave each other and the comfort of it, and circle away, even though it's hard sometimes, so that we can come back and swap information about what we've learnt even if what we do changes us and we risk not recognizing each other when we return.'

That night, we had a going-away party in the barn and danced and drank and laughed and talked until dawn.

I have never uncovered anywhere the same bonds of friendship as I found in certain small sections of Australian society. It has something to do with the old code of mateship and something to do with the fact that people have time to care for one another, and something to do with the fact that dissidents have had to stick together, and something to do with the fact that competition and achievement are not very important aspects of the culture, and something to do with a generosity of spirit that can afford to grow within that unique sense of traditionless space and potential. Whatever it is, it is extraordinarily valuable.

The trip home reinstated a faith in myself and what I was doing. I felt calm and positive and strong, and now, instead of the trip appearing out of character, instead of worrying about whether or not it was a pointless thing to do, I could see more clearly the reasons and the needs behind it.

A couple of years before, someone had asked me a question: 'What is the substance of the world in which you live?' As it happens, I had not slept or eaten for three or four days and it struck me at the time as a very profound question. It took me an hour to answer it, and when I did, my answer seemed to come almost directly from the subconscious: 'Desert, purity, fire, air, hot wind, space, sun, desert desert desert.' It had surprised me, I had no idea those symbols had been working so strongly within me.

I had read a good deal about Aborigines and that was another reason for my wanting to travel in the desert – a way of getting to know them directly and simply.

I had also been vaguely bored with my life and its repetitions – the half-finished, half-hearted attempts at different jobs and various studies; had been sick of carrying around the self-indulgent negativity which was so much the malaise of my generation, my sex and my class.

So I had made a decision which carried with it things that I could not articulate at the time. I had made the choice instinctively, and only later had given it meaning. The trip had never been billed in my mind as an adventure in the sense of something to be proved. And it struck me then that the most difficult thing had been the decision to act, the rest had been merely tenacity – and the fears were paper tigers. One really could do anything one had decided to do whether it were changing a job, moving to a new place, divorcing a husband or whatever, one really could act to change and control one's life; and the procedure, the process, was its own reward.

3

THE TIME had come for me to choose my two camels. I singled out a stubborn but quiet old dowager called Alcoota Kate and a beautiful young wild thing – Zeleika. Sallay approved the choice and wished me well. My friends at Basso's Farm had moved to the city, leaving the house for me to live in until it was sold. It was a stroke of luck – nothing could have been more desirable at that stage. It meant I could hobble my camels out in the wild fenceless back country where they would have plenty to eat, and I could live in a home of my own. No people.

The last day at the tent was a disaster. While I was away Akhnaton had flown off with his friends never to be seen again; I had somehow to work out how to get two edgy camels six miles down a major highway without killing myself and them; Kate had sat on a broken bottle a few weeks earlier and lacerated her brisket, but no one had paid it much attention, simply treating it occasionally with Stockholm tar; Zeleika had a large infected gash in her head; and Dennis and I gave way to our hostile impulses for the last time.

I got them to Basso's at last, after only minor traumas and a near nervous collapse. There was no one but myself to rely on now, no Kurts, Sallays or Dennises to help or hinder. I cleaned their wounds, hobbled them out and watched happily as they munched their way along the dirt track leading to the hills in the east. My camels. My home.

It was one of those brittle-bright days such as only a desert in bountiful season can produce. Crystal water sped down the broad bed of the Charles River, a foot or two deep in some places where it swirled around a giant trunk of a dappled river gum; black-shouldered kites hovered above their hunting ground in the back garden, catching the light on their shimmering wings and in their blood-red predatory eyes; black cockatoos with flamboyant orange tail-feathers screeched their music through the high trees; sunlight exploded, flooding everything with its harsh pounding energy; crickets grated intermittently from the flowering pomegranates and made, together with the drone of the blow-flies in the kitchen, an anthem for hot Australian afternoons.

I had never had a home of my own – having left the barred windows and regimented dormitories of boarding school to enter immediately the communal life of cheap shared houses with large groups of friends. And here I was with a whole castle where I could be queen. This sudden transition from too much bad company to the prospect of none at all was a pleasant shock. Like walking from the din of a busy street into the heavy silence of a shuttered room. I wandered and roamed through my domain, my private space, smelling its essence, accepting its claim on me and incorporating every dust mote, every spider's web into an orgy of possessive bliss. This sprawling, tattered old stone ruin, which was sinking gracefully back into the ground from which it had come; this delightful, roofless pile of rocks with tough thriving fig trees and tall smothering grasses; its permanent guests, the snakes, lizards, insects and birds; its dramatic patterns of light and shade; its secret rooms and recesses; its unhinged doors, and its nestling correctness in the Arunta rock complex; this was my first home, where I felt such a sense of relief and belonging that I needed nothing and no one.

Before that moment, I had always supposed that loneliness was my enemy. I had seemed not to exist without people around me. But now I understood that I had always been a loner, and that this condition was a gift rather than something to be feared. Alone, in my castle, I could see more clearly what loneliness was. For the first time it flashed on me that the way I had conducted my life was always to allow myself that remoteness, always protect that high, clear place that could not be shared without risking its destruction. I had paid for this over and over with moments of neurotic despair, but it had been worth it. I had somehow always countered my desire for a knight in shining armour, by forming bonds with men I didn't like, or with men who were so off the air there was no hope of a permanent relationship. I could not deny this. It lay, crystal clear, beneath the feelings of inadequacy and defeat, the clever, self-directed plan that had been working towards this realization for years. I believe the subconscious always knows what is best. It is our conditioned, vastly overrated rational mind which screws everything up.

So now, for the first time in my life, my aloneness was a treasure which I guarded like a jewel. If I saw people driving up to see me, I would most often hide. This precious happy time lasted for a month or two but, like everything, had to follow the laws of change.

My closest neighbour was Ada Baxter, a handsome Aboriginal woman with a wildly passionate nature and a warm, generous heart. She loved high times and flagons of wine. Her shack, which sat at the back of Basso's, was very different from the impoverished humpies of her relations on the other side of the creek. It had been built for her by one of her succession of white men-friends (to Ada, an association with whitefellas meant status), and in it were the treasured knick-knacks and paraphernalia of a material society which she had partly adopted but which, in essence, was not her own. She came over often to share some booze, or camp on the floor if she thought I needed protecting. Although she could not understand my desire to be alone, her company was never an infringement of my privacy, as it was easy and relaxed and carried with it that ability many Aboriginal people have to touch and be affectionate without stiffness, and to be comfortable with silence. I loved Ada. She always addressed me as 'my daughter', and was as kind and understanding a mother as I could ask for.

One of the potters who had lived there before had told me a very funny story about this remarkable woman. They had all been sitting at home one night, listening to the sounds of drunken battle wafting over from Ada's camp. Suddenly, the shouts became louder and more urgent and my friend went over to see if there was any trouble. He arrived in time to see Ada's boyfriend staggering around the shack emptying a can of petrol on the way, then bending down with shaking fingers, trying to light the stuff. It had all sunk into the dust by then, so there was no real danger, but Ada was not to know that. She had gone to the woodpile, picked up the axe and felled the man with one blow. He dropped flat on his back, blood streaming from the wound into the ground around him. My friend thought for sure Ada had killed him and screamed at the others to run for an ambulance. Being so certain there was nothing he could do for the bloody body, he did what he could for Ada who was by then in shock. With trembling fingers he wrapped her in a blanket and handed her some of his tequila. There was a groan behind him. The man struggled on to an elbow, fixed my friend with a swaying glare and said, 'For Christ's sake, man, can't you see she's had enough?'

Just before moving to Basso's, I had met a group of young white people involved with Aboriginal rights. Like me, they had brought with them the idealism and indignant morality of their various good educations. It was against this small group that the catch-cry, 'Do-gooder trouble-makers from the city' was levelled by many of the locals. If this were true in the beginning, and it often was, it rarely remained so, because life in Alice Springs quickly replaced political and personal naïvety with astuteness. I liked these people, agreed with them and supported them, but I did not want them around me. I had won so much, had gained so much ground all on my own, that I felt, psychologically at least, self-sufficient. I did not want potential friendships complicating things. They did, after all, require energy that I needed to direct at camel trips. But two of them in particular – Jenny Green and Toly Sawenko – sought me out and wooed me with their wit, warmth and intelligence until I began, surreptitiously, to look forward to their visits, and the cheeses and wines they brought, now such a luxury in my austere, monastic life. They gradually and tactfully broke through my reserve until, months later, I had become hopelessly dependent upon them for encouragement and support, until they became so inextricably involved with that era that I cannot think of it without remembering them.

The distorted memories of the next few months are all stored together in my brain like a tangled adder's nest. I only know that from such wonderful beginnings at Basso's, life degenerated into a negative farce, so bad that it almost had me believing in fate. And fate was against me.

I was still spending time with Kurt and Gladdy – for one thing I was manipulative enough to want to use Kurt's yards and facilities and knowledge. This I succeeded in doing by being sweet, apologetic and everything Kurt admired in an underling. But I paid. Oh how he made me pay. There was none of the former tentative camaraderie between us. It had been replaced by total animosity. And there was Gladdy. I wanted to maintain my friendship with her, who was so badly in need of it. She had been talking about leaving Kurt, who was half-heartedly trying to sell the ranch at an astronomical price. Gladdy wanted to stick it out for a little longer, at least until the sale came through, so that she would have some money – as a symbol of having remained unbeaten rather than a desire for the money itself. And there were Frankie and Joanie, two Aboriginal children from Mount Nancy camp, with whom Gladdy and I had spent so much of our time.

Joanie was a beautiful girl of about fourteen with the grace and poise of a natural model. She was also extremely bright and perceptive and, already, well acquainted with despair. I understood her depression, it was the kind engendered by

56

a feeling of helplessness in the face of insurmountable odds. Joanie wanted things from life – things that would remain for ever out of her reach, because of her colour, because of her poverty.

'What have I got to look forward to?' she would say. 'Booze? Getting married to someone who beats me up every night?'

Frankie was slightly better off. He at least had the hope of an acceptable identity as a ringer or station hand – itinerant work at best, but which would allow him a certain amount of self-worth. He was a natural clown, Frankie. And we watched lovingly when he made that transformation from child into young man, with his too-large boots and his copied swagger. He would come up to visit me at Basso's all man-talk and man-action, then suddenly, noticing it was getting dark, sheepishly change back into the boy and ask, 'Hey, you wouldn't mind walking me across the creek, would you? I'm scared at night.'

At first, some of the men at the camp had not understood a woman living alone. Along with one or two desperadoes from town, they sometimes came up in the middle of the night in the hope of some drunken dalliance. I had bought myself a gun, a Savage .222 high-power rifle and 20-gauge shotgun, over-under – a beautiful instrument, but all I knew about it was that the bullet came out one end, while you held the other. I never, but never, loaded it. This, however, poked out of the door with a few curt words behind it, did not fail to make an impression. My friends were horrified when I told them I had actually pointed a gun at someone. Well, not directly at someone, I hastened to assure them, but rather aimlessly through the door and into the dark. I could see they thought I was losing my grip but I defended this grow-ing hill-billy mentality of mine, which seemed perfectly reasonable given the conditions I was living in and given my highly developed sense of aggression and property. I learnt later that the gun episodes caused endless bouts of hilarity tinged with respect down at the camp and I never had any trouble again. In fact over the months their attitude changed totally. I was now protected if anything, watched out for and looked after. And if they thought I was a bit daft, it was with an overlay of good humour. I was, through Joanie, Frankie, Gladys and Ada, getting to know them all better, beginning to overcome my shyness and my white guilt and to learn more and more about the incredibly complex problems – physical, political and emotional – all Aboriginal people have to contend with.

There were approximately thirty camps in and around Alice Springs, squatting on parcels of crown land or on camping reserves on the outskirts. These had been set up over the years as traditional territorial sites for members of different surrounding tribal groups, who visited the town from their home settlements, up to several hundred miles away in the Northern Territory and South Australia. One of the main attractions of town was the easy access to alcohol, but there were other important regional resources to be found. These included Aboriginal Legal Aid, Health Services, Aboriginal Art and Craft Centre, Department of Aboriginal Affairs offices, second-hand car lots specially designed to rip off Aborigines, and other assorted bright lights. There was fairly regular movement between these Alice Springs domiciliary sites and the home settlements, although some people became permanent dwellers and built themselves huts of bush timber frames, second-hand galvanized iron, and whatever other makeshift components they could find in the municipal dump. There were five water taps to serve all thirty camps, and many people were so destitute they lived out of garbage cans, off discarded food they found at the dump, and by cadging hand-outs in the street. Many were alcoholics, so whatever money they got went straight into a flagon of cheap wine. Children and women suffered the most, from malnutrition, violence and disease.

Mount Nancy was the most economically successful, well-organized, socially cohesive camp in town. Small houses (financed by D.A.A.) were beginning to replace the humpies, and an ablution block was being built. The worst camps, by comparison, were those in the dry river-bed of the Todd, right in the centre of town. The people here had no access to water, sanitation or shelter, had nothing to sustain them but alcohol. Because of the river's land tenure, this was a primary camping ground for itinerant Aborigines. They were under threat from the town council which had been trying to extend the leases of the properties bordering the river out into the river-bed itself – a tidy way of getting rid of the camps and making things clean and nice for the tourists, who, after all, spent considerable money buying fake Aboriginal artefacts from the shops.

From what I could see at Mount Nancy, people survived by sharing up what money they could get from part-time cattle work, child endowment, widows' and deserted wives' pensions, and the rare, very rare, unemployment cheque. Gambling was a way of redistributing wealth rather than acquiring it. One of the myths concerning Aboriginal people is that they are chronic 'dole bludgers'. In fact, fewer blacks receive social services than do whites, despite ten times more unemployment.

Even the few part-Aboriginal people who live in town as whites do, suffer from subtle forms of racism. It is a daily experience for blacks in Alice Springs. It reinforces their own feelings of worthlessness and self-hate. The constant frustration in not being able to change their lives makes many of them give up hope, turns them into alcoholics, because that, at least, provides some form of release from an untenable situation, and finally, grants them oblivion.

As Kevin Gilbert writes in *Because a White Man'll Never Do It*:

It is my thesis that Aboriginal Australia underwent a rape of the soul so profound that the blight continues in the minds of most blacks today. It is this psychological blight, more than anything else, that causes the conditions that we see on reserves and missions. And it is repeated down the generations.

Education was always a problem. Schools were mixed, white with black, and tribe with tribe. As if having to read books about Dick, Dora and their cat Fluff, and studying history books stating that Captain Cook was the first person in Australia, or that 'blackfellows' who 'form one of the lowest races of mankind in existence ... are fast disappearing before the onward march of the white man,' was not enough, apart from having to take bricks wrapped in brown paper to school instead of lunches because there was no money and no means to make them, apart from being bawled out at school for not doing homework (is it possible to do homework in a rusted-out car body by firelight?), apart from having perforated ear drums and eye infections and sores and malnutrition, apart from having to deal with the inherent racism of many of the teachers, apart from all that – they might well have to sit next to some kid who might be a traditional tribal enemy.

So it was little wonder that children did not want to experience this totally alien and threatening environment. It taught them nothing they needed to know since the only job they were likely to get was itinerant station work, which did not require the ability to read and write. Little wonder that they were termed hopeless, unable to learn, sow's ears. 'Ah yes,' the whites shook their heads in sadness, 'it's in the blood. They'll never be assimilated.'

Before large mining corporations began lusting after Aboriginal Reserve land, 'assimilation' was virtually a non-policy. It made little difference to the way Aboriginal people actually lived. Now, it is a means of getting Aboriginal people off their land, the only thing they have that grants them any kind of self-worth, and into the town where they cannot find work and where they must depend more and more on white institutions for survival. It also provides the government with a handy P.R. exercise, so that the Prime Minister can speak out against apartheid in South Africa, maintain a clean international reputation, and still carry out a policy which appears on the surface to be antithetical to apartheid but which, on closer inspection, produces identical effects. That is, a policy which ensures that Aboriginal lands go once again into the hands of the whites (in this case multinationals), that a cheap labour source is made available by removing all trace of black ethics and culture, leaving the white races pure. This is exactly what apartheid was set up in South Africa to accomplish. Assimilation is anti-land rights, anti-self-determination, and blacks do not want it. Kevin Gilbert again:

> Every ... Aboriginal, when asked, repeats over and over again that the only way that an answer can come is when white Australia gives blacks a just land base and the financial means to allow communities to begin to help themselves.

The problem of schooling, like so many others, could have been remedied so easily by a little bit of expense on the government's part – the introduction of a modified mobile school. Predictably, instead of increasing the budget to deal with this kind of problem, the present government has made enormous cuts in Aboriginal spending. (The Department of Aboriginal Affairs has recently been conducting a survey of Australian Aborigines. In the housing section, the question was asked, 'How many Aborigines are homeless?' In another section 'homelessness' was defined as not including people living in humpies, lean-tos, tin shelters or car bodies.)

Frankie had a friend called Clivie who was younger but far more worldly-wise. He was an incorrigible and expert thief, which was O.K. with me; in fact, given his condition, it seemed like a fairly sensible thing to be doing except that, uh-oh, he was stealing from me. Poor destitute me, who was saving up at the rate of fifty cents a week to buy things like boxes of rivets and screwdrivers and leather and knives, all very attractive knick-knacks for young boys. This was difficult for me to deal with. On the one hand I knew that their attitude to possessions was totally different from mine; that is, material objects could not be owned by one person, they were a shareable commodity. On the other hand, when things disappeared from Basso's they usually disappeared for good, or were brought back by an apologetic mother, battered and broken. So I constantly chivvied Clivie and Frankie for their light-fingeredness, which caused temporary bouts of apology but essentially did no good at all.

I had returned from town one day, and was quietly walking back to my room from the kitchen. I kept one room locked, with my most treasured possessions inside. Frankie and Clivie were busily trying to get through the window. They were whispering together like jewel thieves. It was all I could do to repress my laughter, but I held it until I'd gained proper control, then I put a very stern look on my face and said, 'And what do you think YOU'RE doing?'

I swear I have never seen anybody leap out of their skins before. It was as if they'd touched a live wire. They turned to me like stunned mullets, Frankie's eyes popping out, Clivie's downcast with guilt. There was a respite in pinching for a while.

Some months later, Clivie went on a real binge. I don't know what brought it on, but he did some pretty stupid things. He stole knives and a gun, I think, and rounded it all off by taking a bottle of whisky from the police department, then going to live on his own in the bush for a couple of weeks – terrified, no doubt, by the possible consequences of his actions. He finally struggled home, was pronounced a delinquent by the welfare department and police, taken from his crippled mother and all his relations, who, the authorities said, were not able to look after him properly, and sent to a boys' home somewhere down south. Clivie was eleven.

During this time, a kind of misery, a feeling of defeat, was building almost unnoticed in my head. The joy of being on my own, of living in a fantasy place, and of dreaming about the trip without ever coming to terms with the reality of it was beginning to pall. It dawned on me that I was procrastinating, pretending, play-acting, and that was the source of my discomfort. If everyone else believed I would eventually take the camels out into the desert, I did not. It was something I could put at the edge of my mind to play with when I had nothing better to do. It gave me a superficial identity, or structure, which I could crawl into when I was down, and wear like a dress.

This unease was put into abeyance by the daily welter of details and little problems. Both of my camels were ill and required constant attention. I would hobble them out at night to feed, get up at seven to track them down (which could take hours), bring them home, doctor them, train Zelly, make half-hearted attempts at getting their gear ready, and so on until it was time to pedal the three miles in to the restaurant, and the three miles back again at midnight.

Zeleika was dreadfully thin – she had lost all her condition after she was brought in on the train following her capture. She had been squeezed in with a dozen or so frightened wild animals, put in a yard, thrown, hobbled, and left to think about it for a few days. She had been terrorized and banged around badly, and as if that wasn't enough, she had then been nose-pegged. Bringing camels in from the wild is a cruel business at the best of times; sometimes half the herd dies either from the exhaustion of the chase or from falls and broken limbs.

Kate had not had to endure this experience. She had been used as a pack animal years before, treated abominably, something which she would never forget, then put out to rest in her dotage with a friend on Alcoota Station. Sallay had picked her up from there, leaving the friend behind. She remembered humans and hated them. She was hopeless as a riding camel, fighting the nose-line all the way, and too old and set in her ways ever to change. However, she was a good pack animal, strong and patient, and I figured I would train Zelly for riding and use old Kate as the work-horse. Although she would never dream of kicking, her great ugly yellow fangs would chomp out in every direction when she was displeased, which was always, until she was persuaded out of that nonsense with a few solid clouts across the lips. Poor Kate, she gave in so easily, but no matter how kind or loving I subsequently tried to be to her, she would never trust or like me. She had a 'personal space' of ten feet, and if any homo sapiens stepped inside that radius she would roar her head off until that person exited that space. She would stand placidly, great mouth open wide, and roar and roar like a lion, only pausing to draw breath. If you stood there for two hours, she would roar for two hours. She was also obscenely overweight. I led her down to the truck weighing-dock one day, and she clocked in at about two thousand pounds – not bad for a stumpy-legged old cow. Her hump was a great mountain of deformed gristle perched on her back, and her massive thighs rubbed together and jiggled when she walked. She was altogether a most awe-inspiring beast.

I brought the vet out within that first week to look over my girls. It was to be the beginning of a long association with the animal doctors of Alice Springs. Hundreds of dollars went into their respective accounts before I left, even though many of them didn't charge me for the consultations, out of pity. There was to come a day when these wonderful men would run and hide when they saw me entering their clinics, or, if caught, would sigh and say, 'Who's dying today, Rob?' and then wince when I told them of the latest developments

5-7   Toly Sawenko (*above*) and Jenny stayed with me at Basso's, three miles north of Alice Springs, after I had left Kurt.

8–9 At Basso's, I spent several months preparing for the trip. *Below*, Jenny with Dookie, whose nose-line is pegged into the flesh of the nostril. The camel is a cud-chewing animal and so cannot wear a bit.

in cameloid problems. But they taught me a great deal in that time, how to throw needles into muscles, how to jab needles into jugulars, how to lance, incise, stitch, disinfect, castrate, patch, bandage and clean and all that with the detached coolness of a hardened professional.

The vet gave the camels a thorough check-up. He told me Zeleika had a broken rib, then, when he saw the look on my face, hastily reassured me that it had knitted and would only cause trouble if she fell again. Her infections could be cleared up easily with antibiotic powder. I then led out the great wobbling mass of Kate, and showed the vet her brisket, which by now was dripping huge amounts of pus. This brisket, or pedestal, is a cartilaginous growth on the chest just behind the front legs. Similar pads on the front and hind legs are the pressure points on which the animal sits. It is covered by a hard skin, like the bark of a tree. I had been treating the wound in it with hosings, disinfectant, antibiotic powder and Stockholm tar. The vet inspected it, paused, thrust his hand in deeper, and whistled. I didn't like the sound of that whistle.

'It looks bad,' he said. 'The infection is spreading up through the flesh in pockets. There could be some glass in there. Still, I'll dose her up with terramycin and see how she responds.'

He then took out an enormous syringe with a needle on it the size of a drinking straw, handed it to me and made me stand two feet away from Kate's neck and throw the needle at her like a dart. I didn't throw hard enough. Kate's roars went an octave higher. I stood back again, aimed and threw with all my might. It sunk in up to the hilt, and I was surprised it didn't stick out the other side, like the bolts on Frankenstein's monster. I then attached the syringe and injected ten c.c.s of the viscous stuff, leaving a large egg-shaped lump.

'Well done,' said the vet. 'Now, do that every three days, twice more, and then give me a call. O.K.?'

I gulped and managed to whimper, 'O.K.' through the trembling of my chin. My hatred of needles was about to be cured for ever.

Whatever dreams I'd had about winning Kate's confidence now flew out the window. Every day I dressed the wound at least twice or gave her shots, causing her pain and reinforcing her hatred of my species. Her protective radius grew to twenty feet for me and stayed at ten for anyone else. There was no improvement. When next the vet came, we decided to lay the old girl out cold with nembutal, and cut and drain the wound. Had I not been so worried over the animal (no one knew the correct dose for a camel, so we had to guess), I would have been able to laugh at the comical way in which Katie reacted to the drug. She went down slowly, her lips all flaccid and foolish, her eyes glazed over as she stared, fascinated, at small blades of grass and ants and things, dribble running out of her great slack jaws – she was stoned out of her mind.

The operation was anything but funny. Although there were no glass fragments that we could see, the infection had gone much deeper than the vet had thought, which necessitated some radical cutting he had hoped to avoid. However, when the job was done and another course of injections prescribed I felt confident that everything would be all right. Kate did not improve. I spent the next several months of my life totally dedicated to her well-being – spending money on her like water, and using huge doses of every antibiotic, herbal remedy, and Afghani cure in the book. I tried every treatment every vet in town suggested. Kate never responded.

During this time, I also had to begin training Zeleika for riding and carrying pack. This was not easy – I had no money to buy equipment, no saddle to put on her back so that I wouldn't fall off every time she bucked, and I had lost most of my nerve at Sallay's. So I rode her bareback, quietly, up and down the soft sand of the creek, not asking her to do too much – just trying to win her confidence and keep her quiet and protect my own skin. She was in such poor condition that I constantly had to balance the need for training against not allowing her to worry herself back into a skeleton. Camels always lose weight during training. Instead of eating, they spend all day thinking about what you are going to do to them. Zeleika also had a lovely gentle nature which I did not want to spoil. I could walk up to her anywhere in the wild, whether she was hobbled or not, and catch her, even though I could feel her muscles tighten into hard lumps with tension and fear. Her only dangerous fault was her willingness to kick. Now, a camel can kick you in any direction, within a radius of six feet. They can strike with their front legs, and kick forward, sideways or backwards with the back. One of those kicks could snap you in half like a dry twig. Teaching her to accept hobbles and side-lines was not an easy business. In fact, it was ulcer-inducing if not death-producing and required infinite patience and bravery, neither of which I was particularly blessed with but I had no choice. To quieten her I had to tie her to a tree on the halter and encourage her to eat rich and expensive hand-feed, while I groomed her all over, picked up her legs, played loud music on a tape recorder and got her used to having things around her feet and on her back, all the time talking talking talking. When she did let fly with one of those terrible legs, it was out with the whip. She soon learnt that this kicking got her nowhere and that it was easier to be nice, even if that niceness didn't come from the heart.

One day, I had tied her to her tree outside Basso's and taken Kate up to Kurt's for a hosing out. When I came back, Zeleika was missing and so was the tree, a young gum sapling about fifteen feet high and one foot thick at the base. It had been completely uprooted. Zelly did not like being away from Kate.

This particular quirk is the most difficult to overcome when training. Camels hate leaving their mates and will use any ruse, any dirty trick, any amount of foul play to get home. It is easy enough to take them somewhere in a group, but getting an animal off on its own is a trial and a battle of wits. This is understandable as they are a herd animal, and equate company with safety. It is very threatening for a camel to be out on his own, especially with a maniac on his back.

Because camels' necks are so strong, the nose-line is essential for a riding animal. It is almost impossible to control them with just a halter, unless you have super-human strength. They cannot take a bit like a horse as they are cud-chewers. The only alternative is a jaw-line, which I sometimes used in training before the peg wound healed, but which cut into their soft bottom lip. So the nose-peg method is best. They are usually given only one of these, which sticks out the side of either nostril. To it is attached a piece of string, strong enough to cause pain when it is jerked, but not so strong that it will not snap long before the peg is pulled through the flesh. This string is attached to the outside of the peg, then split under the jaw and used simply as reins. Once the peg wound has healed, this method causes no more discomfort than a bit does to a horse.

I had learnt how to nose-peg an animal from both Kurt and Sallay – each had totally different methods. Sallay skewered the flesh straight through from the inside with a sharpened mulga stick, then inserted the wooden peg into the hole and dressed it with kerosene and oil. Kurt's method was more sophisticated if not better. He would mark the spot on the nose with a marker pen, punch a small hole in the flesh with a leather punch, widen that hole with a butcher's skewer driven through from the inside up to the hilt, and follow this with the insertion of the peg, which, by the way, looks more than anything else like a small wooden penis. He would then dress it carefully every day, for anything up to two months, with dilute antiseptic and antibiotic powder. I had performed this brutal operation on one of Kurt's young bulls but I hated it. It made me feel sick. However, Zelly's nose was now so infected, despite the constant cleaning, that I thought perhaps there were wood splinters inside it preventing it from healing. So, to our mutual horror, I tied her down, cut the peg with bolt cutters and inspected the wound thoroughly. I discovered that the peg had indeed splintered along the shaft, and was opening the wound as it turned. I had to make another peg and insert it through that tortured flesh. How animals ever forgive us for what we do to them, I will never understand.

Sallay came out to visit me one day to see how I was doing. I took him down to Zelly and he looked her over, commenting on how well she looked and how quiet she was. He then stood back for a minute, rubbed his chin thoughtfully, and shot me a sideways glance.

'You know what I think, girl?'

'What do you think, Sallay?'

He rubbed those expert hands over her belly again. 'I think you've got yourself a pregnant camel.'

'What? Pregnant?' I yelled. 'But that's fantastic. No wait, that's not fantastic. What if she has it on the trip?'

Sallay laughed and patted me on the shoulder. 'Believe me, having a baby camel on your trip would be the least of your worries. When it's born, you just tie it up in a sack, hoist it on its mother's back, and within a few days it will trot along behind with the best of them. In fact, it would be a good thing for you, because you can tie the baby up at night and be sure that the mother won't go too far. Could solve one of your main problems, eh? Well, I hope she is, for your sake. Should be a nice little calf too, if that wild black bull I saw her running with was the father.'

By now I knew I had to make a decision about Kate. She had blood poisoning which had carried the infection to her knee, she had lost half her weight, and her roars now were the protests of a fragile and pitiful old lady. I was attending to her three or four times a day, putting a hose in one side

of that knee and watching an arc of pink muck coming out
of a hole in the other side. I procrastinated over destroying
her for two reasons – I just could not believe a simple cut
could kill a camel, and, with Kate gone there would be no
hope of starting the trip and I would be very nearly back
at square one. I eventually decided that I must put the old
girl out of her misery. I felt terribly guilty. She had really
been too old to go through the rigours of vets and saddles
and the separation from her mate on Alcoota. I believe she
actually pined away – lost her will to live. I had often thought
of sending her back but now it was too late. However, I was
determined not to get soppy about it. It was something that
had to be done, and I was even practical enough to sharpen
up my knives so that I could take her beautiful coat and tan
it. I had never used the gun and was more terrified of botch-
ing the whole thing than of actually killing her – I had successfully steeled myself to that. Jenny, who was spending
more and more time with me at Basso's, and who was
becoming an indispensable friend, offered to be with me that
day. 'It's all right really, Jen. I've got it under control, but
if you want to come out that's fine.'

She came. I was in a cold sweat of trepidation. The day
had an unreal washed-out feeling as we walked together over
the hills. It wasn't until we got to Kate that I realized how
hard I had been holding Jenny's hand. I sat Kate down in
a washaway, pointed the rifle at her head, wondering if divine
retribution would have the bullet ricochet back at my own,
and pulled the trigger. I remember the noise of her hitting
the dust with a thud but I must have shut my eyes. I was
not expecting the momentary wave of hysteria that swept
over me then. Jen practically shouldered me home, made me
tea, and then had to leave for work. I was badly shaken. I
had never done anything like that before. Never destroyed
something that had a personality. I felt like a murderer. The
idea of stripping Kate's hide was unthinkable. It was all I
could do to go back to the carcass and stare, wondering at

what I had done. So that was that. No Katie, no trip. Fate again. And all that time and all that money and all that energy, devotion and care, for nothing. Eighteen months had passed down the plug-hole, for nothing.

4

MY DEPRESSION over the shooting of Kate was com-pounded by my escalating terror of Kurt. He seemed so out of control, so close to the edge, that I believed he had the capacity to kill, if not me and Gladdy, then at least my animals. So I had to play his game. Had to let him believe I was no threat – not worth bothering about. He thought Gladdy and I were plotting something, but he didn't ever say as much; his mind turning over like a mill, machinating ways and means of thwarting whatever plans we were concocting.

This debilitating fear, this recognition of the full potential of Kurt's hatred of me, and the knowledge that Kurt could and would hurt me very badly if I displeased him enough, was the catalyst which transformed my vague misery and sense of defeat into an overwhelming reality. The Kurts of this world would always win – there was no standing up to them – no protection from them. With this realization came a collapse. Everything I had been doing or thinking was meaningless, trivial, in the face of the existence of Kurt.

The fear was like a fungus that slowly grew over me and defeated me in the weeks that followed. I went down down down to that state that I had long since forgotten existed. I would stare for hours out my kitchen window, unable to act. I would pick up objects, stare at them, turn them over in my hand, then put them down and wander back to the window. I slept too much, I ate too much. Tiredness over-whelmed me. I waited for the sound of a car, a voice – any-thing. And I tried to shake myself, slap myself, but the energy and strength that I had so taken for granted had leaked out through my fear.

Yet the strange thing was I snapped out of this melancholy the moment a friend arrived. I tried to tell them about it, but the language to describe such a thing belonged to that feeling, so I joked about it instead. Yet I desperately wanted them to understand. They were evidence that reason and sanity still existed and I clung to them as if I were drowning.

Kurt went away on holiday and Gladdy decided to leave while the going was good. I was happy for her; she looked better already. But I knew how much I was going to miss her, and I was frightened of being left on my own with her husband. One night I was up staying with her, as often happened these days when Kurt was away, and Katie's ghost was still inhabiting my room at Basso's. We had both gone to bed hours before but I could not sleep. I was again overcome by a sense of failure. Not just of the trip but a kind of personal failure – the absolute impossibility of ever winning against brute force and domination. I was worrying it over and over, trying to seek a solution, impossible in that state of mind because of its very nature. And then I thought: of course, the perfect way out – suicide. Now, this was not the ordinary chest-beating, why-are-we-born-to-suffer-and-die syndrome, this was something new. It was cold, rational, unemotional. And I wonder now if that's how people usually come to it. Coldly. It was so simple really. I would walk way out bush, sit myself down somewhere, and calmly put a bullet in my brain. Yes, that would do nicely. No mess, no fuss. Just nice clean simple exit. Because no life was better than half-life. I was planning it out, the best place, the best time, when suddenly Gladdy sat bolt upright in the bed opposite me and said, 'Rob, are you all right? Do you want a cup of coffee?' It was the equivalent of a bucket of iced water thrown over someone in hysteria, waking me to the horror of what I was thinking, the enormity of it. I had never been to that point before, and don't think I shall ever have to again. I worked something out that night in my shaky way.

She left a few days later. I inherited her old dog Blue, a

cattle dog whom she had saved from a pound a few weeks before. As we hugged goodbye, she said, 'You know, the moment I saw you, I knew you were going to play some important part in my life. Odd, isn't it?'

Kurt returned shortly afterwards, and his vengeance was matchless. He now had me so terrorized that I slept with a small hatchet under my pillow. He continued to try to sell the place, or at least appeared to. My brother-in-law, a man with more money than sense and more heart than money, heard about this and, to my complete bewilderment, rang Kurt and offered to buy the place for me. At first it seemed like the answer to all my problems, then I realized that it was a crazy idea. We might not be able to resell and I could be stuck looking after it for years. However, if I could keep Kurt on the hook until Gladdy got herself together enough to see a lawyer, that would be a good thing. So there followed a game of cat and mouse with my tormentor. To convince him that I had every intention of buying, I had to spend most of my time up there, pretending to prepare for take-over. There were no holds barred now. I remember Kurt came down to my room at Basso's one morning at about six, ripped all the clothes off my bed, yanked me out and screamed that if I slept in when I had the ranch, the whole thing would be worthless. The murderous light never left his eyes during those weeks. We were involved in a tacit war, both playing games, both desperate to win. He was forcing me to train the young white bull, Bubby, without benefit of nose-line or saddle, something he would never have done in the old days. This meant that I was thrown at least three times a day, and my nerves were shot to bits. The tension of doing this, coupled with the tension of playing a very dangerous game, was taking its toll.

Then one morning I woke to find that he had disappeared overnight, in a puff of dust, like a genie, had sold the place secretly to some station people at half price and disappeared with all the money. He told the buyers that I went along

74

with the ranch and would teach them all they needed to know about camels. They knew precisely nothing. I went to see them. 'Look,' I explained, 'I do not go along with the place, but if you are willing to give me the two camels I want, I will certainly teach you all I know.'

They were pitifully confused. They didn't know who was ripping off whom, or whom to trust. They acquiesced grudgingly, but kept putting off signing the piece of paper. I knew exactly the two camels I wanted, Biddy and Misch-Misch – two females because bulls were such a nuisance and quite dangerous when in season during winter. Once again I was tied to the ranch and beginning to believe that this process of trying to wheedle camels out of non-cooperative people was never-ending. I foolishly taught them enough camel-managing for them to think they didn't need me, then, predictably, they back-pedalled on the deal, offered me money for the work I had done, and dismissed me. 'O.K.,' I thought, 'just wait until something goes wrong, you bastards, then let's see who comes crawling to whom for what.' And when it came, my stroke of great good fortune, it was a little upward spiral of fate that made up for all the downers put together. Dearest Dookie, that most gentle of beasts, took a turn and frightened the socks, shirt, shoes and trousers off the new owner.

Luckily I was there. I had been up at the ranch most of the day, arguing about pieces of paper and money and so on, and watching smugly as the man made mistakes. My heart was hardened. 'Ha, ha,' I sneered to myself, 'suffer or sign.'

When the time came to hobble the camels out at night I felt I had to show him how to do it for the camels' sakes. If he left the hobble leathers too loose, they would slip down over the hock and possibly damage the animal's legs. First, I took out dear quiet Dookie.

'There, you see, in that hole there, and make sure this is never so loose that it can slip over this lump here, understand?'

'Hmmm, yes I see.'

I let the bull go, and turned to fetch the others. Then I heard a strange rumbling sound behind me and glanced over my shoulder and froze in my tracks. I caught a look at the man's face too. The blood had drained to his boots. Dookie had transmogrified. Dookie was coming for me with a decidedly Kurtish look in his eyes which were rolling back into his head like spun marbles. Dookie was making burbling noises and white froth was blowing out the side of his mouth. Dookie was trying to rut some rocks. Dookie was completely berserk. I had come between him and his girlfriends and for the first time in his young life he was taken over by those uncontrollable urges of a bull in season. He began thrashing his head and neck around like a whip. He was trying to gallop at me in his hobbles. He was going to try to knock me down and sit on me and crush the life and blood out of my body.

'Dookie?' I said, backing off. 'Hey, Dook, this is me,' I gasped as I made a bee-line for the gate. I hopped all five feet of it like Pop-Eye after spinach. Dookie was completely oblivious to the man who was still frozen, cowering against the wall of rocks, on the wrong side of the fence. It was me Dookie wanted.

'Get out of there,' I screamed as Dookie tried to bite off my head at the neck. 'For Christ's sake, man, get me the whip, get me the hobble chain, get me the cattle prodder,' I yelled maniacally as Dookie pinned me to my side of the gate with his twisted neck and tried to squash me into a cardboard replica. He was leaning into the fence now, trying to smash it so he could get at me. I could not believe this. This was some nightmare from which I would wake screaming at any moment. My Dookie was a Jekyll and Hyde, a killer, a mad mad mad mad bull. The man was galvanized into action. He brought out all those instruments of torture. A cattle prod throws a huge number of volts, and this I pressed into Dookie's snapping lips while I beat him as hard as I could across the back of the head with the hobble chain. I could

76

barely hear my own whimpering through the fracas. Dookie did not feel a thing. He was like a windmill with teeth. I got away from the gate for a second and my mind crystallized. I raced for some ropes, a wood plank, and an iron bar weighing fifteen pounds. About five feet from the other side of the fence, Dookie's side, was a gum tree. I walked up my side of the fence till I was in line with it. Dookie followed me bellowing and snorting and thrashing. I bent down to his front legs, threw the rope through the hobbles, cleared the fence, and quickly, oh so quickly, brought the rope around the tree and heaved with all my might. I had him tied to the tree by the legs now and I only hoped that all of it would hold. I then proceeded to bash that creature over the back of the neck with the wood, until it snapped, and then with the iron bar. Down he would go, half conscious, then up again to attack. I had the super-human strength you only get when you are in a flat, adrenalin-pumping panic, and fighting for your life. Suddenly, Dookie sat down with a thump, shook his head a few times, and remained sitting quietly grinding his teeth.

I waited a moment, bar poised in mid-air. 'Are you all right, Dookie?' I whispered. I moved up to his head. No reaction. 'Dookie, I'm going to put this nose-line on you now and if you go crazy again, I swear I'll kill you.' Dookie looked at me through his long graceful lashes. Butter wouldn't melt in his mouth. I quietly put the nose-line on him, asked him to stand up, bent down and undid the rope, took off his hobbles, and led him back into his yard. Like a little lamb he went, limping slightly.

I returned to the man. 'Well, ha ha, that's bulls for you,' I said, trying to will a little colour back into my cheeks. I was drenched in sweat and shaking like a leaf in a high wind. His mouth was still open, gawping. We led each other inside and had a solid hit of brandy.

'Do ah, do bulls often act like that?' he said.

'Oh hell yeeees,' I answered, beginning to see the light at

the end of the tunnel. 'Christ, bulls attack like that all the time.' I had him now, I knew what was coming. I was almost overcome with glee. I tried to slather a look of sisterly concern over my face. 'Yeah, you want to keep your kids away from those bulls, that's for sure.'

By nine o'clock I was running down the creek towards home, whooping and shouting and leaping and laughing hysterically. He had sold me the two bulls for seven hundred dollars – money I didn't have but which I could borrow. They weren't the two I would have chosen, but I was in no position to look a gift-camel in the mouth. Dookie, king of kings, and Bub that incorrigible little joker were mine. I had my three camels.

This miraculous turn of events opened a whole new vista of troubles for me. For a start, no matter how far I hobbled Dookie out bush, he would strain his way back to the ranch and terrorize everybody witless. He was harmless when hobbled and side-lined and legally there was nothing they could do, but I knew they were having a rough time and I felt sorry for them. I tied my boy up during the day, and let him go at night with Bub and Zelly, miles out in the hills, his feet chained together closely and cruelly; at six in the morning I would try to get to him before his previous owners did. The man refused to listen to reason. Twice I caught him driving his car full pelt at Dookie's rump, scaring the animal and making him more aggressive than ever, and possibly damaging those hobbled legs beyond repair. One day the man flew at me in a temper.

'You're just fooling around on a bloody holiday while I have to make a living out of these bloody animals,' he said. 'I'm telling you now, if that bull gets anywhere near my place, I'll kill it.'

I saw red then. I had, after all, taught this idiot all he knew and had he been civil I was quite willing to teach him more. He certainly hadn't done badly on the deal. 'And if anything happens to my Dookie, friend, you will wake up one morning and find all your camels missing. Gone out bush for a holiday.' Counter-threatening came quite easily to me now, even though I secretly and guiltily believed him to be right.

This range-war mentality had been developed over the months, years now, until it governed my attitude to the world at large. I was a battleaxe – a product of the frontier. And there were perfectly good reasons for that.

Fullarton had paid me a little visit to suggest that the town wasn't big enough for two camel businesses, should I be deciding to set one up.

On one occasion some people from town came to look over the place in the hope of buying it before the Aboriginal Lands Council could get its black hands on it. They walked straight through my bedroom as if I didn't exist, without even a how you do or a by your leave. I was furious and told them to get out of my house, and next time to have the civility to ask permission before walking through it and taking photographs. They blustered and shouted in return that they would have me thrown out by the health department.

There were also the occasional police visits to contend with. 'Just checking up on how you're doing,' they would say as they made themselves at home and searched the roofless rooms, god knows for what. Molotov cocktails? Heroin? I don't know. A couple of them even threatened to prevent my going on my trip: 'You haven't got a chance, you know, even men have died out there, so why should you rely on station people and us to come and rescue you?'

By this stage Julie, a friend, was living with me. We had taken up a window-cleaning business in town, pedalling in on our bikes with mops and squeegees and methylated spirits. Jenny was soon to come out too. Now that Kurt was gone I did not have to worry about my friends' safety, and I was beginning to understand that being alone got awfully boring sometimes, and that I needed people, wanted them.

Life was changing for me. I was being softened and set on a different tack by my friends; in fact things were now so comfortable I had almost forgotten about the trip. I had previously lived the life of a miserly savage at Basso's. I ate brown rice which I have always hated, and vegetables from my impoverished garden, and then at night after work, when I had brought home the cold meat given to me by the chefs at the restaurant, Diggity, Blue and I would attack it like wolves, all eating together and fighting over the best bits. But with my friends present, there was a reason for being more civilized, easier, pleasanter. Jen was a brilliant gardener, Toly was a superb fix-it man, and Julie was a wizard cook. We lived almost luxuriously. They loved Basso's as much as I did and each gave it an added dimension which made it more of a home. At first this was slightly difficult for me to accept. When you are used to being the queen, it is hard to consider democracy replacing lone rule.

I realized how deep my resistance to change had gone when we were all sitting having tea one afternoon in the back garden. Some travelling hippies arrived. They'd heard about the place down south and were here to stay for a few days' holiday. My hackles immediately rose and I said they couldn't stay. When they had gone, I turned to the others and said, 'How dare they assume they can just walk right in to someone's private home and stay for a holiday, bloody boring insipid recorder-playing, *Jonathan-Livingston-Seagull*-reading, brown-rice-sandwich-eating weeds. Jesus.'

Jenny and Toly looked at me sideways, eyebrows slightly raised, and said nothing. But looks sometimes speak louder than words and I could see that they were thinking something like, 'Intolerant, hypocritical old boiler, you've become what you most dislike.'

So I mulled that one over for a while. I tried to find out the root cause of this meanness in me, apart from the obvious things, like having to fight, at least in Alice Springs, fire with fire. I was surrounded by people who for some reason found my very presence a threat. And had I not been able to stand up to them on their terms, I would be somewhere back on the east coast, my tail between my legs. But it was more than that. For many outback people, the effect of almost total isolation coupled with that all-encompassing battle with the earth is so great that, when the prizes are won, they feel the need to build a psychological fortress around the knowledge and possessions they have broken their backs to obtain. That fiercely independent individualism was something akin to what I was feeling now – the stiffness, the inability to incorporate new people who hadn't shared the same experience. I understood a facet of Alice Springs, and softened towards it, at that moment.

Over the weeks that followed Gladdy's departure, Blue dog had managed to inveigle his way into not only my heart, but Diggity's also. He was a charming old codger, a dog's dog. His primary preoccupations were eating and sleeping; these were followed, in order of preference, by chasing willing female camp dogs, and fighting male camp dogs. At first both Dig and I ordered him outside, but gradually we relented, until Blue was snoring, scratching and snuffling on our nest along with us, on those freezing desert nights. He had life pretty well cased out. He knew what was important and what was not. His fighting urge came to an abrupt end one day when he was almost killed by a pack of irate camp dogs. He licked his wounds for a week, then, with the admirable wisdom of a dog who has lived long, and experienced much, retired into a noble, graceful old age.

I woke one morning early to find him dying on my back porch. He had been poisoned with strychnine. By the time I had collected my wits, he was dead. I cried as I buried him. Dear old Blue did not deserve such a cruel end. There were two thoughts uppermost in my mind – who would be so sick as to do such a thing, and, thank god it wasn't Diggity. I found out then that it was quite common for dogs to be poisoned this way in Alice Springs. Some unknown person had been doing it for twenty years and the police still had no clues. Had I not lived so long in the town, I probably would have been very surprised. As it was, I merely sighed, and thought, of course, what else could one expect of such a place.

It was once again midsummer, the end of the year, and my room at Basso's which had been so icy in winter was now a furnace. It was actually a series of cave-like rooms, all stone, with arched windows and doorways, straw on the cement floor and virtually without furniture. It was a haven for the most enormous cockroaches I have ever done battle with. They were fearless and would rise on their hind legs if confronted. They had me bluffed. As I went in at night with my candle, they would scuttle and scratch their way back into their various holes with a noise that made my skin crawl and my stomach heave. They are the one creature, apart from leeches, that I simply cannot bear. I laid down large quantities of poisonous powder, something I would not normally do, but they thrived on it. They ate it, chomp chomp, for breakfast, lunch and tea and continued to grow like mutated monsters.

And then there were the snakes. Basso's was home to these exquisite creatures – they courted, bred and died there, refusing to be interfered with by humans. Although deadly, they did not bother me half as much as the cockies; I quite liked them in a respectful, distant sort of way, and I always acted on the belief that if you left them alone, they would leave you alone. But Diggity hated them with passion. I worried for her, because she would chase them and try to kill them and although she was very good at it, it would only take one bite to kill her. One night I was sweltering in my little cave reading a book by candlelight, when Diggity began her snake vibrato, a behavioural signal that was unmistakable. Out from under my bed came a small Western Brown, on his way to do business with the world outside. It didn't bother me too much and shortly I blew out my candle and went to sleep. Somewhere in the night I was woken up by Diggity once again, rigid beside me, hair stiff like a warthog, and teeth bared growling. I lit the candle. On the bottom of the bed on the outside of my sheet was yet another snake, dozing. Dig chased it off. I began to feel extremely goose-pimply then and I was too scared of treading on one of the things to get up and block off the door. It took me a few hours to return to sleep. I awoke at about ten in the morning to see Diggity about to pounce on a huge snake slithering under my bed. Three in one night was just too much. I blocked up all possible snake entry holes in my wall, but it was several weeks before I got a decent night's rest.

One continues to learn things in life, then promptly forget them. And I should have known by now that pride always comes before a fall. I was beginning to feel cocky. I was beginning to feel that I was in control of events, self-congratulatory, complacent. Life was good and bountiful. Nothing else could go wrong, statistics were against it. I had had my various runs of bad luck. My friends were around me. I was in no danger. After all I had been through, the discomfort of not being able to get away from Basso's for even a day seemed only the slightest of prices to pay. Toly was spending most of his weekends with us, and we all adored him. He worked as a teacher at Utopia, an Aboriginal-owned cattle station, 150 miles north. And if he whisked Jen away for days at a time, and if I could never go with them because I was chained to the camels, I tried hard not to be envious. They left big empty spaces when they disappeared. Literally hundreds of times we planned ways in which I could get to Utopia, but always some little thing cropped up and I would be unable to go.

One of the little things that often cropped up was that I could spend a whole day tracking my camels. Their footprints would become all mixed up and it was difficult to sort today's from yesterday's. There were six or seven directions in which they would head out to feed, most of these being rocky places where tracking was not easy. They would secrete themselves away in hidden valleys or dense thickets where I could not see them – they blended in so well with the khaki and reds of the landscape. They had bells on, but I swear they held their necks perfectly still and stiff when they smelt me on the wind. When they saw me, of course, it was all, 'Hail fellow, well met. Clang clang.' And, 'What kept you so long?' And, 'How nice to see you, Rob, what tit-bits have you got in your pockets?' It got to the point where, instead of catching them, I could simply unhobble them and watch them gallop and buck all the way home, or else crawl up behind some hump and get a lift. Dookie had lost all his bull-headed silliness with the hot weather, and the three were now an inseparable team. Zelly was plumping out in all the right places and her udder was swelling nicely. Camel gestation is twelve months but I had no idea when the calf was due. They had well-defined relationships to one another. Zeleika was the street-smart, crafty, unfazable, self-possessed leader. She was wiser than the other two put together in the ways of the wild. She was the Prime Minister, while Dookie was nominally king, but if anything untoward happened he was the first to hide behind her skirts. And Bub was in love with Dookie. Dookie was his hero, and he was quite brave as long as he had Dookie's rear end in front of his nose. He totally lacked any desire or capacity to lead. If Dookie was Hardy, then Bub was definitely his Laurel.

It was on one of these mornings, after I had tracked them down the creek, that something happened which made me believe the world had stopped. Bub was lying on his side. I thought he was sunbathing so I sat next to his head and said, 'Arra (get going), you lazy little sod, it's time to go home,' and put a lolly in his mouth. (They liked jelly-beans and long sticks of licorice best.) Instead of leaping up to see what other goodies I had, he continued to lie there, chewing the sweet half-heartedly, and I knew something was dreadfully wrong.

I got him up and saw that he was standing on three legs. I lifted the foot and checked the soft pad underneath – there was a gash, with a wedge of glass stuck in it. Kurt had had to shoot one of his animals because of just such a wound. These pads were meant for soft sand, not sharp objects, and were the most vulnerable part of the animal. Inside the pad is a squishy, elastic sort of bladder; when pressure is put on the foot, any hole will therefore widen. It is impossible to keep them off a leg, because they need that pressure for circulation. The cut had gone straight through the bottom of the foot, and up through the hairy top surface. I thought he was finished. I sat there and wept on that river-bank for a good half hour. I howled and howled. Camels are such hardy animals, I thought, it's just sheer perverse and cruel fate that has caused this to happen. Who is it up there who hates me? I shook my fist and howled some more. Diggity licked my face and Zelly and Dook bent down to offer their condolences. I had Bub's big ugly head in my lap. He continued to eat jelly-beans, lapping up the attention and playing Camille admirably. I pulled myself together, took the glass out of the foot as carefully as possible, and led him slowly home. The vets I knew were out of town, I discovered when I pedalled in to the clinic, and a new inexperienced boy was doing the locum for them. He came out to Basso's to look at Bubby, stood six feet away from the camel, said, 'Hmm, he's got a cut in his foot all right.' And gave me some injections for tetanus. Not much help. I had met two women at the restaurant, Kippy and Cherie, who were terminal animal lovers and who managed a veterinary practice in Perth. I pedalled in to work that night and told them what had happened. They came out the next day, their last in town, lanced the top hole so that it would drain, and prescribed hot water and Condy's crystals. The foot was to be immersed in a bucket of the stuff and I was to massage the wound, cleaning it out thoroughly. Wonderful women, they gave me hope again.

Toly and Jenny then built me a large holding yard out the back of Basso's, with old star pickets, scraps of wire and netting, and various other assortments of stuff which we picked up here and there. It was an excellent yard. I kept Bubby in there, treated his foot three times a day and prayed. I had now modified the treatment, with the help of the town surgeon, to inserting an infant's nasal feeding tube into the top of the cut and dousing out the whole wound with strong antiseptic. This went on for a few weeks, and I could never be sure if the foot was healing or if rotten flesh was growing in there like mushrooms. Some days I had hope, others I was once again in the pits, whimpering for Jenny, Toly, Julie or the town surgeon to come and pull me out. Bub did not enjoy the treatments and neither did I. 'Keep that bloody foot still, you little mongrel, or I'll chop it off at the knee.' He gradually came round. Soon the foot looked healthy enough for me to let him go with the others, who had been hanging around the house like bad smells, putting their long necks into the kitchen, or standing expectantly, eyes greedily bulging every time we sat in the garden for a cup of tea. My friends were falling in love with them as much as I was, though they wrongly accused me of projecting human attributes on to them. We laughed at them for hours. They were better to watch than a Marx Brothers movie.

And then one bright sunny day it happened. They disappeared. Into the wild blue yonder, just like that, poof. No camels, no adorable do-no-wrong beasties. They had deserted me, the ungrateful, cunning, fickle, deceitful two-timing traitors – pissed off. Headed for the hills as fast as their hobbled legs could carry them. It was quite usual for them to wander short distances but this time it was serious. Maybe they were bored, and looking for adventure. But I suspected Zeleika was the culprit. She was going home thank you very much, leading the others back to her herd where there were no such things as saddles and work. She was not as easily conned and bribed with hand-outs and cuddles as the others. Not as spoilt. And she had not for a minute forgotten the sweetness of freedom.

I headed out as usual that morning with Dig to find their tracks. It took me about an hour to pick them up – they were heading almost due east, out into the wild hills. I followed for a couple of miles, thinking that they would be just around the next corner and imagining I could hear bells tinkling not too far away. There is a little wedge-bill bird in that country that sounds just like a camel-bell, and it often had me fooled. It was getting very hot, so I took off my shirt, put it under a bush and told Dig to wait there for me until I got back, which I thought would be about half an hour at most. She was already panting and thirsty. She hated being left behind but it was for her own good, and she obeyed. I was now into rough uninhabited country – there was no one and nothing for countless miles. I was vaguely wondering what on earth could have induced the camels to wander this far, this fast. But I wasn't worried. I was hot on their trail – their droppings were still moist. I could see from the tracks that one of them had broken a leather strap and was dragging a chain. And I walked. And I walked. And I walked. I crossed the Todd River and immersed my boiling body in a cool pool and drank as much as I could. I wet my trousers and wound them around my head. And still I walked. My speed slowed down now as I was in stonier country. And all the while I was thinking, 'What's happening here? Has someone chased them? What's going on, for Christ's sake?' I walked thirty miles that day, tantalized by the belief that they were just a minute ahead of me, but I heard nothing but phantom bells dinging inside my own skull, and saw nary a camel. I returned late at night to find poor Diggity almost fretted away, still sitting under the bush, her pink tongue dry as a bone, and a groove of worried dog-prints a hundred yards in the home direction, and a hundred yards in my direction. But she had stayed, faithful creature, despite what must have been an unbearable anxiety and an equally unbearable thirst. She

87

was so relieved to see me, she almost turned herself inside out.

The next day I left better prepared. I reached yesterday's point fairly quickly – it was only about eight miles as the crow flies – to find that the tracks petered out a mile or two later into rocky escarpments. I went home and rang up all the station owners out in that direction. No, they had not seen any camels, they usually shot them anyway. But they would keep a look-out for mine.

Then I found some generous people in town with a light aircraft who offered to take me up into the clouds to look for them. Julie came with me. I knew vaguely where they would be, I thought, then realized that if they could go that far in one day, they could go seven times as far, in any direction, in the week that had passed. I felt despondent. We flew in a grid pattern, much lower than regulations ordained, for about an hour. Not a sign.

'There they are,' I screamed, strangling the co-pilot from behind.

'No, donkeys.'

'Oh.'

And as I sat, straining my eyes out the window of the plane, something rose to the surface which had been buried since the moment I decided on this trip, more than two years before. I didn't have to go through with it. Losing the camels was the perfect excuse. I could pack my bags and say, 'Oh, well, I did my best,' and go on home, free of this obsession, this compulsion. I had never really considered doing it of course. I had conned myself into believing I would but no one would be crazy enough to do such a thing. It was danger-ous. Now, even my camels would be happy, and that would be that.

And I recognized then the process by which I had always attempted difficult things. I had simply not allowed myself to think of the consequences, but had closed my eyes, jumped in, and before I knew where I was, it was impossible to renege. I was basically a dreadful coward, I knew that about myself. The only possible way I could overcome this was to trick myself with that other self, who lived in dream and fantasy and who was annoyingly lackadaisical and unpractical. All passion, no sense, no order, no instinct for self-preservation. That's what I had done, and now that cowardly self had discovered an unburnt bridge by which to return to the past. As Renata Adler writes in *Speedboat*:

> I think when you are truly stuck, when you have stood still in the same spot for too long, you throw a grenade in exactly the spot you were standing in, and jump, and pray. It is the momentum of last resort.

Yes, exactly, only now, after all this time, I had discovered that the grenade was a dud, and I could hop right back to that same old spot which was safety. The excruciating thing was that those two selves were now warring with each other. I wanted desperately to find those camels, and I wanted desperately not to find them.

The pilot snapped me back to the present dilemma.

'Well, what do you want to do? Shall we call it a day?'

I would have said yes, but Julie talked us into one more run.

And on that final turn, there they were. Julie spotted them, we took a position and flew back to the runway. And that was the point at which all my disparate selves agreed to do the trip.

5

WHILE IT seemed relatively easy to fix the position of the camels from the air, once on the ground and surrounded by a confusion of little creeks, hills and washaways that I had not noticed from the plane, actually finding the beasts was quite difficult. Jenny and Toly came with me. We drove the long-suffering old Toyota as far as we could into the stony scrub, then set out on foot with the dogs who immediately took off after phantom leopards and moon-tigers. This desire of Diggity's to hunt everything except camels was a bone of contention between us. I had been trying to train her to help me track them but she was not remotely interested. Her all-consuming passions were kangaroos and rabbits and these she would chase for hours on end, bounding over clumps of spinifex, head turning this way and that in mid-air like Nureyev. She was beautiful to watch but never actually caught anything.

I had decided to cut across as many sandy creeks and washaways as possible, hoping to find their tracks easily. We walked to the top of a hill to see if we could spy them but there was nothing but the still, olive-green witchetty bushes, and miles of broken red rock and dust. I wanted to go down a different side of the hill to meet up with another creek-bed, so down we traipsed, stumbling along the curves of the spurs where the going was easiest. The sun was almost directly overhead. And when we got to the bottom of the hill, and into this new creek which I thought would take us out into the flatter lands beyond, something very peculiar happened. There were fresh human footprints going up the creek in the opposite direction. Everyone stopped short. For a tiny flash of a second, I thought, 'Now who on earth could be out here in the middle of nowhere walking down this very creek on a summer's day at noon?' Then, the knowledge that they were our own prints, that not only had we arrived back at the place which should, by all rights and reckonings, be 90 degrees to our right, but that we had somehow ended up going in the opposite direction, hit me like a smack on the back of the head. I sat down. I felt as if bits of computer tape and smoke and sparks would come out of my ears any minute. What happened to north, south, east and west? Where did they go? Only seconds before I had had such a firm and confident grip on them. There was some ill-concealed snickering and nudging going on behind me.

It was a good lesson perhaps, but it chilled me to the bone. I had visions of my ending up a baked carcass, all golden crisp, lying in some ditch in the middle of the desert, or arriving back in Alice Springs after months of wandering, thinking I was in Wiluna. Someone had just given me a medical pamphlet on the symptoms of dying of thirst (a sensitive, well-thought-out gift, I felt, and always handy) and it looked like just about the worst way you could go, physical torture in medieval dungeons included. I didn't want to die of thirst ever. I realized how much I had relied on tracking or Diggity to get me home in the past, instead of training myself to take mental bearings. This, along with many other survival mechanisms, would definitely have to be worked on.

When we did at last find the camels, they were overcome with guilt, shame, and a profound desire to go home. They had lost most of their hobble straps, two of their bells, and had spent two or three days walking up and down a fenceline which they found stood between them and the general direction of Basso's. Camels are home bodies. When they fixate on a place or an area, you can be 99 per cent sure that they will always try to get back to it. Dookie and Bub had obviously overridden Zelly who wasn't about to take off on her own. They hung around me like flies, shuffling their feet, looking embarrassedly at the ground, or coyly through their elegant lashes, acting apologetic and loving and remorseful, then I rode them back. Bub's foot was almost completely healed.

Now that the trip was real, now that I knew it was actually going to happen, I was horrified by the amount of work I had to do to prepare. And I was at a complete loss as to how I could lay my hands on the money to buy equipment and so on. The camels took up so much of my time that it was impossible to get more work in town. I could borrow money from family or friends but I decided against that. I had always been poor, always lived on a shoe-string, and if I did borrow the money it could take me years to pay it back. Besides, I hated being in debt, and it seemed unfair to ask my family to donate money to a project which, I knew, already had them worried half into the grave. And most of all, I wanted to do the thing on my own without outside interference or help. An attempt at a pure gesture of independence.

While I was sitting at Basso's, fretting, worrying and chewing my nails up to the elbow, a young man, a photographer, arrived with a friend of mine. He took a few photos of us and of the camels but, for an event which had such far-reaching effects, the meeting was inauspicious to the point where I had forgotten about it the next day.

But Rick came again, this time for dinner with a group of people from town. And once more, I was so preoccupied that only a few things stand out in my memory. He was a nice enough boy – rather Jimmy Olsenish I thought – one of those amoral immature photojournalists who hop from trouble spot to trouble spot on the globe without ever having time to see where they are or be affected by it. He had the most beautiful hands I had ever seen on anybody – long tapering fingers that wrapped around his cameras like frogs' feet; and I remember vaguely some tepid arguments concerning the morality of and justification for taking clichéd photographs of Aborigines in the creek-bed for *Time* magazine when you knew precisely nothing about them, and didn't much want to. And, oh yes, I remember he stared at me a lot, as if I were a little bit touched. Just those few things, nothing more remains.

He also talked me into writing to *National Geographic* for sponsorship. I had tried this years before, only to receive a polite refusal. But when they left that night, I wrote what I drunkenly considered a brilliant letter, and thought no more about it.

Before I went to Alice Springs, I had never held a hammer, had never changed a light-bulb, sewn a dress, mended a sock, changed a tyre, or used a screwdriver. I had never, in all my life, done anything which required manual dexterity, patience, or a sense of functional design. And here I was, confronted with the problem of designing and building a complete pack, not to mention saddles. Kurt, Sallay and Dennis had taught me a lot but not enough. I was soon to discover that the method known as trial and error was a vastly overrated way of learning to do something. I could not afford either the wastage of materials or the loss of time and my sanity. I was still broke, still scrimping and saving to buy necessities, so that even one ruined rivet got me where it hurt most – in the pocket. I had to weld a saddle frame for Zeleika which would fit, then make three leather pads stuffed with barley straw and lash them to the frame. I needed girths, breast-plates, cruppers and various extra bars and hooks to attach the gear to. The other two saddles had to be redesigned and on top of all that there were six canvas bags, four leather bags, water canteens, bedrolls, specially designed pack covers that could be lashed to the whole thing, map holder and more to think about. It drove me to distraction and despair. Luckily, Toly came to my rescue. He had a natural gift for making things work. How I envied his brain. For hour after hour I would sit outside, fiddling and whimpering over bits of canvas and webbing and leather and copper rivets and plastic and so on, often screaming with frustration and throwing bits of stuff around in a blind fury of incompetence

93

and impatience. Toly said to me one day, after one of these outbursts had ended in temper-tantrum tears which soaked into his shoulder, 'Rob, the secret of this business is that you must learn to love the rivet.'

Of all the things I had to cope with before and after the trip, this learning to make and fix things was the most excruciating. It was a slow and agonizing process but gradually the fogs of ignorance and clumsiness cleared. I began to look at machines without experiencing instant brain-fade, and to work out how they functioned. This no-woman's-land of tools, machinery and so on began to make sense to me. It was all still fiddly, time-consuming and boring, and it still gave me ulcers, but it was no longer completely unintelligible. I have Toly to thank for that. If I never actually learnt to love the rivet, I at least learnt how to tolerate it.

The many and various pressures on me were beginning to manifest themselves in bouts of moodines, despair, whingeing, and the wringing of hands. Jen and Toly thought I might crack if I didn't get away for a while, and eventually talked me into taking a week's holiday. It took them a few days to convince me that it was possible, and that the camels would not necessarily die just because I wasn't there to fuss over them. We put Zeleika in the yard; Jen and Toly would go out each day while I was away to collect feed for her, and I was placated into believing that I had nothing to worry about. But wouldn't it be my luck, after spending all that time with them without even a day's break, that that was the week Zeleika decided to give birth. I received the telegram and sped back to Alice as if I was being chased by wasps, to find the most endearing, beautiful, glossy, black, spindly, lovable little calf, tottering around after his mum, who stubbornly refused to let anyone near him. It took me a day or two to convince Zelly that I wasn't going to harm her firstborn; it took a little longer with Goliath. He had his mother's brains and his father's easy good looks and he was born a fighting handful – cheeky, pushy, self-centred, demanding, petulant, arrogant, spoilt, and delightful. He eventually settled down enough for me to be able to put the halter Jen had made for him on his head permanently. And from that day I began picking up his legs, tickling him all over, placing bits of cloth on his back and tying him up, for just ten minutes at a time, to a tree in the yard. I let Zelly go and kept the calf inside – a perfect arrangement for all concerned except Goliath who would bellow his lungs out until his mother came back to feed him.

Everything seemed to be coming together at a break-neck, if erratic pace. The two bulls had to be castrated as I would be travelling in winter and didn't fancy another bout with either Dookie or Bub. I had decided to leave in March, the beginning of autumn. As it looked as if the Lands Council was at last getting Basso's, and as Jenny and Toly had to get back to Utopia, we planned a trial run there with the camels and gear, for January, merely a month ahead. Sallay cut the bulls for me. It was done without anaesthetic and had me quivering and wringing my hands with sympathetic pain. The bulls were trussed up with ropes like plucked chickens, rolled over and then slash slash, scream scream, the gruesome job was done. Two weeks later it became apparent that Dookie was at the gates of death with an infection. I called on my friend the vet, and he came out to remove the huge lumps of stuff with emasculators. We drugged the camel, like Kate, until he was unconscious, then the vet showed me what to do. He pulled out the tubes, now swollen to the size of yams, and cut them off as high as he could. Dookie came immediately to consciousness with the pain. Then came the interminable terramycin shots. The vet agreed with me that a walk to Utopia would help the wounds to drain so preparations were now in earnest.

Both the camels and I were totally inexperienced at packing up and going on long journeys. My panic and irritability reached absurd heights. The weather didn't help – 130 degrees in the sun. The gear on which I had lavished so much fetishistic care looked, in the cruel light of practicality, ridiculous. I was gibbering by the time we decided to leave. We had planned it for six in the morning while the air was still breathable and didn't scorch the lungs like butt ends. At eleven I was still running around like the proverbial headless chicken, and Toly and Jenny were alternately trying to placate and keeping well out of my way. Eventually it all looked correct. The saddles were on, all nicely padded with sheepskins and blankets. The pack was distributed evenly and it looked relatively workable.

I tied the animals, who were by now extremely toey, together, and went inside for a final cup of tea and a last loving glance at Basso's. Ada was with us and in tears, which did nothing for my confidence. 'Oh my daughter, please don't go, stay here with us. You're going to perish out there for sure.' A camel commotion started up outside and I bounded out of Ada's arms to see, to my horror, that the three were in a complete tangle and terrified out of their wits. It was a total shambles. Ropes and camels' heads and bits of ripped pack were jumbled together in a turk's-head knot. It took half an hour to sort it out. At last we were on our way, and we hugged Ada and waved confidently as we moved out into the blazing sun.

Inside three hours, we were back again. Zeleika had stumbled and almost pulled the saddle off Dookie who was in front of her, and two of the canvas bags had ripped because I had not thought of reinforcing the ring handles with leather from the inside. I spent another full day working out how the animals should be tied together: the answer was, with a rope running from the neck of the one in front to the halter of the one behind, the rope passing through the girth, and a nose-line only attached to the saddle in front to keep them from hanging back. So that solved that problem. The canvas bags Toly helped me fix. We were off and once again we waved confidently to Ada who was once again in tears.

It took us eight days of unspeakable hell to walk to Utopia,

10–11   Toly, Jenny and I made a trial run with the camels 150 miles
north of Alice Springs to Utopia, an Aboriginal-owned cattle station.

12   At last I set off through the Macdonnell Ranges, the oldest mountains in the world, from Glen Helen, 80 miles west of Alice Springs.

150 miles away through vicious and distorting summer. The first day was almost comical in its absurdity. The road leading out of Alice was narrow, twisted and perilous with huge lorries hurtling along it, and if there was one thing that camels hated it was anything bigger than them that moved. So I decided to cut through the back country and meet up with the road further along where it wasn't so diabolically dangerous. Fine. Only to do that we had to penetrate dense scrub, scale rocky escarpments, stumble over huge boulders and sweat and struggle and panic. If Jenny and Toly remained infuriatingly calm and placid it was only because they didn't fully understand how unlikely it was that we might make it. Nor how devoid of warning are most cataclysmic events. To my utter amazement, and to their gloating triumph, we made seventeen miles that day unscathed. This minor victory did nothing to alleviate my pessimism – we still had a long way to go.

The next day it became apparent that two of the saddles would have to be drastically altered. Dookie's shoulder was rubbed white, and one of the pads of Zelly's saddle kept slipping out. She was a bag of bones by then – she was worrying herself into a skeleton. I did not know that our method of travel was extremely hard on the camels. We were breaking camp at four in the morning, walking until ten, resting in the shade until four, then continuing until eight at night. This was not only tiring them but breaking into their favourite feeding times. They were unused to going without water, and were drinking five gallons a day each and more if they were given it. I was beginning to think all those stories about desert animals were preposterous myths. Jenny and Toly took turns in bringing up the rear with the Toyota. We wouldn't have made it without that vehicle. I dumped Dookie's saddle in there and for the rest of the trip he had an easy time of it.

Living on one's nerves and expecting every moment to produce a horrendous catastrophe is one thing – doing it in

130-degree heat is quite another. Hell must be something like that. By nine o'clock the heat would be so immense, so overwhelming that it would bend the mind a little, but we pushed on religiously for ten a.m., knowing that what we were experiencing at nine a.m. was relatively icy. Then we would begin searching for a spot to rest in – usually some cement drain-pipe beside a melted and shimmering tarred road – and there we would gasp for the allotted number of hours, with wet towels thrown across our burning bodies and sucking on oranges and tepid water canteens. It was not easily forgettable. Toly and Jenny were marvellous. They did not once complain (probably because they couldn't get a complaint in edgeways) and, to my constant amazement, they seemed actually to be enjoying themselves.

We arrived at Utopia to the welcoming sound of children shouting and hundreds of emaciated mangy camp-dogs howling. The last part of the trip had been almost pleasant, walking along wide white sand-rivers with tall gums to shade us, and dipping our broiled bodies in bore tanks. It had ironed out everything that was wrong with the saddles, gear and me, albeit the hard way, and as such it was a godsend. The work of readjustment and redesign would be enormous I knew, but not insurmountable.

I spent several weeks at Utopia, a beautiful, rich, 170-square-mile cattle property which had been given over to the Aboriginal people under the more generous Labour Government. Contrary to negative press reports, they were managing the property very well, although none of them could hope to get rich as the proceeds had to be divided up among about four hundred people. There were half a dozen whites there, mostly involved in teaching or health work. It was one of the most successful Aboriginal communities in the Territory. The country was flat, grassy, covered in tall scrub in places, dotted with lakes, and through it ran the Sandover River, an enormous white sandy bed which swelled to a red raging torrent when the rains came.

I lived in two silver ovens, laughingly referred to as caravans, with Jenny and Toly, repeating the fiasco of the preceding weeks only on a higher, more finely tuned level of borderline panic. I struggled and dithered with saddles until I thought them perfect or useless. I lost camels, tracked them and found them again. I practised holding my ostentatious compass when nobody was looking. I stared bewildered at topographical maps and tried not to think of certain medical pamphlets. I made lists of lists of lists, then started all over again. And if I did something that wasn't on a list, I would promptly write it on one and cross it out, with the feeling of having at least accomplished something. I walked in my sleep into Jenny and Toly's room one night and asked them if they thought everything was going to be all right.

And I was accused by a visiting politico of being a bourgeois individualist. 'Oh my god, not a bourgeois individualist,' I thought, as I slunk away to my room, to brood in front of the mirror and bite my nails. For one who had associated herself with the left for years, it was the political equivalent of having V.D. I had never been a political animal, even in the heyday of the 1960s, although I had tried. I lacked two essential ingredients. Courage and conviction. This had left me feeling vaguely guilty, a carry-over from when people (including myself) had carried banners stating that if you weren't part of the solution, you were part of the problem.

I had a long session with the mirror that afternoon, trying to find out if I was a bourgeois individualist or not. Perhaps if I had taken along a company of people and made it a communal camel trip, it would have met with approval? No, that would merely have been liberalism, wouldn't it? Revisionist at best. Heaven forbid. You can't win.

All right then, what is an individualist? Am I an individualist because I believe I can take control of my own life? If so, then yes, I was definitely that. All right, bourgeois. 'A person preferring safety, comfort, illusion, to the hazards and adventures of revolution.' Well, I supposed it all depended on what you defined as the revolution. And what you considered safe and comfortable. At least part of the revolution had become an effort to puzzle out the very nature of our collective madness. But this was very close to neurosis and paranoia. Which, as everybody knew, was bourgeois.

This preoccupation with whether I was a good guy or a bad guy gradually faded over the next week or so as I watched, antennae out, my Marxist friend perform. He was incredibly bright, with a brain twice the size and weight of a pumpkin. I found him attractive and at the same time he frightened me. I was insanely jealous of his I.Q. and the way in which he could use the traditionally masculine language of the political intelligentsia to win any argument, and to produce an impenetrable aura of dominance and power around him. He saw any entry into the morbid internal landscape as, traditionally at least, the realm of the female. He saw it as counter-productive.

Of course, then I understood – anything that smacked of mental struggle, any confession of weakness that might be termed 'indulgence' was bourgeois, reactionary, anti-political. Maybe this was why (and I had seen this so often, and marvelled at it, puzzled over it) many politically oriented men – that is, rational, clever, articulate, intellectual, competent, dedicated, revolutionary, verbally aggressive men – found it so difficult to face, or come to terms with, or admit, their own sexism. Because it involved the painful self-indulgence of turning inward, of recognizing in oneself the enemy. While I knew that it is essential for women to become politically articulate, I also believed it might be a good idea for men to understand and use what has, up to now, been the perceptive language commonly attributed to the female.

As it turned out, my friend's plans for Utopia met with some successes and some failures: the successes because many of his ideas for social change were brilliant and applicable, the failures because he approached Aboriginal people and their situation with a missionary zeal and allowed his political eals for making a Utopia of Utopia to override a true perception of what was actually happening there, and what the people themselves wanted and needed. When his relationship with the people became difficult and complex for him, when the older ones did not trust him or like him, he translated this as their being 'reactionary'. And because of his subtle verbal bullying, he missed out on valuable information that would have been given him by, in particular, Jenny, who usually remained totally silent when he was in the room discussing the future of Utopian blacks. She was made to feel like an inarticulate dodo, and our friend never knew what a wealth of experience and ideas he could have tapped.

He left months later, defeated, and wrote me a long letter saying that at last he understood what I was doing, and that sitting on a sandhill somewhere, contemplating my navel, was not so bad after all. But that was not what I was doing. Once again, I got that nasty, creeping-up-behind-me feeling that I was biting off more than I wanted to chew. Why was everyone so goddamn affected by this trip, adversely or otherwise? Had I stayed back home, studying half-heartedly or working in gambling clubs or drinking at the Royal Exchange Pub and talking about politics – that would have been quite acceptable. I would not have been up for all these astounding projections. So far, people had said that I wanted to commit suicide, that I wanted to do penance for my mother's death, that I wanted to prove a woman could cross a desert, that I wanted publicity. Some begged me to let them come with me; some were threatened, jealous or inspired; some thought it a joke. The trip was beginning to lose its simplicity.

I was at Utopia that I received a return air ticket to Sydney and a cable saying, 'Of course we are most interested ...' from *National Geographic*. Now, all this time I had known, or rather, one of me had known, that they would accept my proposal. How could they not? I had written such a cajoling,

confident letter. Of course I must take the money and run
I had no choice. I needed hand-made water canteens, a new
saddle, three pairs of stalwart sandals, not to mention foo
and pocket money. I also knew at some level that it mean
the end of the trip as I had conceived it: knew that it w
the wrong thing to do – a sell-out. A stupid but unavoidab
mistake. It meant that an international magazine would b
interfering – no, not overtly, but would have a vested intere
in, would therefore be a subtle, controlling factor in, wh
had begun as a personal and private gesture. And it mean
that Rick would have to be around occasionally to tak
pictures – something I put out of my mind immediately, sa
ing that he would only come for a day or two at a time, an
then only three times during the trip. I would hardly noti
his presence. But I knew that this would alter irrevocab
the whole texture of what I wanted to do, which was to b
alone, to test, to push, to unclog my brain of all its extraneou
debris, not to be protected, to be stripped of all the soci
crutches, not to be hampered by any outside interferen
whatsoever, well meant or not. But the decisions had alrea
been made. Practicality had won the day. I had sold a gre
swatch of my freedom and most of the trip's integrity f
four thousand dollars. That's the breaks.

The night before I was to wing my way south, we
gathered in the caravan with the object of fitting me out f
the journey. Julia, a friend of Jenny's, was there too, and
played dressing-up with their clothes. All I had were o
baggy men's bowling trousers, ten-year-old bright re
patent-leather dancing pumps, shirts you could spit throug
sarongs with holes in the wrong places, derelict runnir
shoes, and a couple of dresses stained with all manner of cam
excreta. We agreed that arriving at a posh hotel for a cor
ference with the heads of *National Geographic* dressed like th
would be a bit too authentic. They might decide I was a b
risk, too much of a loony tune. So I tizzed myself up in tig
jeans and whip-chic high-heeled suicide boots. It did nothi

or my confidence. I gathered my maps together and tucked
hem impressively and efficiently under my arm, so as to
ppear capable and sure of what I was doing, then realized
hat I didn't know very much about the country I was about
o go over, should they ask me any embarrassing questions.
decided to fake it.

I suffered during that dress rehearsal. My friends clapped
ands to foreheads and groaned theatrically. I hadn't even
lanned out the route coherently yet. And I suffered. I
uffered that sickening, palm-sweating, pre-exam terror all
he way to Sydney and right through the two hours with
Rick, right up to the moment when I walked into the bar
o meet these extraordinary Americans who were going to
ive me money for nothing – and then I switched into cool,
uave little-miss-has-it-all-together-and-you-might-be-
ucky-enough-to-get-some 1977. The interview took fifteen
ninutes and then everyone agreed that it was a fascinating
dea and I obviously knew a great deal about the country
nd yes, *Geographic* would send me the cheque very soon and
ow charming to meet you my dear, we look forward to
eeing you in Washington when you come to write the story
nd what a marvellous book it would make have you
hought of writing a book dear and good luck goodbye.

'Rick, do you mean to tell me they've actually said yes?'
'Yes, they've said yes.'
'Rick, do you mean to tell me it's that easy?'
(Laughing) 'You were great. Really. You didn't look
cared at all.'

My hysterical cackle kept up for about two hours. I was
n an untouchable high. I had sprouted metaphorical wings.
he trip was real. The last hurdle had been cleared with flying
olours. I hooted and clapped Rick on the back. I drank mar-
aritas and tipped waiters. I beamed at elevator men. I sur-
rised hotel maids with my cheery hellos. I swung down
King's Cross like a million dollars. And then I slowly col-
apsed. Like a bicycle tyre with a slow leak.

What had I done?

Rick was flabbergasted at the mood change – from th
dizzy heights of joyous success to the gloomy pits of hideou
doubt and self-hating in one hour. Rick tried to comfor
Rick tried to placate, Rick tried to reason. But how coul
I tell him that he was part of the problem? That he was
nice guy to talk to but I didn't particularly want him or hi
Nikons or his hopelessly romantic notions along on my trip
I can deal with pigs so easily, but nice people always confoun
me. How can you tell a nice person that you wish they wer
dead, that they'd never been born, that you wish they woul
crawl away into some hole and expire? No, not that, merel
that you wish fate had never caused you to meet. In retro
spect, I should never have allowed myself to see Rick as
fellow human being at all. I should always have regarded hir
as a necessary machine without feelings, a camera in fact. Bu
I didn't. Rick was part and parcel of my trip willy-nilly an
I kicked myself for allowing it to happen. I should have lai
down the law then and there. I should have said, 'Rick, yo
may come out three times for three or four days at a stretc
and I want you involved in this thing as little as possible an
that's that.' But as usual I let the situation play itself out.
allowed my brain and will to put off till tomorrow wha
should have been done today, and said nothing.

Rick had not been through the preparations, did not com
prehend what had gone before, did not perceive that I wa
as feeble a human being as any other, did not understand wh
I wanted to do it, and therefore projected his own emotiona
needs on to the trip. He was caught up in the romance c
the thing – the magic – a side-effect I had not expected, bu
one which I had seen in many people, even my close friend
And Rick wanted to record this great event, my traipsin
from point A to point B. My mistake in choosing Ric
became apparent to me. I should have chosen some hard ca
loused typical photographer whom I could be nasty, viciou
and cruel to without a trace of conscience. Rick had an ou

standing quality, apart from his practised lovableness, and that was his naïvety. A fragility, a kind of introverted sweetness and perceptiveness that is rare enough in men, and virtually unique in successful photographers. I liked him. And I realized that he needed this trip perhaps as much as I did. And that was the burden. Instead of getting away from all responsibility to people, I was obviously heading straight into a heavy one. And I felt robbed.

I flew back to Alice in a lather of conflicting emotions. Was I being too precious about this thing? Why shouldn't I share it with people? Was I a selfish mealy-mouthed little child? A bourgeois individualist even? Suddenly it seemed as if this trip belonged to everybody but me. Never mind, I said, when you leave Alice Springs it will all be over. No more loved ones to care about, no more ties, no more duties, no more people needing you to be one thing or another, no more conundrums, no more politics, just you and the desert, baby. And so I pushed it all down into the dim recesses of my mind, there to fester and grow like botulism.

I came home to a monumental flood. The 150 miles to Utopia was a red swirling river and I tried twice in four-wheel drives to get there.

I eventually made it, walking the last six miles in water up to my thighs. When it rains out there, it rains. The camels had disappeared once again, and it had been too wet for anyone to follow them. We waited a few days, and after tracking them with the vehicle, we spotted them high up on a hill, freaked out of their tiny minds, and stir-crazy with fear. Camels cannot handle mud. Their feet are not designed for it. They bog in it hopelessly or their feet skid out from under them and they can crack their pelvises. Conditions like this always worry them. Besides, they were away from home and in times of stress I believe they felt it strongly. They had been heading south, back to Alice Springs.

The cheque arrived. I set a departure date. I commissioned a traditional Afghani pack saddle from Sallay. I bought equipment and food. I arranged transport for the camels back to Alice Springs. My family wrote saying they would come out and say goodbye. People gave me gifts for the journey and everyone, everyone, seemed to be involved in a mounting excitement. As if we all suddenly believed it was true, that I was actually going to do it, after having just played a two-year game of pretend, or as if we had participated together in a dream, and had just woken up to find it real. The preparations had been, in a sense, the most important part of the event. From the day the thought came into my head 'I am going to enter a desert with camels' to the day I felt the preparations to be completed, I had built something intangible but magical for myself which had rubbed off a little on to other people, and I would probably never have the opportunity to do anything quite as demanding or as fulfilling as that ever again.

I tracked the camels back to the ranch. New people had bought it and they were more than willing to let the beasties stay in the yards for a few days. Dookie, Bub and Goliath had never been on a cattle truck before, so were gullibly easy to load. I left Zelly till last, knowing she would balk and hoping she would eventually follow the others. I breathed a sigh of relief at the end of it. I had never loaded camels either and I wasn't sure whether I should tie them down or not. I carpeted the floor with sand and envisaged broken camel legs sticking through the bars at the side. We hadn't gone ten miles when Dookie decided he didn't like hurtling along rough dirt roads in trucks at fifty m.p.h. any more and tried to jump out. Whoops. For the rest of the journey I sat precariously on the roof of the cabin, alternately bashing him over the head screaming, 'Whoosh, whoosh!' and stroking his sweaty neck and crooning loudly above the whistling of the wind, 'Take it easy, little camel, it will all be over soon, do stop bellowing now please, there's a good boy.'

'AAAAHHHHHHHHHHHHH! WHOOSH, WHOOSH, YOU BASTARD!'

Their shit had turned to water by the time we got there. So had mine.

I had given myself a week in Alice to tidy up all last-minute details. That involved getting together in one enormous pile all my fifteen hundred pounds of baggage, picking up the saddle from Sallay and seeing if it fitted, and buying all the perishable foodstuffs.

It also meant spending a week with my family, whom I hadn't seen in over a year, and arranging with Rick when I would see him on the track and how, and saying countless goodbyes. In short, it was one hell of a hectic week.

Rick came laden with every trapping under the sun. The people from whom he had bought his four-wheel-drive Toyota in Melbourne had seen him coming a mile off. 'Hey, boys, here's a live one.' They had sold him every survival gadget they had, from a winch the size of a bull to a rubber dinghy with paddles that took half an hour to inflate.

'Rick, what on earth ... what's THAT for?'

'Well, they told me it might flash flood out here, so I thought I'd better get it. I don't know. I've never been in a desert before.'

We were all at Sallay's at the time, and after we had picked ourselves off the ground where we had been rolling convulsed and pointing at Rick, we teased him unmercifully.

He had also bought me a two-way radio, and a huge gleaming contraption that looked like one of those chrome-plated exercise bicycles that plump people use.

'Richard, I'm going to be walking twenty miles a day. Why would I need an exercise bicycle?'

I didn't want a two-way radio, and I definitely didn't want this stationary bike either. It was for generating power, should the batteries fail on the radio. Imagine sitting out in the middle of nowhere, pedalling as hard as you could saying 'help' into a microphone. I'd feel silly.

An argument ensued, with me saying that I refused to take either of these machines, and everyone else saying things like,

'But you must,' or 'If you don't, I'll worry myself sick,' or 'Oh, my heart,' or 'What if you break a leg?' or 'Please take it, Rob, for us. Just to make us feel better.'

Emotional blackmail.

I had thought long and hard about a radio, and had decided that it was somehow not right to take one. It didn't feel right. I didn't need it, didn't want to think of it sitting up there, tempting me, didn't want that mental crutch, or physical link with the outside world. Foolish I suppose, but it was a very strong feeling.

I eventually gave in grudgingly to taking the set, but refused the pedal part point blank. I was angry with myself then, for allowing other people to stop me doing things the way I wanted to do them, for whatever reason. And angry because that other one of me, the boring practical self-preserver, had said, 'Take it, take it, you idiot. You want to die out there or something?'

It was another tiny symbol of defeat. Of the trip not really being mine at all. I stashed it away with all the others.

Meanwhile, I watched my family. My father and sister. Between us, it seemed, there had always been invisible ropes and chains that we had chafed at, fought against, thought we had escaped from only to find them as strong as ever. We were bound together, since the death of my mother, by guilt and the overwhelming need to protect one another, mostly from ourselves. It was never stated between us. That would have been too cruel – the opening of old wounds. And, in fact, we had managed to bury it successfully, hide it behind set patterns of relating. And if sometimes one of us cracked with the pressure of it, we hastily explained it in terms that would not hurt, that would protect, that would cover up. But now a certain awareness pleaded from behind blue eyes, and begged for recognition in the set of three similar faces. It was like electricity. A need to lay a ghost, I suppose, before it was too late (i.e., before I karked in the desert). It was painful. We none of us wanted to make the same mistake twice, of leaving too much unsaid, of not at least trying to state the unstateable.

My sister and I lived totally different kinds of lives at that stage. She was married with four children. We appeared on the surface as different as chalk and cheese, but we had that closeness that only two siblings who have shared a traumatic childhood can have. And it was between us that the conspiracy was strongest and most clearly stated and accepted. The need to protect Pop. The duty. To save him pain at any cost. It is odd that both of us spent most of our lives doing just the opposite.

And as I watched our reactions, as I saw his eyes mist over when he thought no one was looking, or glance away in confusion when he knew someone was, I got an inkling of just how much emotional charge was being focused on this trip. I began to see how much it meant to him and how much it would take out of him. Not just because he was proud of it. (He had spent twenty years in Africa, walking across it in the 1920s and 1930s, living the life of a Victorian explorer. He could now refer to me as a chip off the old block.) Nor simply because he was frightened. But because all the stupid meaningless pain our family had suffered might somehow be symbolically absolved, laid to rest through this gesture of mine. As if I could walk it away for all of us.

This is all conjecture. But the time for me was excruciatingly sad. There was a poignancy in the air, though well masked, as always, with our roles and our patterns, now a little shaky, a little transparent, and our jokes.

Sallay offered to truck the camels as far as Glen Helen, a spectacular red sandstone gorge, seventy miles west of Alice. That way, I could miss the bitumen road and the tourists and the curious townsfolk. I arranged to meet him at the trucking yards at dawn on my last day. Pop and I rose at three a.m. to walk the camels down. It was still dark and we weren't talking much, just enjoying moonlight and night noises, and each other's company.

After about half an hour of this he said, 'You know, Rob, I had a strange dream about you and me last night.' I could not remember Pop ever telling me anything as personal as a dream before. I knew it was difficult for him to talk like this. I put my arm around him as we walked along.

'Yes, what was it?'

'Well, we were sailing in a lovely boat together on the most beautiful tropical turquoise sea, and we were very happy, and we were going somewhere. I don't know where it was, but somewhere nice. And then suddenly, we were on a mud-bank, or a sea of mud rather, and you were so frightened. But I said to you, don't worry, darling, if we can float on water, we can float on mud.'

I wondered if the dream meant the same to him as it did to me. It didn't matter, it was enough that he had told me. We hardly spoke again.

The night at Glen Helen was normal enough. Sallay cooked chapaties, Iris made us laugh, Pop and I went for walks, the kids had rides, my sister and brother-in-law Marg and Laurie wished they could spend more time out bush and Rick took pictures. To my complete surprise, the minute my head touched the swag I fell asleep.

But oh how different the dawning. We all woke up with tight forced smiles which soon enough disintegrated into covert then overt weeping. Sallay loaded the camels for me and I couldn't believe I had so much stuff, or that any of it would stay there. It was ridiculous. I could feel anxiety and excitement bulging the back of my eyeballs, and playing violins in my stomach. I knew they all had that sinking feeling that they would never see me alive again, and I had the sinking certainty that I would have to send messages from Redbank Gorge the same day, saying, 'Sorry, muffed it on the first seventeen miles, please collect.'

Josephine started bawling which started Andree which started Marg which started Pop, and there were hugs and good lucks and 'Watch out for those bull camels like I told you,' from Sallay, and feeble little pats on the back, and Marg looked deep into my eyes and said, 'You know I love you, don't you,' and Iris was waving, and then everyone was waving, 'Goodbye, sweetheart, goodbye, Rob,' and I grabbed the nose-line with cold sweaty shaking hands, and walked up over the hill.

'I walk, I lift up, I lift up heart, eyes, to down all the glory of that magnificent heaven.'

I could not remember how the rest of it went but the words were dinging around in my head like an advertisement jingle or an Abba tune. It was just how I felt. As if I were made of some fine bright, airy, musical substance and that in my chest was a source of power that would any minute explode, releasing thousands of singing birds.

All around me was magnificence. Light, power, space and sun. And I was walking into it. I was going to let it make me or break me. A great weight lifted off my back. I felt like dancing and calling to the great spirit. Mountains pulled and pushed, wind roared down chasms. I followed eagles suspended from cloud horizons. I wanted to fly in the un-limited blue of the morning. I was seeing it all as if for the first time, all fresh and bathed in an effulgence of light and joy, as if a smoke had cleared, or my eyes been peeled, so that I wanted to shout to the vastness, 'I love you. I love you, sky, bird, wind, precipice, space sun desert desert desert.'

Click.

'Hi, how's it goin'? I got some great shots of you waving goodbye.' Rick had been sitting in his car with the windows up, listening to Jackson Browne, waiting for me to come round the bend.

I had almost forgotten. I plummeted back to earth, my grandiose emotions crashing into shards of fussy practical detail. I looked at the camels. Dookie's pack was all skew-whiff. Zeleika was pulling at her nose-line to see where

Goliath was and Goliath was straining at his rope which was pulling off Bub's saddle, trying to get to his mother.

Rick took hundreds of photos. At first I felt uncomfortable and camera-shy. And if one vain little voice said, 'Don't show that gold filling when you smile,' or 'Watch those double chins,' she was soon defeated by the sheer impossibility of remaining self-conscious in the face of the burgeoning quantity of film exposed. The camera seemed omnipresent. I tried to forget about it. I was almost successful. It wasn't that Rick was asking me to do anything, or interfering physically, it was just that he was there and his camera was recording images and giving them an isolated importance, which made my actions stilted and unspontaneous, as if I were just out of sync with myself. Click, observer. Click, observed. And whatever else could be said in their favour – cameras and Jackson Browne just didn't fit in this desert. I began right then and there to split into two over Rick. On the one hand I saw him as a blood-sucking little creep who had inveigled his way into my life by being nice and by tempting me with material things. On the other hand I was confronted with a very warm, gentle human being who genuinely wanted to help me and who was excited by the prospect of an adventure, who wanted to do a good job, and who cared.

The day grew hotter, and Dookie's pack got worse and worse so that I had to stop constantly to try to rearrange it. My neck had a crick in it from glancing back at the animals. The great spirit had fled, leaving me to my own resources. Make me or break me indeed. I knew so little. It was preposterous thinking I would make it unscathed two thousand miles to the ocean. Good season or no, the desert is no place for a dilettante. I combated these feelings by thinking of it as nothing more than a series of steps, of days, one after the other, and if nothing went wrong during one, why should it on the next? Tiddly pom.

I had arranged to meet Jenny and Toly and a few friends

from town at Redbank Gorge. That would be the final contact with people until I got to Areyonga, an Aboriginal settlement seventy miles along. I was exhausted by the time I arrived. It is one thing to walk seventeen miles, quite another to do it when you are so tense that your muscles have set hard like cement.

We spent the night and the whole next day in that impossibly beautiful place. We camped in silver sand, near the entrance of the water-filled gorge. Rick's rubber raft came in handy for shipping camera gear up the mile-long ravine while we tried to swim through it in water that was black, crystal and freezing. This gorge was only a couple of feet wide in places, with red and black cliffs that rose sheer out of the water for a hundred feet or more. Then it would open out into a gloomy cavern or a fissure where the sun shot spears of yellow into the green, transparent water. Rick was the only one who made it the whole mile, out to the sunny cliffs at the other entrance. We built him a driftwood fire half way on one of the tiny beaches of a cave-pool, so he would make it unfrozen on his way back. That night he drove back to Alice, to catch a plane that would take him to his next assignment somewhere out there in the big wide world. We arranged to meet again at Ayers Rock, three weeks away, because *Geographic* had insisted on a full pictorial coverage of this well-known Australian landmark. I felt resentful about having to see him again so soon.

On the following morning, I went through two and a half discouraging hours of loading up. I knew I had far too much stuff, but at that stage I was sure I needed all of it.

Bub carried four petrol drums containing water for the camels, each weighing fifty pounds. Over these were four canvas bags filled with food, all manner of tools, spare bells, spare leather, clothes, mosquito net, raincoats for them, etc. The swag I attached to the back of the saddle. Zeleika carried much less weight than the other two, as she would need all her spare energy for feeding the calf. Two hand-made five-gallon water drums were designed to fit into the front section of her saddle. Behind this and hanging on a bar were two tin trunks filled with food and the various odds and sods that I would need for camping at night, such as kerosene lamp, cooking utensils. The pretty goat-skin bags went over the water drums and Diggity's dog biscuits were secured to the top. Dookie, being the strongest, had the most to carry. Four water drums, a large hessian sack containing oranges, lemons, potatoes, garlic, onions, coconuts and pumpkins, two large red-leather bags with yet more tools and paraphernalia, two more canvas bags including a cassette-recorder and the offending radio set, and at the back of his saddle, a five-gallon bucket with washing things in it. All of them carried spare ropes, straps, hobbles, halters, sheepskins, etc. Everything was strapped down securely with ropes running around the gear then lashed to the saddle-frame.

I put my pillow on Bub's saddle so I could ride comfortably, and slung my rifle and a small bag carrying all the precious things like cigarettes and money over the front of this saddle. My maps (which were 1 : 250,000 series, topographical) I wrapped in a cylindrical pipe and stuffed into one of Bub's packs. The compass I carried around my neck. I had a knife strapped to my waist and a few spare nose-lines in my pocket. Hmmm. Only two and a half hours for fifteen hundred pounds – I was going to spend this whole trip heaving baggage.

I decided to put Bub in front since he had the best saddle for riding, should I get footsore. He was also the most easily spooked, and I wanted him where I could have complete control of him should he decide to shy. Zeleika came next so I could keep an eye on her nose-line and berate her if she started pulling back on it. Dookie came last, a slight and an ignominy he could scarcely bear. I let Goliath go, so he could eat as he walked along. I was planning to tie him to a tree at night as Sallay had suggested. This meant that the very real danger of the camels disappearing in the night, when they were hobbled out to feed, would be minimized. I left a halter on him, with a length of rope hanging from it, so he would be easy to catch.

It was done. I was on my own. For real. At last. Jenny, Toly, Alice Springs, Rick, *National Geographic*, family, friends, everything, dissolved as I turned for the last time, the early morning wind leaping and whistling around me. I wondered what powerful fate had channelled me into this moment of inspired lunacy. The last burning bridge back to my old self collapsed. I was on my own.

Part Two
Shedding Burdens

6

ALL I REMEMBER of that first day alone was a feeling of release; a sustained, buoyant confidence as I strolled along, Bub's nose-line in my sweaty palm, the camels in a well-behaved line behind me and Goliath bringing up the rear. The muffled tinkling of their bells, the soft crunching of my feet in the sand and the faint twittering of the wood-swallows were the only sounds. The desert was otherwise still.

I had decided to follow an abandoned track that would eventually meet up with the main Areyonga road. Now, the definition of a track in Australia is a mark made across the landscape by the repeated passage of a vehicle or, if you are very lucky, initially by a bulldozer. These tracks vary in quality from a corrugated, bull-dust-covered, well-defined and well-used road to something which you can barely discern by climbing a hill and squinting in the general direction you think the said track may go. Sometimes you can see where a track is by the tell-tale blossoms of wildflowers. Those along the track will either be growing more thickly or be of a different type. Sometimes, you may be able to follow the trail by searching for the ridge left aeons ago by a bulldozer. The track may wind around or over hills and ridges and rocky outcroppings, straight into sand-dunes, get swallowed up by sandy creek-beds, get totally lost in stony creek-beds, or fray into a maze of animal pads. Following tracks is most often easy, sometimes frustrating, and occasionally downright terrifying.

When you are in cattle or sheep station country, the following of tracks can be especially puzzling, mainly because one always assumes that a track will lead somewhere. This is not necessarily so since station people just don't think like that. Also there is the problem of choice. When you are presented with half a dozen tracks all leading off in the general direction you want to go, all used within the last year, and none of them marked on the map, which one do you choose? If you choose the wrong one it may simply stop five miles ahead, so that you have to back-track, having lost half a day's travel. Or it may lead you to an abandoned, waterless windmill and bore, or slap-bang into a new fence-line, which, if followed, will begin leading you in exactly the opposite direction to where you thought you wanted to go, only now you're not quite sure because you've made so many turnings and weavings that you are beginning to lose confidence in your sense of direction. Or it might lead you to a gate made by some jackaroo who thought he was Charles Atlas and which you haven't got a hope in hell of opening, or if you can open it without suffering a rupture, then closing it is impossible without using the camels as a winch, which takes half an hour to do and you're already hot and bothered and dusty and all you really want in life is to get to the next watering place and have an aspirin and a cup of tea and a good lie down.

This is complicated further by the fact that whoever those people are who fly in planes and make maps of the area, they need glasses; or perhaps were drunk at the time; or perhaps just felt like breaking free of departmental rulings and added a few little bits and pieces of imaginative topography, or even, in some cases, rubbed out a few features in a fit of solitary anarchic vice. One expects maps to be always but always 100 per cent correct, and most of the time they are. It's those other times that can set you into a real panic. Make you doubt even your own senses. Make you think that perhaps that sand-ridge you swore you sat on back there was a mirage. Make you entertain the notion that you are sun-struck. Make you gulp once or twice and titter nervously.

However, that first day held none of these problems. If the track petered out into dust bowls with drinking spots in the middle of them, it was relatively easy to find where it continued on the other side. The camels were going well and behaving like lambs. Life was good. The country I was travelling through held my undivided attention with its diversity. This particular area had had three bumper seasons in succession and was carpeted in green and dotted with white, yellow, red, blue wildflowers. Then I would find myself in a creek-bed where tall gums and delicate acacias cast deep cool shadow. And birds. Everywhere birds. Black cockatoos, sulphur-cresteds, swallows, Major-Mitchells, willy-wagtails, quarrian, kestrels, budgerigar flocks, bronze-wings, finches. And there were kunga-berries and various solanums and mulga apples and eucalyptus manna to eat as I walked along. This searching for and picking wild food is one of the most pleasant, calming pastimes I know. Contrary to popular belief, the desert is bountiful and teeming with life in the good seasons. It is like a vast untended communal garden, the closest thing to earthly paradise I can imagine. Mind you, I wouldn't want to have to survive on bush-tucker during the drought. And even in the good season, I admit I would prefer my diet to be supplemented by the occasional tin of sardines, and a frequent cup of sweet billy tea.

I had learnt about wild foods from Aboriginal friends in Alice Springs, and from Peter Latz, an ethnobotanist whose passion was desert plant-foods. At first, I had not found it easy to remember and recognize plants after they had been pointed out to me, but eventually the scales fell from my eyes. The Solanaceae especially had me confused. These are a huge family, including such well knowns as potatoes, tomatoes, capsicums, datura and nightshades. The most interesting thing about the group is that many of them form a staple diet for Aboriginal people, while others which look almost identical are deadly poisonous. They are tricky little devils. Peter had done some tests of various species and found that one tiny berry contained more vitamin C than an orange. Since these were eaten by the thousands when

Aboriginal people were free to travel through their own country, it stands to reason that their modern-day diet, almost totally devoid of vitamin C, is just one more factor contributing to their crippling health problems.

I was a little nervous my first night out. Not because I was frightened of the dark (the desert is benign and beautiful at night, and except for the eight-inch-long, pink millipedes that sleep under the bottom of the swag and may wish to bite you when you roll it up at dawn, or the careless straying of a scorpion under your sleep-twitching hand, or the lonely slithering of a Joe Blake who may want to cuddle up and get warm under the bedclothes then fang you to death when you wake up, there is not too much to worry about) but because I wondered if I would ever see the camels again. I hobbled them out at dusk, unclogged their bells and tied little Goliath to a tree. Would it work, I asked myself? The answer came back, 'She'll be right, mate,' the closest thing to a Zen statement to come out of Australia, and one I used frequently in the months ahead.

The process of unloading had been infinitely easier than putting the stuff on. It only took an hour. Then there was wood to be gathered, a fire and lamp to be lit, camels to be checked on, cooking utensils, food and cassette player to be got out, Diggity to be fed, camels to be checked on, food to be cooked and camels to be checked on. They were munching their heads off happily enough. Except Goliath. He was yelling piggishly for his mother, who, thank god, was taking no notice whatsoever.

I think I cooked a freeze-dried dish that night. A vastly overrated cardboard-like substitute for edible food. The fruit was O.K., you could eat that straight like biscuit, but the meat and vegetable dishes were tasteless soggy tack. I fed all my packets to the camels later on, and stuck with what was to be my staple diet: brown rice, lentils, garlic, curry, oil, pancakes made with all manner of cereals and coconut and dried egg, various root vegetables cooked in the coals, cocoa, tea, sugar, honey, powdered milk, and every now and then, the ultimate in luxury, a can of sardines, some pepperoni and Kraft cheese, a tin of fruit, and an orange or lemon. I supplemented this with vitamin pills, various wild foods, and the occasional rabbit. Far from being deficient, this diet had me so healthy, I felt like a cast-iron amazon; cuts and gashes vanished in a day, I could see almost as well at night as I could in sunlight, and I grew muscles on my shit.

After that first lack-lustre meal, I built the fire up, checked again on the camels, and put my Pitjantjara learning tapes into the cassette. *Nyuntu palya nyinanyi. Uwa, palyarna, palu nyuntu*, I mumbled repeatedly at the night sky now thick and gorgeous with billions of stars. There was no moon that night.

I nodded off with Diggity snoring in my arms as usual. And from that first night, I developed a habit of waking once or twice to check on the bells. I would wait until I heard a chime, and if I didn't I would call to them so they turned their heads and chimed, and if that didn't work, I would get up and see where they were. They were usually no more than a hundred yards from camp. I would then fall instantly back to sleep and remember waking up only vaguely in the morning. When I woke well before dawn, one fear at least had diminished. The camels were huddled around my swag, as close as they could get without actually crushing me. They got up at the same time I did, that is, over an hour before sun-up, for their early-morning feed.

My camels were all still young and growing. Zeleika, the oldest, I thought was maybe four and a half or five. Dookie was going on for four and Bub was three—mere puppies, since camels can live until they're fifty. So they needed all the food they could get. My routine was built around their needs and never my own. They were carrying what I would consider a lot of weight for young animals though Sallay would have scoffed at such an idea. He had told me how a

123

bull camel had stood up with a ton on its back and that up to half a ton was usually carrying capacity. Getting up and down was the hardest thing for them. Once they were up, carrying the weight was not so difficult. The weight, however, had to be evenly balanced or the saddle would rub, causing discomfort and eventually producing a saddle-sore, so at this stage the process of loading up was fastidiously checked and rechecked. On the second morning I got it down to just under two hours.

I never ate much in the mornings. I would build a cooking fire, boil one or two billies of tea, and fill a small Thermos with what was left. Sometimes I craved sugar and would pile two tablespoons into the billy then wolf down several tablespoons of cocoa or honey. I burnt it up quickly enough.

My main problem now seemed to be whether the gear would hold together, whether the saddles would rub, and how the camels handled the work. I was a little worried over Zeleika. Diggity was doing fine but occasionally got footsore. I felt great, if knock-kneed with exhaustion by the end of a day. I decided to cover approximately twenty miles a day, six days a week. (And on the seventh she rested.) Well, not always. I wanted to keep a fair distance covered in case something went wrong, and I had to sit somewhere for days or weeks. There was a slight pressure on me not to take it as easy as I would have liked. I didn't want to be travelling in summer and I had promised *Geographic* I would be at journey's end before the year was out. That gave me six months of comfortable travel, which I could stretch to eight if needs be.

So, by the time everything was packed away and the fire smothered, the camels would have had a couple of hours of feeding. I would then bring them in nose-line to tail, tie Bub with his halter to the tree and ask them to whoosh down please. The cloths and saddles went on first, front to back, the girths done up, by pushing them underneath the animal and behind the brisket. The nose-lines were taken off the tail

124

and attached to the saddle. Next the loading, first one object, then its equivalent on the other side. It was all checked
and checked again, then I asked them to stand up, and the
girths were tightened and the holding ropes run through
them. All set to go. One more check. Departure. Hey ho.

But wouldn't it be my luck that on the third day, when
I was still a puppy, a cub-scout in the ways of the bush, and
still believing blindly that all maps were infallible and certainly more reliable than common sense, I found a road that
wasn't meant to be there. While the road I wanted to be there
was nowhere to be seen.

'You've lost a whole road,' I said to myself, incredulously.
'Not just a turning or a well or a ridge, but a whole bloody
road.'

'Take it easy, babe, be calm, she'll be right, mate, settle
down settle DOWN.'

My little heart felt like a macaw in a canary cage. I could
feel the enormity of the desert in my belly and on the back
of my neck. I was not in any real danger – I could easily have
set a compass course for Areyonga. But I kept thinking, what
if this happens when I'm two hundred miles from anywhere?
What if, what if. And I felt very small and very alone suddenly in this great emptiness. I could climb a hill and look
to where the horizon shimmered blue into the sky and see
nothing. Absolutely nothing.

I re-read the map. No enlightenment there. I was only fifteen or so miles from the settlement, and here was this giant
dirt highway where there should only be sandstone and roly-
poly. Should I follow it or what? Where the hell did it lead?
Was it a new mining road? I checked the map for mines but
there was nothing marked.

I sat back and watched myself perform. 'O.K. First of all,
you are not lost, you are merely misplaced, no no, you know
exactly where you are so stifle that impulse to scream at the
camels and kick Diggity. Think clearly. Then, make camp
for the night here, there is plenty of green feed, and spend

the rest of the afternoon looking for that goddamn track. If you don't find it, cut across country. Easy enough. Above all, do not flap around like a winged pigeon. Where's your pride? Right.'

I did all that, then went off scouting, map in hand, Diggity at foot. I found an ancient trail that wound up through the mountains, not exactly where the map said it should be but close enough for a margin of credibility at least. It went for a couple of miles off course then came out to meet up with, yes, yet another major highway that had no right to exist. 'Shit and damnation.' This I followed for another half mile in the general direction of Areyonga, until I came across a bullet-ridden piece of tin bent over double and almost rusted away, but with an arrow that pointed at the ground and the letters A   ON   upon it. I skipped back to camp in the gathering twilight, apologized profusely to my poor dumb entourage, and fixed lesson one firmly in my brain for future reference. When in doubt, follow your nose, trust your instincts, and don't rely on maps.

I had been alone for three days in country that people seldom visited. Now I was crawling down a wide dusty deserted boring road, an occasional beer or coke can winking at me from the bushes. The walking was beginning to take its toll on all of us. Diggity's feet were pincushioned with bindy-eye prickles, so I heaved her up on to Dookie's back. She hated it, and stared off into the distance, sighing dramatically, with that long-suffering look common to brainwashed dogs. My own feet were blistered and aching, and my legs cramped up as soon as I stopped walking. Zeleika had a large lump which distended her milk vein and her nose-peg was infected. Dookie's saddle was rubbing him slightly but he stepped high and seemed, unlike the others, to be thoroughly enjoying himself. I suspected he had always wanted to travel.

This worry over the camels was unrelenting. Without them I would be nowhere, and I treated them like porcelain.

126

Camels, so everyone says, are tough, hardy creatures, but perhaps mine were so pampered that they had turned into hypochondriacs; they always seemed to have some little thing wrong with them, which, doubtless, I blew out of all proportion. But I had been burnt once with Kate, and I wasn't about to take risks with their health.

Areyonga is a tiny missionary settlement wedged between two sandstone mountain faces of the Macdonnell Ranges. As settlements go, it is a good one. It is laid out traditionally, that is, a small village of houses where the whites live, a general store which Aborigines are being trained to run themselves, a school, a clinic, and the Aboriginal camps sprawling around the outskirts looking like Third World refugee centres. All the whites, about ten I think, could speak the language fluently and were pro-Aboriginal.

After 160 years of undeclared war on Aboriginal people, during which time wholesale slaughter was carried out in the name of progress, and while the last brutal massacre was taking place in the Northern Territory in 1930, the colonialist government set up this and other Aboriginal reserves on land neither the cattlemen nor anyone else wanted. Because everyone believed that the indigenous people would eventually die out, allowing them to keep small sections of their land was seen as a temporary measure which would make life safer for the settlers. The blacks were rounded up like cattle by police and citizens on horseback wielding guns. Often, different tribes were forced to live on one small area; as some of these groups were traditionally antagonistic, this created friction and planted the seeds of cultural decay. The government allowed missionaries to rule many of these reserves and to confine and control the people. Half-caste children were taken forcibly from their mothers and kept separate, as they were seen as having at least a chance of becoming human. (This was still happening in Western Australia until very recently.)

Even these pitifully inadequate reserves are now under

threat, because large mining concerns, notably Conzinc Rio-tinto, have their eyes on them for further exploitation. Already, many companies have been allowed to mine what was once Aboriginal territory, bulldozing it into a scarred dust-bowl and leaving the people destitute, their land destroyed. Many reserves have been closed down and the people sent to the towns where they cannot find work. Although this is called 'promoting assimilation', it is another method of transferring Aboriginal land to white ownership. However, Pitjantjara people are slightly better off than most other central desert and northern tribes, because uranium has not yet been mined in their country and because the area is so remote. Many of the old people do not speak English, and the people on the whole have managed to keep their cultural integrity intact. It also became apparent to me that the majority of whites now involved with the Aborigines are fighting alongside them to protect what is left of their lands and their rights, and eventually to reach the point where the blacks are autonomous. Whether this is possible, given the rural white backlash, the racist attitudes of Australians generally and the genocidal policies of the present government, and given that the rest of the world seems neither to know nor care what is happening to the oldest culture in the world, is a doubtful question. The Aborigines do not have much time. They are dying.

I arrived a mile outside the settlement by mid-afternoon, to be met by hordes of excited children, giggling, shouting and raving Pitjantjara. God knows how they knew I was coming, but now, from Areyonga all the way down the line, the inexplicable communication network called 'bush telegraph', or 'keeping one's ear to the ground', would tell people I was on my way.

I had been hot, irritable and tired when I arrived, but now these delightful children lifted my spirits with their cacophony of laughter. How easy they were. I had always felt slightly uncomfortable around most children, but Aboriginal

3   Exploring a cave in Uluru, Ayers Rock.

14–15   Leaving the Olgas, where I camped for a week, I rode the temperamental Bubby, with Zeleika and Dookie behind and Goliath trailing. By now unsaddling time was down from one hour to twenty minutes.

6–17 It took twice as long to saddle up before setting off again in the morning—above at Lassiter's Cave. Each night I hobbled the camels so that they could not stray far.

18–19   In a rare downpour of rain, Dookie slipped and pulled a muscle, and had to be coaxed the 30 miles to Docker River, where I was greeted by excited Pitjantjara children.

kids were different. They never whined, whinged or demanded. They were direct and filled with joie de vivre and so loving and giving with one another that they melted me immediately. I tried out my Pitjantjara. Stunned silence, then hoots of laughter. I let them lead the camels. There were children on my back, children clinging to camel legs and camel saddles and children ten deep on every side. The camels had a very special attitude to them. They would let them do anything, so I didn't have to worry about anyone getting hurt. Bub especially adored them. I remember how, at Utopia, when he was tied to his tree during the day, he would see the kids bounding towards him after school, and would immediately sit down and start to doze off in pleasant expectation of being jumped on, bounced on, pulled, tugged, pushed and walked on by the small people. By the time I got to the village proper everyone was out to meet me, all asking questions in lingo because word had already spread that the *kungka rama-rama* (crazy woman) could speak it fluently. I could not. It didn't seem to matter.

The camels were like a key in relating to Pitjantjara people. I could not have picked a better way to travel through their country. It was a stroke of genius. They had a special relationship with these animals as they had been the one tribe to use them constantly for walkabout right up to the mid-1960s, when cars and trucks eventually took over. The whole of the first section of my trip would be through their tribal territory, or what was left of it, a large reserve controlled by white bureaucrats and dotted with mission and government settlements.

I stayed three days in Areyonga, talking to people and generally getting the feel of the place and living with a school teacher and his family. I would have dearly loved to stay down at camp but was too shy to force myself on to people who might not want a whitefella hanging around, poking her nose into their business. One thing I particularly noticed, on all the settlements and camps I saw, was that many of the old people were blind. Trachoma, a chronic form of conjuncti-vitis, diabetes, ear infections, heart trouble and syphilis are just some of the diseases which ravage Aboriginal populations, living without proper housing, medical facilities or correct diet. Infant mortality has been reported by some at 200 per 1,000, though official estimates are not so high. The figure is increasing. Professor Hollows, an eye specialist, organized a national survey of eye-diseases amongst Aborigines. He stated, 'It is clear that Aborigines have the worst ethnic blind-ness rate in the world.'

Despite these facts, the present Fraser government has seen fit to cut back violently on the Aboriginal Affairs budget. These cut-backs have almost devastated the work of Aborigi-nal health and legal aid organizations.

It is equally extraordinary that the Australian Broadcasting Commission was asked by the Federal Director General of Health to cancel a film about Aboriginal blindness in the Northern Territory because it might damage the tourist trade there.

Or how's this: the Queensland premier, Mr Bjelke Peter-son, asked the federal government to stop Professor Hollows's anti-trachoma team from working in that state, because two of the Aboriginal field workers were 'enrolling Aboriginal people to vote'.

The rest of the time I spent worrying over the camels. Zeleika's suspicious lump was suspiciously bigger. When I inspected her peg, I found the inner knob fractured. Oh no, not again. I tied her down, twisted her head around and in-serted a new one. I could hardly hear myself think through her bellowing, and did not notice Bub sneaking up behind me. He nipped me on the back of the head, then galloped away behind Dookie, as startled as I was by his audacity. Camels stick together.

When we were all rested, and when I thought most of our problems were ironed out, we headed off for Tempe Downs station, forty-odd miles to the south, over an unused path through the ranges. I was a bit windy about my ability to navigate through these hills. The people at Areyonga had sapped my confidence by insisting that I call them on the two-way radio when I made it to the other side. No one had used the track for ten years and it would be invisible at times. The range itself was a series of mountains, chasms, canyons and valleys that ran all the way to Tempe, perpendicular to my direction of travel.

It is difficult to describe Australian desert ranges as their beauty is not just visual. They have an awesome grandeur that can fill you with exaltation or dread, and usually a combination of both.

I camped that first night in a washaway, near the ruin of a cottage. I awoke to the muttering of a single crow staring at me not ten feet away. The pre-dawn light, all pastel misty blue and translucent, filtered through the leaves and created a fairy-land. The character of such country changes wonderfully throughout the day, and each change has its effect on one's mood.

I set off clutching map and compass. Every hour or so, my shoulders would tighten and my stomach knot as I searched for the right path. I got lost only once, ending up in a box-canyon and having to back-track to where the path had been obliterated by a series of cattle and donkey tracks. But the constant tension was sapping my energy and I sweated and strained. This went on for two days.

One afternoon, after our midday break, something dropped off Bub's back and he flew into a flat panic. I now had Zeleika in the lead, because of her sore nose, and Bub at the rear. He bucked and he bucked and the more he bucked, the more bits of pack went flying and the more frenzied he became. By the time he stopped, the saddle was dangling under his quivering belly, and the goods were scattered everywhere. I switched into automatic. The other camels were ready to leap out of their skins and head for home. Goliath was galloping between them and generally causing havoc. There was not a tree in sight to tie them to. If I blew this, they might take off and I would never see them again. I couldn't get back to Bub so I whooshed the lead camel down and tied her nose-line to her foreleg, so that if she tried to get up, she would be pulled down. I did the same with Dook, clouted Goliath across the nose with a branch of mulga so that he took off in a cloud of dust, and then went back to Bub. His eyes had rolled with fear and I had to talk to him and pacify him until I knew he trusted me and wouldn't kick. Then I lifted the saddle with my knees and undid the girth on top of his back. Then I gently took it off and whooshed him down like the others. I found a tree a little further on, and beat the living daylights out of him. The whole operation had been quick, sure, steady and precise, like Austrian clockwork – perfect. But now, whatever toxins had been stirred up by the flow of adrenalin hit my bloodstream like the Cayahogan River. I lay by the tree, trembling as hard as Bub. I had been out of control when I beat him and began to recognize a certain Kurtishness in my behaviour. This weakness, my inability to be terrified with any dignity, came to the forefront often during the trip, and my animals took the brunt of it. If, as Hemingway suggested, 'courage is grace under pressure', then the trip proved once and for all that I was sadly lacking in the stuff. I felt ashamed.

I learnt a couple of other things from that incident. I learnt to conserve energy by allowing at least part of myself to believe I could cope with any emergency. And I realized that this trip was not a game. There is nothing so real as having to think about survival. It strips you of airy-fairy notions. Believing in omens and fate is all right as long as you know exactly what you are doing. I was becoming very careful and I was coming right back down to earth, where the desert was larger than I could comprehend. And not only was space an ungraspable concept, but my description of time needed reassessment. I was treating the trip like a nine-to-five job. Up bright and early (oh, the guilt if I slept in), boil the billy, drink tea, hurry up it's getting late, nice place for lunch but I can't stay too long ... I simply could not rid myself of this regimentation. I was furious with myself, but I let it run its course. Better to watch it now, then fight it later when I was feeling stronger. I had a clock which I told myself was for navigation purposes only, but at which I stole furtive glances from time to time. It played tricks on me. In the heat of the afternoon, when I was tired, aching and miserable, the clock would not move, hours lapsed between ticks and tocks. I recognized a need for these absurd arbitrary structures at that stage. I did not know why, but I knew I was afraid of something like chaos. It was as if it were waiting for me to let down my guard and then it would pounce.

On the third day, and to my great relief, I found the well-used station track to Tempe. I called Areyonga on my radio set, that unwanted baggage, that encumbrance, that infringement of my privacy, that big smudgy patch on the purity of my gesture. I screamed into it that I was all right and got nothing but static as a reply.

Arriving in Tempe, I had a pleasant lunch with the people who ran the station, then filled my canteen with precious sweet rainwater from their tanks and continued on my way.

7

Soon after leaving Tempe, I crossed a wide river-bed, slapping my bare feet on hot river pebbles and soft sticks and delighting in the crunch of glittering sand between my toes. Then I saw my first sandhills. This country had had bush-fires through it the previous season which had been followed by heavy rains, so the colours of the landscape were now brilliant orange, jet black and sickly bright lime Day-glo green. Whoever heard of such a desert? And above all that, the intense hot dark blue of a perennially cloudless sky. There were new plants everywhere, tracks and patterns I had not noticed before, patches of burnt bushes sticking up like old crows' feathers from wind-rippled ridges, new bush foods to be searched for and picked. It was delicious new country but it was tiring. The sand dragged at my feet and the repeti-tion of the dunes lulled me into drowsiness when the first excitement wore off. The stillness of the waves of sand seemed to stifle and suffocate me.

However, I had at least learnt to live with the flies by then and didn't even trouble to scrape them away from my eyes, where they swarmed in thousands. The camels were black with them, and they followed us in clouds. In cattle country they were always worse than in the clean free desert. Ants work later shifts; in that blessed hour before the mosquitoes took over from the flies, masses of the horrid little creatures would crawl up my trouser legs while I was having a hard-earned cup of tea. This depended on where I camped of course and I soon learnt to stay away from nice flat claypan. The other nuisance in finding a good camping spot was prickles. Dry country has an infinite variety of prickles – there are little hairy ones that get caught in blankets and jumpers and saddle-cloths, there are tough cruel ones that get stuck in dogs' paws, and there are giant monstrous ones that stick in bare flesh like tacks.

I had approximately two weeks' travel before I could expect to reach Ayers Rock, and I was not looking forward to my arrival. Rick would be there to bring me back to reality. And I knew that the Rock was tamed, ruined by busload upon busload of tourists. By the time I got near Wallera Ranch, two days after Tempe, the tourists were beginning to drive me crazy. In overrigged vehicles they would come in droves to see Australia's natural wonder. They had two-way radios, winches, funny hats with corks on them, stubbies (beer bottles) and leather stubbie-holders with emus, kangaroos and naked women tooled upon them, all this to travel down a perfectly safe road. And they had cameras. I sometimes think tourists take cameras with them because they feel guilty about being on holiday, and feel they should be doing something useful with their time. In any case, when otherwise perfectly nice people don their hats and become tourists, they change into bad-mannered, loud, insensitive, litter-bugging oafs.

I must make a distinction here between travellers and tourists. I did meet some lovely people on the road, but they were rarer than hen's teeth. At first I treated one and all with pleasant politeness. There were ten questions invariably asked me, and I unfailingly gave my pat reply. I posed for the inevitable snap snap of Nikons and the whirr of Super-eights. It got so that I was stopped every half hour and by three in the afternoon, the dangerous hour for me, a time when my senses of humour and perspective fail me badly, a time when I cannot even be nice to myself, let alone these fools who would pile out, block my path, frighten the camels, hold me up, ask stupid boring questions, capture me on celluloid so that they could stick me on their refrigerator doors when they got home, or worse still, sell me to newspapers when the heat was on, then drive off in a cloud of choking blinding dust, not even offering me a drink of water – by three in the afternoon I would begin to get mean. My rudeness made me feel a little better but not much. The best policy was simply to keep off the road or feign deafness.

Those two weeks were strangely disappointing. The initial buzz had worn off and little niggling doubts were starting to worm their way into my consciousness. I was feeling ambiguous about it all. Nothing portentous or grand was really happening to me. I had been expecting some miraculous obvious change to occur. It was all nice of course and even fun sometimes, but hey, where was the great clap of the thunder of awareness that, as everyone knows, knocks people sideways in deserts. I was exactly the same person that I was when I began.

Some camps on those nights were so desolate they stole into my soul, and I longed for a safe nook out of that chill empty wind. I felt vulnerable. Moonlight turned the shadows into inimical forms and I was so glad of Diggity's warmth as we snuggled beneath the blankets that I could have squeezed her to death. The rituals I performed provided another necessary structure. Everything was done correctly and obsessionally. Before I went to bed, everything was placed exactly where I wanted it for the morning. Before the trip I had been hopelessly vague, forgetful and sloppy. My friends had made cracks about how I would probably forget to take the camels one morning. Now it was the opposite. The food was packed away, billy filled with water, tea, cup, sugar and Thermos out, nose-lines on the tree. I would roll out the swag, just so, by the fire and study my star book.

Stars all made sense to me now that I lived under them. They told me the time when I awoke at night for a piss and a check on the bells. They told me where I was and where I was going, but they were cold like bits of frost. One night, I decided to listen to some music and put Eric Satie into the cassette. But the noise sounded alien, incongruous, so I turned it off and sucked on the whisky bottle instead. I talked to myself, rolling the names of the stars and constellations around on my tongue. Goodnight, Aldebaran. See you, Sirius. Adios, Corvus. I was glad there was a crow in the heavens.

Wallera Ranch was not a ranch at all but a watering-hole for tourists. I went into the bar for a beer, there to be met by a group of typical ockers, all talking, as is their wont, about sex and shielas. 'Oh great,' I thought, 'just what I need. Some intellectual stimulation.' One of them, an ugly weedy pimply little brute, had been a milkman in Melbourne and was entertaining his mates with obviously untrue, gruesomely detailed stories of his countless conquests of sex-starved housewives. Another had been a tourist bus driver who said driving was a terrible 'ball-drainer' because all the women were always after his body. God knows there was enough of it. His beer gut was popping the buttons on his shirt. I left.

I was heading into wild camel country now. Their tracks were everywhere and the quandong trees were eaten almost bare. Sallay had put the fear of god into me about the renegade bulls, who were now coming into season. 'Shoot first and ask questions later,' he had warned, over and over. So I loaded the gun and slung it back on Bub's saddle. Then I thought, 'Christ, with my luck, it will go off and shoot me in the foot,' so I took the bullet out and kept a few rounds in my pocket.

That evening, I camped in a washaway at the foot of some hills. The feed was lush – roly-poly, mulga, salt-bush, camelthorn, acacia and so on. For me there were yalka (like tiny onions) to be dug up and roasted in the coals. 'This is very pleasant,' I said to myself, trying to quell a growing unease. I thought the animals were a bit touchy too, but put that down to projection. I found it difficult to get to sleep that night, and when I did eventually drop off, I was assaulted by psychedelic dreams.

I woke earlier than usual, and let Goliath go for a munch. By the time I had packed up, they had taken off (straight back to Alice) and when I caught up to them, two miles out into the bush, they seemed frightened. 'Must be wild camels around,' I informed Diggity, though I could see no tracks. On the way back, I stumbled on a deserted Aboriginal camp made of mulga branches and almost hidden by undergrowth.

I spent that night with the Liddles at Angus Downs station. They stuck me in the shower, fed me up and when I spoke of the previous night's experience, Mrs Liddle said that you couldn't put a pin between the ghosts around that camp.

Next morning, I fiddled with the pack, designed Zeleika an elastic nose-line hoping she would not hang back on it, put Bub back in the lead, and headed off for Curtin Springs, where I spent a couple of days trying to restuff Dookie's saddle. The pack was not yet perfect.

After that the tourists became just too much, so I set a compass course for the Rock and headed off across the dunes. Trudging across that solidified sea of sand was exhausting me, so I decided to ride Bub. And then I saw the thing. I was thunderstruck. I could not believe that blue form was real. It floated and mesmerized and shimmered and looked too big. It was indescribable.

I slid down the sandhill and pushed Bub quickly across the valley through a forest of desert oaks and up the next incline. I held my breath until I could see it again. The indecipherable power of that rock had my heart racing. I had not expected anything quite so weirdly, primevally beautiful.

I entered the tourist village in the afternoon, and was met by the head ranger of this vast national park. A nice man, whose job was not as enviable as it appeared on the surface. He had to protect that delicately balanced country from an ever-increasing number of Australian and overseas tourists, who not only had no knowledge of desert ecology and the effect their very presence had on it, but who insisted on picking wildflowers, throwing cans out of their car windows, breaking trees for firewood, lighting fires where they had no business to and then not dousing them out, and driving off the perfectly good road leaving wheel ruts that would last for years. He offered me a caravan to rest in, which I accepted, showed me a good place to hobble the camels, and told me he wouldn't mind if I later camped by the Olgas for a few days.

The great monolithic rock was surrounded by fertile flats for a radius of half a mile which, because of the added run-off water, were covered in lush green feed and wildflowers so thick you couldn't step between them. Then the dunes began, radiating away as far as the eye could see, orange fading into dusty blue.

The bush fire had swept through this country too, which, although making it now look prettier and greener, I thought might cause problems with the camels. Many desert plants, when they first shoot up out of the ground looking so deliciously edible, protect themselves with various toxins. While I knew Zelly would know what to eat and what not to eat, I wasn't too sure about the others. Many an early exploratory expedition had failed because camels had been poisoned. So that my animals wouldn't stray too far, Zelly and Goliath now took turns at being tied from the hobbles, with a forty-foot rope to some trees. This was because Zeleika was unequivocally the leader, and without her the others would go nowhere. But it also meant that she would not be there with them to teach them what to eat. I hoped that there was enough good feed around so they wouldn't attempt anything new. They were in fact very careful about this, as I was to discover later.

I sat up on the first sandhill watching the gathering evening changing the bold harsh daylight colours to luminous pastels, then deeper to the blues and purples of peacock feathers. This was always my favourite time of day in that country – the light, which has a crystalline quality I have not seen in any other place, lingers for hours. The Rock did not disappoint me, far from it. All the tourists in the world could not destroy it, it was too immense, too forceful, too ancient to be corruptible.

There were very few of the Pitjantjara mob left here. Most had moved away to more private tribal areas, though a few remained to protect and look after what is an extremely important site in their mythic culture. They were making a meagre living by selling artefacts to the tourists. Uluru they called it. The great Uluru. I wondered how they could stand watching people blundering around in fertility caves, or climbing the white painted line up the side, and taking their endless photos. If it had me almost to the point of tears, how much more must it have meant to them. There was one miserably small fenced-off section on the western side which read, 'Keep out. Aboriginal sacred site.'

I asked one of the rangers what he thought of the blacks. 'Oh they're all right,' he replied, 'they're nuisance value more than anything else.' I was coming to expect this, and there didn't seem much point in stating the obvious, that it was the tourists who were the nuisance value – that they were invading sacred land, that did not, could not ever, belong to them, and which they could not even begin to understand. At least the man did not despise them.

Rick arrived the next day, all bouncy and enthusiastic and full of energy. I had been out exploring and wandering through the bloodwood forests of the southern side. He announced that he had a surprise for me and led me back to the caravan. There on my bed, leg bandaged and crutches resting by the pillow, was my dear friend Jen. My initial reaction was one of great relief, surprise and happiness. The next one was a petty little voice saying to me, 'Are your friends going to follow you all the way?' I did double takes like strobe lighting. Jenny, being an acutely sensitive person, read this in my face as clearly as if I had screamed it at her, although I tried desperately to hide it. It set the tone for the rest of that difficult day – a subtle intricate unspoken tension, which both of us preferred to take out on Rick, rather than each other.

Jenny had fallen off her bike at Utopia and had lain in the dust for some time, unable to move, staring at her own bones beneath her ripped flesh. This had naturally enough set off several shock waves and dwellings upon the frailty of human life, from which she had not yet recovered. She was not up to handling the conflicting emotions that reverberated through the caravan that night like drums in a canyon. None of us was.

Rick showed us the slides of the departure from Alice on his projector. We sat there, Jen and I, like those sideshow clown heads – mouths open, heads swivelling. They were gorgeous photos, no complaints there, but who was that *Vogue* model tripping romantically along roads with a bunch of camels behind her, hair lifted delicately by sylvan breezes and turned into a golden halo by the back-lighting. Who the hell was she? Never let it be said that the camera does not lie. It lies like a pig in mud. It captures the projections of who-ever happens to be using it, never the truth. It was very tell-ing, to see how the batches of images changed radically as the trip progressed.

At first, I found it difficult to talk, to tell them anything, because it seemed that nothing much had in fact happened to me. I had just walked down a road leading a few camels, that's all. But as we sat together that night, in the heavy air of the caravan, my brain started to crack open sideways, spew-ing forth bits of cement and chicken wire and I knew that the trip was responsible. It was changing me in a way that I had not in the least expected. It was shaking me up and I had not even noticed. It had snuck up from behind.

The next two days buzzed and sizzled. Jenny was in tears waiting for the plane to take her back to Alice Springs, I felt like pummelled dough and Rick took pictures of us. We de-spised him for it – saw it as a form of parasitism, voyeurism. We were unable or unwilling to see that it was simply his

141

way of handling a situation in which he felt totally out of his depth. And then I was left with him.

It did not help that the magazine had insisted that he get new and exciting shots of the Rock. I posed in caves and walked back and forth across sand-dunes. I led the camels over escarpments and I rode them through wildflowers. 'What about honest journalism?' I shouted, and set my face into cement-like grimaces as I stamped along. Poor Richard, how I made him pay. I think he was truly frightened of me at times. But he was certainly game. I put him on Dookie for a ride, while I rode Bub, who started to shy and pig-root. I yelled at Richard to hang on, but through the fracas, I could hear the steady clicking of his camera. I have noticed this trait in many photographers – the ability to be much braver when they are looking through a lens than when they are not. Interesting.

I had been looking forward to seeing the Olgas for years now. They were the sisters to Ayers Rock, and they looked like great red loaves of bread that some giant had dropped out of the sky. From the Rock, they were a cluster of lavender pebbles along the horizon. I wanted to spend a few days there, away from the tourists, wandering, exploring and just enjoying the lack of pressure, and the time to myself so I could sit and think and sort out my tangles, without worrying about having to get somewhere, or be concerned for anyone else. I wanted to get away again, recapture that feeling of freedom that I had thought would be permanent when I left Redbank Gorge. It was not to be.

I walked the twenty miles, through country that should have mended me but which I did not allow even to penetrate. I was depressed, I felt cheated and put upon, and my face looked like a viola. I hated Rick and blamed him for everything. Besides, he didn't like the desert, couldn't see it. He didn't belong and he couldn't light fires, or cook, or fix trucks. He was like a fish out of water and he thought the countryside boring. He would listen to music or read until

I came into view, then he would take his photos using the magnificent earth as a backdrop.

The other difficulty was that, while my reaction to tension is to let it build up then explode it away in a fit of fury, Rick's was to sulk. I had never met such a terminal sulker. I would rather he had hit me than sulked because I couldn't stand it. By the end of the day I would practically grovel at his feet in an effort to get him to talk, or fight, or something. Anything. And Diggity adored him. 'Betraying brat,' I thought, 'and you usually have such good taste in people.'

We arrived at the Olgas that night in a tight silence, and set up camp directly beneath them. They glowed orange, then red, then iridescent pink, then purple, then turned into a black cut-out against glowing moonlight. Rick called the ranger at Ayers Rock, to test his radio, but not only could he not contact him, a mere twenty miles away, but he had a crackly conversation with a fisherman in Adelaide, five hundred miles to the south.

'Oh wonderful. Wonderful. Just as well we brought radio sets, eh, Rick? I mean when I'm bleeding and croaking out in the middle of woop-woop a mile from the nearest station, it's nice to know I can always have a pleasant chat to someone in Alaska. Wouldn't you agree, Richard? Richard?'

Richard remained silent.

That night I couldn't stand any more. I grabbed Rick by the hand, sat him down beside me by the fire and said:

'O.K., mate, you win. I can't take any more. We'll have to work something out because this is just plain ridiculous. Here we are in the middle of a most magical desert, involved in something which should be giving us joy, and we're acting like children.'

Richard continued staring into the fire, a stricken look around his eyes, and his bottom lip protruding, just a fraction. I tried again.

'It's like this story about the two monks you know. They're not allowed to have anything to do with women.

Anyway, they're walking along together and they see this woman drowning out in a stream. And one monk jumps into the water and carries her to the bank. Then they keep on walking for a while in silence and suddenly the second monk can't hold it back any more and he says, "How could you touch that woman?" And the first monk looks up surprised and answers, "Oh, are you still carrying the woman?" Well you see what I mean, Richard, we're both the second dumb monk and it's stupid and destructive and it's driving me to drink. I've got enough to worry about, and life is too short to treat like a dress rehearsal. So, either you leave right now, I send the money back to *Geographic* and we forget the whole thing, or we reach some better understanding of what we both want and how to go about getting it, O.K.?'

We talked. We talked for hours and hours about every subject under the sun, ending up laughing and being friends which was a great relief. I understood and liked him much better – he would turn out all right, that one. There were many lights hidden under his bushel.

I had also said he could come along with me to Docker River, five days away, and although I desperately wanted to be on my own again, it seemed churlish to send him away, given that he wanted to get photographs of Aborigines, and this would probably be one of the few places he could do so. Although I felt disturbed by this prospect (I knew Aboriginal people were thoroughly sick of having lenses stuck up their nostrils by insensitive tourists) I thought that any press coverage they could get, at this stage in their demise, would be a good thing, providing it was done with their consent. Besides, the relief of having Rick talking to me again, of having dissipated the tension, was worth almost any concession.

I did not perceive at that time that I was allowing myself to get more involved with an article about the trip than the trip itself. It did not dawn on me that already I was beginning

144

o see it as a story for other people, with a beginning and n ending.

We spent a few days at the Olgas which, although pleasant nough, how could they not be in such a place, for me were louded by a feeling of being bound, kept back, hemmed n. I constantly imagined what it would be like, how much better it would be, if I were on my own. I was no longer blaming Richard, however, but myself. I knew I had to take full responsibility for his being there, had to come face to face with the fact that this trip would not, could not, be what I had planned and wanted it to be. And instead of seeing the potential that was there, I mourned for the loss of my precious expectations.

A day out on the track, and the pressure was starting to build again. This because, after I have loaded fifteen hundred pounds of junk, walked twenty miles, unloaded the junk, gathered firewood, lit a fire, cooked a meal for two, and cleaned up after the meal for two, I get a wee bit titchy. Perhaps it's the low blood sugar level, I don't know. I do know that anyone who crosses me after such a day had better expect an explosion, especially if all that person has done is take pictures of me doing all those things, instead of helping me with them.

I seethed with secret rage one night, then threw a bundle of garlic at my companion and yelled, 'Peel that if you haven't got a broken arm.' We were back at square one, with Richard in the sulks, and me thinking up ways I could murder him without getting caught.

I left camp the next morning with Richard telling me he would be along in an hour, to which I grunted something monosyllabic and continued on my way. I walked for one hour, then two, then two and a half. No Richard. 'Oh Jesus, I'm going to have to go back, the car must have broken down.'

I had back-tracked five miles when the first and only car we had seen drove up and stopped. I asked them if they

145

would mind driving a little way along and seeing if they could find Richard's tracks into the scrub, and letting me know if he was all right. They drove all the way to the Rock and returned without seeing Rick. It was well into the afternoon by then, and I was beginning to really worry.

'Snakebite?' I thought. 'Heart attack?'

I was about to leave these new friends when the Toyota came charging over the hill with Rick inside, listening to Joan Armatrading.

'Where *were* you?'

Richard looked from face to face and with a dawning comprehension, and a certain sheepishness, said, 'I was just back at camp reading my book, why?'

I could feel my lips compress into a furious white line. The others swapped glances, coughed delicately, and drove off. Rick apologized. I said nothing. My anger had set cold and hard. It felt like a fist in my chest.

Then the rain came. Great angry thundering clouds swarmed and bustled out of nowhere, and it hailed and poured a deluge. It rained cats and dogs, elephants and whales, and I stumbled through it, cold and wet and holding my anger to me like a baby. I was worried as usual over the camels. And I was exhausted. Exhausted by the work and worry, exhausted by the anger, and exhausted by my thoughts, which went round and round in circles, always returning to the central fact that I was involved in a pointless ludicrous farce.

And of course that was the night that dear little Goliath decided he didn't like being caught and tied to a tree any more. I chased him for over an hour at a run. I entered a new realm of exhaustion. I was covered with freezing mud and shaking with fatigue by the time I grabbed him. Then I crawled back to camp, drank a third of a bottle of whisky in ten minutes and through hysterical weeping over which I had no control, raved at Richard before collapsing in an incoherent, shattered heap.

That night injected two new elements into our relationship. The first was tolerance – that is, the necessity to compromise. It set the real basis for an unlikely friendship, which, although it was to have its ups and downs, was there to stay. The second was sex.

Ah. Yes. Silly me. Inevitable I suppose, but in retrospect, one of the worst mistakes I made in terms of my freedom during the trip. It deepened my commitment to Richard in some ancient and subtle way – I could no longer discount his feelings as easily as I might have otherwise. Rick Smolan, photographer extraordinaire, New York Jewish survivalist, conman and manipulator par excellence without even knowing it; talented, generous, strange young man who felt awkward and hid behind Nikons, this was the creature with whom my trip was becoming hopelessly entangled; who I was to feel robbed me of its original meaning and essence, who had changed from someone I barely noticed to a millstone round my neck and my cross to bear. The first confusing oscillatory element that was to be so characteristic of this trip had struck. It allowed Rick to 'fall in love'. Not with me, but with the camel lady.

However, we were much kinder to one another after that night. While Rick began really trying, I began to come to terms with the fact that he either had to be completely out of the thing, or completely involved in it. I could not have it both ways. He began slowly changing from that day, letting the desert work on him, coming to a recognition of it, and of himself as a consequence.

We passed Lassiter's Cave – poor Lassiter, that gold-hungry mug who lost his camels and perished in the sandhills, holding a nose-peg which he must have ripped from his frightened bolting camels, and leaving behind an unsolved mystery concerning his supposed discovery of a gold outcropping so rich he would have been a billionaire, if he had only made it back. The Pitjantjara mob, who up till then had had virtually no contact with whitefellas, had tried to keep

147

him alive, but, like so many other luckless explorers, he had not been able to keep up the pace and died a miserable death only tens of miles from safety. Many of the old Pitjantjar people remember him. I tried hard not to think about tha nose-peg in his hands.

We were a day or two short of Docker, when the firs major disaster of the trip occurred. I was carefully leading my camels through a river that had once been a track, wher Dookie, the last in line, slipped and landed flat in the water I went back to him and asked him to stand up. I tapped him behind the shoulder and asked him again. He looked at me pitifully and groaned to his feet. The rain was blinding me and running down me in cold torrents. He could hardly use his front right leg.

We camped that day in a deep luminous glassy green light. I had no idea what was wrong with the leg. I prodded, rubbec and examined from shoulder to foot. It was tender but there was no swelling that I could see. I made hot compresses bu did not know what else I could do. Was it a broken bone a torn ligament, what? The point was that Dookie could no walk. He sat in the creek-bed, miserable, and refused to move. I cut him feed and brought it to him and massagec the shoulder again. I hugged him, fussed over him, and al the while I felt sick and tired and beaten. A thought was in vading me which I tried to keep away. That I might have to shoot my boy, that the trip might be ended, that it wa all just a stupid pathetic joke. I was glad Richard was there

At last, the rains cleared. Everything was rinsed clean anc sparkling. We rested two days, then limped into Docker where as usual there were hundreds of excited children to mee us. The community adviser gave us a caravan to live in, anc Rick decided to stay until we knew what Dookie's fate woulc be. In the end I waited there six weeks, not knowing whethe the leg would heal or not. Rick stayed for two. It was no a happy time.

It is amazing to me how human beings can remain calm

controlled and sensible on the surface, when internally they are cracking up, crumbling, breaking down. I can see now that that time in Docker was the beginning of a kind of mental collapse, though I would not have described it in such a way then. I was still functioning after all. The whites there were kind and did their best to entertain and look after me, but they could not know that I needed all my energy just to remain in that caravan and lick my wounds. They could not know that they were gutting me with their invitations that I was too morally weak to resist, that my endless smiles hid an overwhelming despair. I wanted to hide, I slept for hour after hour and when I woke up it was into nothingness. Grey nothingness. I was ill.

Whatever justifications for photographing the Aborigines I had come up with before, now were totally shot. It was immediately apparent that they hated it. They knew it was a rip-off. I wanted Rick to stop. He argued that he had a job to do. I looked through a small booklet *Geographic* had given him to record expenditures. In it was 'gifts to the natives'. I couldn't believe it. I told him to put down five thousand dollars for mirrors and beads, then hand out the money. I also realized that coverage in a conservative magazine like *Geographic* would do the people no good at all, no matter how I wrote the article. They would remain quaint primitives to be gawked at by readers who couldn't really give a damn what was happening to them. I argued with Rick that he was involved in a form of parasitism, and besides, since everyone saw him as my husband, whatever they felt for him, they felt for me too. They were polite and deferential as always, and they took me hunting and food-gathering, but the wall was always there. He came up with all the old arguments, but was torn, I knew, because he recognized it was true.

It was coming time for him to leave and he felt thwarted – he had not done his job. One night we had heard wailing from down at camp. Without my knowledge, he snuck out of the caravan early the next morning and went down there to take pictures. He was not to know that he was recording a secret ceremony and sacred business, but he was lucky he didn't get a spear through his leg. I did not know this until after he had gone, but I could feel the people set against us. Not overtly, never overtly, but it was there, a feeling, which I thought was simply because they could see through me. It seemed that one of my main aims, to be with Aboriginal people, was now unattainable.

I had hobbled the camels seven miles out of town, where the feed was best. Dookie I let roam loose. Each day I drove out to check on them, cut feed for Goliath for whom I had built a rope enclosure, and stare at Dookie who did not seem to be improving. I decided to fly back to Alice in the mail plane to consult a vet, or Sallay, or obtain a portable X-ray. I cannot describe the feeling of defeat, landing at the Alice airport. I had sworn never to go back, but now it looked as if I would never be free of the place, even physically. I consulted everyone, tried to get the X-ray unit from health departments, hospitals, even dental clinics. All to no avail. The response was always the same. All you can do is wait and see.

I flew back. Richard left, leaving me the car.

The routine over the next few weeks was abysmally tedious. I would force myself to get up in the morning, after having read a crummy science-fiction book all night to prevent me from thinking, then drive out to the camels. This was sometimes made more pleasant by taking along hordes of children. But the day I had my first encounter with a wild bull, I was on my own.

'God, Diggity, Dookie looks bigger all of a sudden, it must be all this green feeee ... oh no. Oh Jesus. It's happened.'

There cavorting with my Zelly, and stirring up my boys were ... My own camels were so toey, I thought they might take off with them if I waited too long. Luckily there was a young Aboriginal man just down the road. He drove round

150

and round the bulls, so they couldn't get at me, while I dashed out, feeling terrified out of my wits, and tied Zelly quickly to a tree. So far so good. Then I hurtled back to the settlement at the speed of light. Nothing like a bit of danger to get the blood flowing again. I grabbed my rifle and a couple of men and hurtled back again. I had hardly used the thing, and was still frightened of it, still shut my eyes involuntarily when I pulled the trigger. I rested my arm on the truck, shot, missed, shot, wounded, shot, shot, shot, shot, killed.

We then chased the other bulls in the vehicle, and the men shot them with piffling little .22s. It took many wounds to kill them, and it seemed that each bullet caused me almost as much pain. It was terrible, shocking, to see such proud beasts fall. How people kill for pleasure is totally outside my realm of understanding. And then the remorse.

Glenys, a nurse working for the Aboriginal health service, arrived a few days later. I immediately liked her. We went out often, hunting with the women, digging for maku (witchetty grub) and honey-ant and going on bunny bashes, in which the women find a warren, dig deep down into the earth with their crowbars and extract, if they're lucky, handfuls of rabbits, who then have their necks expertly cricked, and are slung on the back of the truck to be taken home and roasted in the coals. I loved these expeditions – twenty women and children would cram into and on to the Toyota, all laughing and talking, and we would drive thirty-odd miles to a special place. The skinny mangy camp dogs would follow at a gallop, yapping and yelping, and arrive hours later half dead with exhaustion, just as we would be ready to leave.

Glenys and I decided to drive to Giles, a weather station one hundred miles west. There was a large Aboriginal camp there and a handful of whites to run the station. When we arrived, some young men came out and invited us into their canteen. We knew the inevitability of the conversation, and neither of us particularly wanted to go through that again. Glenys was part-Aboriginal, and felt their nigger jokes more strongly than I did. I had learnt to turn a deaf ear. We told one of them we would be going down to the camp.

'See if you can't knock down a few coons with that roo bar while you're there, haw haw.'

I threw the truck into reverse and spattered him with gravel as I spun the wheel. Glenys leant out the window and swore at him. His jaw actually dropped.

When we got to camp, we went and had a talk with some women. After a while, there was some whispering and conferring going on amongst them. An old lady then came up and asked us if we would like to learn to dance. Of course the answer was yes. We were led to a clearing away from the view of the camp. The oldest women, beautifully ugly old hags, squatted down at the front while the younger women and girls formed a mass behind them. Glenys and I sat in front. There was much touching and laughing and reassurance. I did not speak enough Pitjantjara to understand all they were saying, but it didn't matter. The mood was transmitted. Then the chanting began. It was led by the old ladies, different ones leading at different times. Others found sticks and tapped them one upon the other on the red earth in rhythm. I didn't know whether to join in, did not know the rules of conduct. But as it went on, that droning, dust-woven, meditative music, I felt transported and close to tears. The sound seemed to rise from the ground. It belonged so perfectly, it was a song of unity and recognition, and the old crones were like extensions of the earth. I wanted to understand so much. Why were they doing this for us, these smiling women? I melted into a feeling of belonging. They were letting me into their world. They asked me if I wanted to dance. I felt stupid and clumsy and afraid to get up. Eventually an old woman took me by the hand and to the strange clicking rhythm and the droning melody, she danced and made me copy her. I tried my best. There were hoots of laughter from behind. Tears rolled down faces and sides were clenched in a delight of laughter. I laughed with them, and my old teacher hugged me. She showed me again the difficult bodily tremor that came at the end of each cadence. At last I got it and then we danced in earnest, hopping and shuffling in grooves in the dust, and shaking at the end, and turning and going back and then slowly skipping in a circle. Hours passed. Gradually an unspoken group decision that the dance had ended thinned out the women. Soon everyone was moving away. We stood there, not knowing what was expected of us. We were about to leave too when one of the old women came up to us, puckered her toothless mouth, and said, 'Six dollar you got six dollar.' Her knobbly old hand was outstretched, the others turned and watched. I was dumbfounded, speechless. I had not thought ... I gathered my speech and told her we didn't have any. I emptied my pockets to show her. 'Two dollar, you got two dollar.' Glenys fumbled and gave her all the change she had. I promised her I would send her the money, then my friend and I left.

We didn't talk much on the way home. I did not know then that it was merely a rule of etiquette to give some little gift at the end of a dance. I felt it as a symbolic defeat. A final summing up of how I could never enter their reality, would always be a whitefella tourist on the outside looking in.

And so it dragged on, that gradual decaying of my little hopes and dreams. While Dookie's shoulder began slowly to heal (I had diagnosed it by then as a torn muscle), I asked round Docker if any of the old men would like to come with me to Pipalyatjara. I wanted to cut across country for the next hundred and some-odd miles, but knew this would be through sacred country, dotted with sacred sites where women were not allowed to go. I could not do it without an old man. It would be the worst form of trespassing, but I desperately wanted to get away from the tracks. Without actually saying yes, they didn't say no either, a common form of politeness amongst Aborigines called courtesy bias. I knew

153

they didn't trust me, even though I had no camera. I ha
found out from the irate community adviser what Rick ha
done, knew that I was an accomplice and found it hard t
look at them. Taking photos of secret business was far wors
than desecrating a church could be to the staunchest c
Christians. The Aborigines there sorted travellers into tw
sections, tourists and people; I realized that to them I ha
become a tourist.

There were only half a dozen whites at Docker. The
were good people. From the community adviser to th
mechanics to the store managers, they invited me to barbe
cues, on picnics and out hunting, but they could not penetrat
my gloom.

By the time I was ready to leave, it was decided that non
of the old men wanted to come. That meant 160 mile
of dirt track, which, although I could expect to see ne
vehicles, I did not look forward to. I didn't know whethe
to continue. It all seemed rather pointless. I had sold the trip
misunderstood and mismanaged everything. I could not b
with Aboriginal people without being a clumsy intruder
The journey had lost all meaning, lost all its magical inspirin;
quality, was an empty and foolish gesture. I wanted to giv
up. But to do what? Go back to Brisbane? If this, the hardes
and most worthwhile thing I had ever attempted, was ;
miserable failure, then what on earth would succeed? I lef
Docker, more unhappy, more negative, more weakenec
than I had ever been.

8

As I left the settlement, alone, I was aware only of a flat-
ness, a lack of substance in everything. My steps felt
achingly slow, small and leaden. They led me nowhere.
Step after step after step, the interminable walking dragged
out, pulling my thoughts downward into spirals. The
country seemed alien, faded, muted, the silence hostile,
overwhelming.

I was twenty miles out, tired and thirsty. I drank some beer.
I was about to turn off and make camp when through the
beer-hazed afternoon heat came striding three large strong
male camels in full season.

Panic and shake. Panic and shake. They attack and kill, remember. Remember now, one – tie up Bub securely, two –
whoosh him down, three – take rifle from scabbard, four –
load rifle, five – cock, aim and fire rifle. They were just thirty
yards away and one was spurting a cylindrical arch of red
blood. He didn't seem to notice it. They all came forward
again.

I was scared deep in my bones. First, I could not believe
it was happening, then I believed it was never going to stop.
My ears thumped, cold sweat stuck to the hollow of my back.
My vision was distorted by fear. Then I was past it, not thinking any more, just doing it.

Zzzzt. This time just behind his head and he turned and
ambled away. Zzzt. Near the heart again, he slumped down
but just sat there. Zzzt. In the head, dead. The other two
trundled off into the scrub. Shake and sweat, shake and sweat.
You've won for now.

I unsaddled the camels and hobbled them close, glancing
round constantly. It was getting dark. They came back.

Braver now, I shot one, but only wounded it. Night cam
too quickly.

The fire flickered on white moonstruck sand, the sky wa
black onyx. The rumbling sound of bulls circled the cam
very close until I fell asleep. In the moonlight, I woke u
and maybe twenty yards away was a beast standing in fu
profile. I loved it and didn't want to harm it. It was beautifu
proud. Not interested in me at all. I slept again, drifting o
to the sound of bells on camels, peacefully chewing their cuc

Came dawn, I was already stalking, gun loaded and read
They were both still there. I had to kill the wounded on
I tried to. Another cylinder of blood and he ran away nippin
at his wound. I could not follow. I knew he would die slowl
but I could not follow, I had my own survival to think o
There he was, the last young bull, a beautiful thing,
moonlight camel. I made a decision. This one of the thre
would be allowed to live until he did something direct t
jeopardize my safety. Happy decision. 'Yes, maybe he'll ta
along right to Carnarvon. And I'll call him Aldebaran an
isn't he magnificent, Diggity, what a match for Dookie.
don't have to kill him at all.' I snuck around to catch th
camels. He watched me. Now, last camel to catch, Bub. O
he galloped in his hobbles, the new bull pacing lazily besid
him. I couldn't catch him with the other bull so close. I trie
for an hour, I was exhausted, I wanted to kill Bubby, to dis
member him, rip his balls out, but they'd already gone. I too
the rifle and I walked to within thirty feet of the now excite
and burbling young bull. I put a slug right where I kne
it would kill him. It did not, and he bit and roared at h
wound. He didn't understand this pain, I was crying. I fire
again into his head and he sat down, gurgling through h
own blood. I walked up to his head, we stared at on
another – he knew then. He looked at me, I shot him in th
brain, point blank.

Bubby was puzzled. He walked up to the carcass and dran
some blood. It was all over his nose, like clown's lipstick

156

and he threw his lips around. He allowed himself to be caught, I didn't hit him. I walked on.

I entered a new time, space, dimension. A thousand years fitted into a day and aeons into each step. The desert oaks sighed and bent down to me, as if trying to grab at me. Sandhills came and sandhills went. Hills rose up and hills slipped away. Clouds rolled in and clouds rolled out and always the road, always the road, always the road, always the road.

So tired, I slept in the creek and thought of nothing but failure. I could not even light a fire. I wanted to hide in the dark. I thought it was surely longer than two days, I had walked so far. But time was different here, it was stretched by step after step and in each step a century of circular thought. I didn't want to think like this, was ashamed of my thoughts but I could not stop them. The moon, cold marble and cruel, pushed down on me, sucked at me, I could not hide from it, even in dream.

And the next day and the next day too, the road and the sandhills and the cold wind sucked at my thoughts and nothing happened but walking.

The country was dry. How could the camels be so thirsty and thin. At night, they came into camp and tried to knock over the water drums. I hadn't enough to spare, I rationed them. The map said 'rockhole'. Thank god. I turned off the track somewhere in that haze of elastic time and walked in. More sandhills, then a stretch of gibberflat, wide and dry and desolate with one dead bird, and two empty holes. Some string somewhere inside me was starting to unravel. An important string, the one that held down panic. I walked on. That night I camped in those sandhills ...

The sky was leaden and thick. All day it had been grey, smooth, translucent, like the belly of a frog. Spots of rain pattered on me but not enough to lay the dust. The sky was washing me out, emptying me. I was cold as I hunched over my meagre fire. And somewhere, between frozen sandhills, in a haunted and forgotten desert, where time is always measured by the interminable roll of constellations, or the chill call of a crow waking, I lay down on my dirty bundle of blankets. The frost clung like brittle cobwebs to the black bushes around me, while the sky turned thick with glitter. It was very still. I slept. The hour before the sun spills thin blood colour on the sand, I woke suddenly, and tried to gather myself from a dream I could not remember. I was split. I woke into limbo and could not find myself. There were no reference points, nothing to keep the world controlled and bound together. There was nothing but chaos and the voices.

The strong one, the hating one, the powerful one was mocking me, laughing at me.

'You've gone too far this time. I've got you now and I hate you. You're disgusting, aren't you. You're nothing. And I have you now, I knew it would come, sooner or later. There's no use fighting me you know, there's no one to help you. I've got you, I've got you.'

Another voice was calm and warm. She commanded me to lie down and be calm. She instructed me to not let go, not give in. She reassured me that I would find myself again if I could just hold on, be quiet and lie down.

The third voice was screaming.

Diggity woke me at dawn. I was some distance from camp, cramped, and cold to my bones. The sky was cold, pale blue and pitiless, like an Austrian psychopath's eyes. I walked out into the time warp again. I was only half there, like an automaton. I knew what I had to do. 'You must do this, this will keep you alive. Remember.' I walked out into that evil whispering sea. Like an animal, I sensed a menace, everything was quite still, but threatening, icy, beneath the sun's heat. I felt it watching me, following me, waiting for me.

I tried to conquer the presence with my own voice. It croaked out into the silence and was swallowed by it. 'All we have to do,' it said, 'is reach Mount Fanny, and there is certain to be water there. Just one step and another, that's

158

ll I have to do, I must not panic.' I could see what had to
be Mount Fanny in the hot blue distance, and I wanted to
be there, protected by those rocks, more than anything I'd
ever wanted. I knew I was being unreasonable. There was
more than enough water to get by on to Wingelinna. But
the camels, I'd been so sure they'd do a week comfortably.
I hadn't planned on the sudden dryness – the lack of green
feed. 'But there'll be water there, of course there will.
Haven't they told me so? What if there's not? What if the
mill's run dry? What if I miss it? What if this thin little piece
of string that keeps me tied to my camels breaks? What
then?' Walk walk walk, sandhills for ever, they all looked
the same. I walked as if on a treadmill – no progress, no
change. The hill came closer so slowly. 'How long is it now?
A day? This is the longest day. Careful. Remember, it's just
a day. Hold on, mustn't let go. Maybe a car will come. No
cars. What if there's no water, what will I do? Must stop
this. Must stop. Just keep walking. Just one step at a time,
that's all it takes.' And on and on and on went that dialogue
in my head. Over and over and round and round.

Late in the afternoon – long creeping shadows. The hill was
close. 'Please please let me be there before night. Please don't
let me be here in the dark. It will engulf me.'

It must be over the next sandhill surely. No, then the next
one. O.K., all right, the next, no the next, no the next. Please
god, am I mad. The hill is there, I can almost touch it. I started
to yell. I started to shout stupidly at the dunes. Diggity licked
my hand and whined but I could not stop. I had been doing
this for ever. I walked in slow motion. Everything was slow-
ing down.

And then, over the last sandhill, I was out of the dunes.
I crouched on the rocks, weeping, feeling their substance
with my hands. I climbed steadily, up the rocky escarpment,
away from that terrible ocean of sand. The rocks were heavy
and dark and strong. They rose up like an island. I crawled
over this giant spine, where it emerged from the waves, in

159

a fuzz of green. I looked back to the immensity of where I had been. Already the memory was receding – the time, the aching time of it. Already, I had forgotten most of the days. They had sunk away from memory, leaving only a few peaks that I could recall. I was safe.

'The mill will be easy to find. Or the rockhole, it doesn't matter. There will be water here somewhere. Everything will be O.K.' Panic melted and I laughed at myself for being so absurd, an effect of emotional and physical exhaustion, that was all it was. I was all right. I was going to be all right. The threads bound together and I touched Diggity. 'Diggity's here, it's O.K. It's too dark to find the mill tonight, Dig, but there's a green patch of roly-poly here, that will make them happy, eh, little one? We'll find the mill tomorrow, the birds and tracks will lead us to it. And I'll give the camels a big drink, but right now I'll make a roaring fire and have some tea and feed you, my little friend.'

I slept deeply and dreamlessly, woke early and rose as easily and cleanly as an eagle leaving its nest. There was no trace of the previous day's fatigue, or the previous night's enemy. My mind was rinsed clean and sparkling and light. Everything around me was bursting with life and vibrance. The colours danced and glistened in the crisp dawn light. Early morning birds, hundreds of them. My spirits high, I packed up quickly, expertly even, like a precision machine. I felt bigger somehow, expanded. I walked a hundred yards around the corner, and there was the mill. The camels drank, Diggity drank and I had a freezing invigorating bath.

About half a mile from the mill, I walked slap bang into a herd of forty camels. The gun came out smoothly and quietly. I had watched them descend like quiet ghosts, from their drinking spot high up in the hills. I looked at them, and they looked at me, sharing the same path. I knew I wouldn't have to shoot this time, but play it safe, that's the rules of this particular game. I smiled at them. They were more beautiful than I could describe. The big boss bull kept them

20-1   Mr Eddie, an elder of the Pitjantjara tribe, travelled with me from his home settlement to Warburton. *Below*, Bubby and Dookie were constantly looking for hand-outs.

22 Bubby was not above stealing my supper from the pan as it cooked.

slightly ahead, and glanced back constantly, to size up the situation. They stopped, I stopped – impasse. I shouted, hooted and laughed at them. They looked faintly quizzical. I waved my arms in the direction of the big bull and said, 'Shoo ...' in a loud and authoritative shout. He looked infinitely bored. I fired some shot-gun pellets into the air and he recognized that sound. He rounded up his family, nipping at their heels, and they gathered momentum, until forty beautiful wild free camels were bucking and galloping down the valley into an echo and a vortex of dust, and then they were gone. I was remembering exactly who I was now.

That night, I was about to turn in when I heard cars purr in the distance. Such a foreign, incongruous sound. I didn't need them any more, didn't want them. They would be an intrusion. I was even slightly afraid of them, because I knew I was still half crazy. 'Yea or nay for human company tonight, Dig? Well let's let the fire do the talking. But will I make sense to them? What if they ask me questions? What will I say? Best thing is just to smile a lot and keep the trap shut, eh, little dog, what you reckon?' I fossicked around in my head, trying to find the pleasantries of conversation that had been blasted into fragments by the previous week's experience. I muttered them to Diggity. 'Oh god, they've seen the fire, here they come.' I checked myself nervously for signs of dementia.

Aborigines. Warm, friendly, laughing, excited, tired Pitantjara Aborigines, returning to Wingelinna and Pipalyatara after a land rights meeting in Warburton. No fear there, they were comfortable with silence. No need to pretend anything. Billies of tea all round. Some sat by the fire and chatted, others drove on home.

The last car, a clapped-out ancient Holden, chug-a-chugged in. One young driver, and three old men. They decided to stay for the night. I shared my tea and blankets. Two of the old men were quiet and smiling. I sat by them in silence, letting their strength seep in. One I especially liked.

A dwarfish man with dancing hands, straight back, and on his feet, one huge Adidas and one tiny woman's shoe. He handed me the best bit of his part-cooked rabbit, dripping grease and blood, fur singed and stinking. I ate it gratefully. I remembered that I had not eaten properly for the past few days.

The one I didn't like so well was the voluble one who could speak a little English and knew all about camels and probably everything else in the world as well. He was loud, egotistical, not composed like the others.

Early in the morning, I boiled the billy and started to pack up. I talked to my companions a little. They decided that one of them should accompany me to Pipalyatjara, two days' walk away, to look after me. I was so sure it was going to be the talkative one, the one who spoke English, and my heart sank.

But as I was about to walk off with the camels, who should join me but – the little man. 'Mr Eddie,' he said, and pointed to himself. I pointed to myself and said 'Robyn', which I suppose he thought meant 'rabbit', since that is the Pitjantjara word for it. It seemed appropriate enough. And then we began to laugh.

Part Three
Little Bit Long Way

9

FOR THE next two days Eddie and I walked together, we played charades trying to communicate and fell into fits of hysteria at each other's antics. We stalked rabbits and missed, picked bush foods and generally had a good time. He was sheer pleasure to be with, exuding all those qualities typical of old Aboriginal people – strength, warmth, self-possession, wit, and a kind of rootedness, a substantiality that immediately commanded respect. And I wondered as we walked along, how the word 'primitive' with all its subtle and nasty connotations ever got to be associated with people like this. If, as someone has said, 'to be truly civilized, is to embrace disease,' then Eddie and his kind were not civilized. Because that was what was so outstanding in him: he was healthy, integrated, whole. That quality radiated from him and you would have to be a complete dolt to miss it.

By now the country had changed dramatically. I was well away from the dreaded pits and hollows of sandhill country. Vast plains covered in yellow grasses like wheat fields swept up to the foot of chocolate-brown rocky mountains and ranges. These were covered at the base by pale green and yellow spinifex and bushes, which slowly gave way to the bare stony outcroppings at the top. Small washaways contained most of the trees, and every now and then just one single bare red sandhill, stuck up in the middle of the yellow. Bright green peeked out of the valleys and chasms, and all of it capped with that infinite dome of cobalt blue. The sense of space, clean bright limitless space was with me again.

However, after all that had happened to me, all that madness and strain, I desperately needed to talk in depth with someone. Because, while my panic and fear had now been supplanted by a frenetic happiness, I was still shaken to the core. Still teetering. I had to recover my ordinary self and make sense of the experience somehow. I was a third of the way through my trip, and Glendle, the community adviser at Pipalyatjara, would be the first and perhaps last friend I was likely to meet. I was longing to see him, to speak in English about all that had been going on. But Eddie kept telling me he had 'gone'. I found out later that he attached the word 'gone' to the ends of many sentences; it roughly implied direction so I need not have worried. But the thought of Glendle being away was too much to bear.

When Eddie walked a little behind I could feel him looking askance at me – feel his puzzled eyes on the back of my head.

'What's wrong with this woman? Why doesn't she just relax, she keeps repeating, "Is Glendle there, Eddie, is he there *now*?"'

'Glendle gooooooone,' he said, waving his little hand in the air. Whenever he said that he raised his eyebrows and widened his eyes in a comical look of surprised seriousness, but I found it hard to smile. I turned and walked on, trying to control the trembling chin and the tears that threatened to bounce out of my eyeballs at any second and stream down my face.

'Please, please, you've got to be there, Glendle, I need to talk and get it all straight. I've never needed a friend like this before. Please, please be there.'

We camped that night three miles out of Wingelinna, Eddie's home settlement. He instructed me to stay in camp while he went in to get his possessions. He came back with a rusty tin, containing a bottle of liniment, a bottle of aspirin and some desert herb. Oh, and a red jumper.

We headed on to Pipalyatjara the next morning, with me feeling anxious and Eddie singing. I wasn't following maps, so I had no idea how close the settlement would be. Suddenly I noticed a tin shed on my right. I must have been staring

lead ahead to have missed it. On its walls were children's
drawings and paintings.

'Could that possibly be a school? Pipalyatjara doesn't have
a school, does it? Glendle's the only white person here, isn't
ne?' I stopped and blinked. I was completely disoriented. I
couldn't remember whether drawings on the walls meant a
school or not. I didn't know if I was crazy enough to be mak-
ng absurd assumptions. And yet it looked like a bush school.
Yes, of course, it had to be, what else. A shadow came to
he door, hesitated and came strolling out rolling a cigarette.
He was a rather hippieish young man, and he said in a quiet
and cultivated voice, 'Hello there, we've been expecting you.
How's it been going?'

I gulped. I wanted to throw my arms about him, prostrate
myself before him, and dance a jig. He spoke English. But
still didn't know how mad I was. And if I was crazy I didn't
want him to realize it. So I just stared dumbly, with a great
honking lop-sided grin splitting my face open and garbled,
Glendle?'

'Just turn the corner and you'll see some caravans, he's in
one of those.' He smiled and offered me a smoke. I was too
embarrassed for him to see my shaking hands, and too afraid
hat I might give myself away by saying or doing something
incomprehensible, so I just shook my head and walked on,
wondering if he had picked anything up.

And then it struck me that people don't really mind if
you're crazy out there. In fact, they half expect it and are
usually slightly troppo themselves. Besides, there aren't
enough people to go around for anyone to worry about
whether they are dealing with a fruit-cake or not.

I knew Glendle's caravan immediately. Who else would
have a wind-chime stuck to a tree in his front yard? The only
tree for miles and a dead one at that. Not that there was a
yard of course, just that invisible demarcation that all dwell-
ngs radiate. He came out and we hugged and then hugged
some more and then we hugged again and I couldn't speak

so I got busy making the camels comfortable, and then we three went inside for the inevitable Australian ritual of tea-drinking. I started gibbering then, and I didn't stop raving blessed English for a minute. Or laughing.

That high lasted four days. Glendle was a most perfect, perceptive and loving host. He even gave up his crisp-sheeted bed, while he and Eddie slept outside. He swore he preferred sleeping outside and it was only laziness that prevented him from doing so more often, which was probably true. So I accepted gratefully. Not that I hadn't fallen in love with my swag by then, but experiencing the luxury of a bed again was kind of interesting. Diggity was overjoyed.

That night Glendle cooked tea. Eddie had set up camp outside and old men and women were constantly coming up to see him and talk to Glendle and me. I was once again struck by these old people. They were softly spoken, chuckled constantly and seemed totally in control of their actions. And I wished I understood more Pitjantjara. While I could pick out 'camel' often, and get the gist of most conversations I couldn't pick up on abstracts. But I could tell that there were many camel yarns being swapped there that night.

Throughout the days that followed it seemed that there were always people coming up to the caravan to say hello, borrow cups and billy, share a mug of tea, air and resolve grievances, or discuss policies. It was nice, but I wondered how Glendle ever got anything done. He was burdened with endless paper-work dished out by bureaucrats, and he hated it. A community adviser's job may be enviable in some ways, but is essentially thankless. His major role is to formalize the distribution of money to individuals, which task is usually done through the medium of a store, where the people cash their cheques and buy goods at inflated prices. The profits are used to buy those things for the community that the Aboriginal council thinks should be purchased. Trucks for example, or bore parts. He co-ordinates all the systems such as health and education services and acts as a liaison officer between bureaucracies and the people. This, of course, makes him the primary flak-catcher, because Aborigines have little concept of budgets, how and why the money gets there, and the bureaucrats know nothing about the Aboriginal way of life.

The job has other soul-destroying aspects, as I learnt from Glendle. No white person can fully enter Aboriginal reality and the more you learn, the more you're aware of that vast gap of knowledge and understanding. It takes a long time to perceive the various complications and rules attached to such a position, and by that time you are usually burnt out. Some advisers out there became initiated by the old men. This, they thought, would bring them much closer to the people and an understanding of them. It certainly did, but it also set up other problems. In becoming initiated, they found they had conflicting duties and responsibilities to various groups, thus making it difficult to be fair to all.

The job is made more difficult by the fact that the adviser is more aware than the Aborigines of the possible consequences of their decisions, and wants to protect them. Not becoming a paternal-style protectionist means seeing catastrophic mistakes being made, and not being able to do a thing about it except advise, because you know that the only way the people can learn to deal with the white world is to make such mistakes. There will not always be kind-hearted whitefellas around to save the situation and be a buffer zone. At some point the people must become autonomous. A fine line.

And Glendle was tired – boned out. Trying to get things started, against the pressure of governments and with the lack of money, support and facilities, depressed and frustrated him at times. While he was besotted with the country and its people, and while he enjoyed a mutually respectful relationship with them, the work took its toll, as it does on almost everyone involved for any length of time with Aboriginal rights, whether it be out on some settlement or in a legal

169

office in town. There is always just too much to fight. The positive steps are so minuscule, so piffling in the face of the enormity of what is being done to them.

Pipalyatjara, unlike many other settlements, was lucky in that it did not have a multi-tribal population. It did not have the phenomenon of regularly occurring inter-tribal fight between individuals and groups. Traditionally throughou Australia each tribe had perhaps several tribal neighbours Some of these were important economic and ritual partners whilst others were regarded as antagonists because of either a history of conflicts or dissimilar customs and beliefs. Nevertheless, their traditional relationships were not taken into account at all when government field officers established the first outposts and settlements. Here in Pipalyatjara, because of the homogeneity, conflict between individuals was strictly controlled by traditional laws and methods for its resolution The settlement was originally set up years ago as an outstation – an alternative to Wingelinna which had been a mining centre. It was hoped that other outstations would spring up like satellites, once Pipalyatjara had been established.

The real importance of this approach to Aboriginal settlement is that it allows groups to get away from the institutionalizing pressure of those areas of maximum Western impact – the mission and government settlements. This movement contains an element of withdrawal; the people go of their own volition back to their traditional life-style and traditional lands, where they are able to enact traditional ceremonies, teach their children traditional skills and knowledge, but at the same time take what they see as important from Western culture, if they so desire. It is a life-style which maximizes identity and pride, and minimizes the problems of cultural conflict. The typical outstation ranges from a camp with no Western artefacts at all, not even a gun, to a camp supplemented with services chosen by the occupants These may include airstrip, water bore, wireless, and caravans containing teaching and medical facilities with perhaps one o several whites teaching in these. This outstation movement eems to be gaining momentum throughout tribal Australia where it is politically possible.

Whilst in Pipalyatjara, I learnt that the Pitjantjara people were trying to have their land turned from leasehold to free-hold. The attitude of the elders at first had been to dismiss the whole question. As far as they were concerned they didn't own the land, the land owned them. Their belief was that the earth was traversed in the dream-time by ancestral beings who had supernatural energy and power. These beings were biologically different from contemporary man, some being a synthesis of man and animal, plant, or forces, such as fire or water.

The travels of these dream-time heroes formed the topography of the land, and their energies remained on earth embodied in the tracks they followed, or in special sites or landmarks where important events had taken place. Contemporary man receives part of these energies through a complex association with and duty towards these places. These are what anthropologists call totems – the identification of individuals with particular species of animals and plants and other natural phenomena. Thus particular trees, rocks and other natural objects are imbued with enormous religious significance for the people who own a particular area of country and have the knowledge of ceremonies and stories for that country.

There is no confusion in the minds of Aboriginal people as to who are the traditional caretakers of country. Land ownership' and responsibility is handed down through both the patriline and matriline. People also have some claim to the land on which they were born or conceived, and there are other more complex relationships between clans whereby the responsibility for land is shared.

The connection between the dream-time, the country, and the traditional caretakers of country is manifested in the complex ceremonies that are performed by clan members. Some are increase ceremonies, ensuring the continued and plentiful existence of plants and animals and maintaining the ecological welfare of the landscape (indeed of the world); some are specifically for the initiation of young boys (making of men); and some are to promote the health and well-being of the community and so on. This detailed body of knowledge, law and wisdom handed down to the people from the dreamtime is thus maintained and kept potent, and handed on through generations by the enacting of ritual. Every tribal person has a knowledge of the ceremonies for his/her country and an obligation to respect the sacred sites that belong to them (or rather, to which they belong).

Ceremonies are the visible link between Aboriginal people and their land. Once dispossessed of this land, ceremonial life deteriorates, people lose their strength, meaning, essence and identity.

In the Pitjantjara case, the old men and women set the issue of freehold and leasehold aside as a triviality and it is doubtful whether the government bureaucrats had the slightest idea why. To those old people, the concept of owning land was far more impossible than owning a star or an allotment of air would be to us.

Apart from the fact that I am no authority on the subject, trying to describe Aboriginal cosmology briefly is like trying to explain quantum mechanics in five seconds. Besides, no amount of anthropological detail can begin to convey Aboriginal *feeling* for their land. It is everything – their law, their ethics, their reason for existence. Without that relationship they become ghosts. Half people. They are not separate from the land. When they lose it, they lose themselves, their spirit, their culture. This is why the land rights movement has become so essential. Because, by denying them their land, we are committing cultural and, in this case, racial genocide.

Dinner with Glendle that night was the usual, pancakes made with wholemeal, bug-infested flour, eggs and milk – a terrible leaden affair that bloated the belly after two bites

Sometimes he'd put the horrible mess into a baking dish and stick it in the oven and call it soufflé. Soufflé à la inner tube.

The wholemeal flour venture at Pipalyatjara had been one of Glendle's failures. Since the intervention of the whites, white flour, tea and sugar have become staples for many Aboriginal people, and although Glendle didn't worship the magical properties of wholemeal, brown rice sandwiches with Dr Suzuki soya butter, given the fact that people were dropping like flies from diabetes, malnutrition and heart disease he thought he would inject at least some particle of nutritional sense into the diet. But they hated it. So he mixed wholemeal flour with white flour, to be sold at their store. They still hated it. Eventually, some of the old people came up to Glendle and told him to keep his porridge, they wanted their old-style, fluffy dampers back again. Defeat. Well, not quite. One old lady remained addicted to it.

We spent many of those nights having long heart-to-hearts. I could feel myself knitting together again, sorting it out, putting it into perspective, clearing my confusion. And I talked about Richard. I had still not rid myself of the burden of him and poor Glendle copped the lot. At the end of one particularly long and vitriolic rave, he just looked at me for a while and said, 'Yes, but you're missing one important fact. Rick is a good friend to you – has done a lot for you. And anyway, it was you who invited him along, not the other way around. Can't have your cake and eat it too you know.'

God knows, it was a simple enough statement of fact, but it had an effect on me. From that one conversation my obsession with Rick and *Geographic*, and my anger with them, began to fade.

The time spent there was so pleasant, so relaxing, and I was learning such a lot that I was sorely tempted to stay for the rest of the year, for the whole of summer in fact, then continue on my way when the cool weather returned. There were so many things to weigh up. For a start, I had arranged to meet Rick in Warburton, and anyway, what would

Geographic say? I didn't care much. But the feed was not all that good here, and the camels were mainly eating a particular bush which gave them horrid green diarrhoea. And I felt restless and wanted to push on and this eventually outweighed the pleasure of being with people I cared for.

Eddie was sticking to two things like glue. Me and my rifle. His eyesight was terrible so he could not have used it very well, but the gun never left his side. I had radioed Rick and arranged to have one the same brought out to Warburton. The old man would walk down with me to check the camels of an evening and he would carry the rifle on his shoulder and sing to himself. I felt, well, flattered I suppose, that he should want to look after me in this way. On one of these evenings we passed a group of women coming towards us. One skinny old lady in a faded dress ten sizes too big for her detached herself from the group and wandered over to about eight feet in front of us. Eddie squinted and then broke into a delighted grin. They shared a polite and obviously respectful exchange, eyes and mouths smiling at each other. I couldn't understand what was said, but I imagined that she was some old and dear friend that he'd grown up with. We walked off and he continued to smile that special happy smile to himself. I asked him who it was, and he turned to me beaming, and said, 'That was Winkicha, my wife.' There was such pride and pleasure in his face. I had never seen that particular quality of love shown so openly between a man and wife before. It staggered me.

That meeting between Eddie and his wife was the first insight in a series which made me realize that, contrary to what most white male anthropologists would have us believe, women hold a very strong position in Aboriginal society. While men and women have separate roles, necessitated by environment, these roles are part of a single function – to survive – and both are mutually respected. With their dexterous food-gathering, the women play a greater part in feeding the tribe than do the men, whose hunting might only bring in the occasional kangaroo. The women also hold their own ceremonies and play a large part in the protection of their land. These ceremonies exist parallel with the men's but it falls to the men to be the enforcers of the 'law', and the caretakers of the 'knowledge', made manifest in sacred objects called 'tjuringas'. If there is sexism amongst Aborigines today, it is because they have learnt well from their conquerors. The difference in status between black women in Alice Springs and black women here was unbelievable.

I remember one story, which I have never had verified, but which rings true, concerning a myth belonging to some tribe in Western Australia. In the beginning, the women had everything. They had the power to procreate, they supported the tribe and kept them alive with their knowledge of bush foods, and they had a natural superiority. They also had the 'knowledge' which they kept hidden in a secret cave. The men conspired to steal this knowledge, so that things would be more balanced. (Now here comes the crunch.) The women heard of this, and instead of stopping them, realized that this was the way things had to go, for the sexes to remain in harmony. They allowed the men to steal this 'knowledge' which has remained in their hands until today.

I asked Eddie if he would like to come with me to Warburton, the next settlement, two hundred miles to the west. I was bitterly disappointed when at first he didn't seem to want to, protesting that he was too old for that sort of thing now. Besides, he didn't have proper shoes, but that was no problem as I could easily get him a pair at the store. I did think he might be right about his age. He was very old, and I wondered if the twenty miles per day routine might prove too much for him. Of course, he could always ride Bub. When I voiced my doubts to Glendle, he laughed and assured me that Eddie could out-walk both of us. He also said he was certain the old man would come as he had noticed a definite twinkle in his eye at the suggestion, and he thought I was a most fortunate woman, as Eddie was a respected elder of the tribe. The next morning, Eddie came to tell me that he had decided to accompany me after all. He needed a few things so we went to the store to purchase them – new shoes and socks, and a tarpaulin for Winkicha while he was away. The store was typical, a small galvanized iron shed, selling the basics – tea, sugar, flour, the occasional fruits and vegetables, soft drinks, clothes, billy cans. It was refurbished with goods once every couple of weeks by a road-train or a light aircraft from Alice.

On the following morning, we got ourselves ready for the walk to Warburton. I had discarded much of my junk at Pipalyatjara, so the pack was lighter and easier to load. This process of paring down possessions continued all the way through the trip, until I had only the barest of essentials. Glendle gave me packages of luxuries that he'd ordered from Alice, small plastic bags of white wine and extra packets of tobacco. Eddie took nothing but his tin of medicines. I had noticed from our time together on the track that he suffered from some pain in his shoulder. I put it down to arthritis but on the morning of our departure, while Glendle was sick in bed and Eddie and I were fiddling around outside the caravan making last-minute arrangements, an old man came up and spoke to him. They walked to a spot about fifty yards away, and in full view of myself and all the others who had gathered to say goodbye, Eddie bent over a 44-gallon drum, while the old man proceeded to wave his hands over him, rub his shoulder and so on. I went in to Glendle to ask what it was all about. He told me it was the nankari (Aboriginal doctor) fixing Eddie up for the trip. He told me he would probably suck a pebble from Eddie's shoulder, which might have been 'sung' there by an enemy. Eddie returned in five minutes and produced the pebble that had been extracted.

There are many cases of Aboriginal people who sicken and die because they believe they have been 'sung'. When this happens, the 'sung' person must go to a nankari for treatment. That is his only hope.

While it was impossible for me to leap outside the limitations imposed by my culture's description of what is possible, I have no doubt whatever that nankaris have an equal amount of success in healing the sick in a tribal situation as do Western doctors in curing detribalized people. The more enlightened white health-workers are now working hand in glove with nankaris and midwives in trying to cope with the various diseases and ailments that affect Aboriginal people.

Once again, all the checks and double checks and final adjustments necessary for departure had put me on overdrive, but five minutes out of the settlement, the calming rhythm of walking and the reassuring sound of the bells clanging behind, and Eddie's presence, settled me down.

We stopped in at Wingelinna to say goodbye to the people there, which took an hour or so. I was itching to get away, still caught in my Western nets, trying to fight them and having little success. At last all the farewells were completed and we began walking into the afternoon sun. We hadn't gone a mile before a car pulled up with some young men – another half an hour. Itch itch itch. On again, then another car, and so on. Late in the afternoon, Eddie informed me he needed pituri, a tobacco-like plant that Aborigines chew. He pointed to a valley in the ranges a mile or two off the track. We walked in silence through the hushed, lush valley. Eddie picked the plants he wanted while I watched. The vague uneasiness and fidgetiness of having the projected pattern of the day rearranged was soon soothed by the meditative way in which we searched for them. This valley was so delicate, so silent, and we didn't speak a word while we padded reverently through it. Once out of it, however, and back into the brutal afternoon sun which scorched my face, no matter how far I pulled my hat down, I again experienced that mental chafing at the bit. I tried hard to wrestle with it, push it out of my mind for good, but I was being torn by two different time concepts. I knew which one made sense, but the other one was fighting hard for survival. Structure, regimentation, orderedness. Which had absolutely nothing to do with anything. I kept thinking wryly to myself, 'Christ, if this keeps up it will take us months to get there. So what? Is this a marathon or what? This is going to be the best part of your trip, having Eddie with you, so stretch it out, idiot, stretch it out. But but ... what about routine ...?' and so on.

The turmoil lasted all that day, but gradually faded as I relaxed into Eddie's time. He was teaching me something about flow, about choosing the right moment for everything, about enjoying the present. I let him take over.

After a few days, my Pitjantjara was improving but it was still useless in fast conversation. This didn't seem to matter at all. It's amazing how well one can communicate with a fellow being when there are no words to get in the way. Our greatest communication lay in the sheer joy in our surroundings. The sound of birds which he taught me to mimic, the gazing at hills, the laughter at the antics of the camels, the hunting for meat, the discovery of things to eat. Sometimes we would sing together or alone, sometimes we shared a pebble to kick down the road – all this was unspoken and perfectly clear. He would quietly chatter and gesticulate to himself and the hills and plants. Outsiders would have thought us on a par for craziness.

We left the track that evening – Eddie had decided to take me through his country. For a week we wandered through that land, and all the while Eddie seemed to grow in stature with every step. He was a dingo-dreaming man, and his links with the special places we passed gave him a kind of energy, a joy, a belonging. He told me myths and stories over and over at night when we camped. He knew every particle of that country as well as he knew his own body. He was at home in it totally, at one with it and the feeling began rubbing off on to me. Time melted – became meaningless. I don't think I have ever felt so good in my entire life. He made me notice things I had not noticed before – noises, tracks. And

I began to see how it all fitted together. The land was not wild but tame, bountiful, benign, giving, as long as you knew how to see it, how to be part of it. This recognition of the importance and meaning of Aboriginal land strikes many whites who work in that country. As Toly wrote in a letter recently:

There is a peculiar power and strength in the country here which in many ways expresses itself in Aboriginal people and which I feel can belong to me too. It keeps unfolding and unfolding and is inexhaustible. What you make of it depends on you.

I remember that time now, as one of delightful calm. But it is a blur, it is undifferentiated. When I try to separate the days, I find that I cannot. I can remember certain incidents with crystal clarity, but when and where they happened I have not the faintest idea. I did discover, however, that the old goat could walk fifty miles to my ten. He gave me pituri to chew when I was tired which tasted unutterably foul but made me feel like running the next thousand yards, as if I'd smoked eighty cigarettes all at once. He made an ash from certain bushes which he mixed with the plant, so that it stayed in one glob when he chewed it. He would stick this glob behind his ear to be used later, like bubble gum. I offered him wine at night but he refused it, laughing, then acted out an old man being drunk. He told me to stick to my wine and he'd stick to his pituri.

Eddie never interfered with the handling of the camels, which pleased me greatly. Camels are really one-man (woman) animals and don't take to being ordered about by strangers. Besides, I treated them like glass, spoilt them and fussed over them, and I knew Eddie's feelings towards them would not be nearly as sentimental as my own. The only time I got faintly titchy with the old man was when he insisted that I should whoosh down Bub so he could ride him for ten minutes, then whoosh him down so he could get off, then do the same thing a mile later. He got titchy in return because, no doubt, he couldn't understand why anyone would have camels if they didn't work them: which was quite reasonable but didn't take into account the fact that they were adored pets rather than beasts of burden, in my eyes at least.

At night, while I busied myself with unsaddling, Eddie would build us a temporary wind-break, a wilcha. This was done expertly and quickly with a minimum expenditure of energy. I think deft is the word. He would drag old trees into a semicircle or three sides of a rectangle, clear a space of prickles for us to sleep in, and build the warming fire. No matter how many blankets I gave him, he never put these over him, but underneath. And after our meal and our talk, he would make sure I was comfortable, virtually tucking me into my swag, then he would curl up, head on his hands and fall asleep. All through the night, he would wake up, check on me and restoke the fire. He accepted the junky food I had with me but would have loved, I know, a kangaroo half-cooked in the coals. This is a delicious meat, and it is cooked by first singeing the hair and rubbing it off, then burying it in a mixture of sand and coals and leaving it for an hour. The insides are still bloody and red, but the meat and the offal sweet and juicy. There are strict rules governing the killing and cooking of kangaroo, in fact of all desert foods. Stories abounded of people who broke the law, by not killing correctly, and suffered terrible accidents because of it.

I had two knives with me, one for leather work and one for skinning and cutting up meat. Eddie asked me one day why I had two, when one would do. I explained to him that the sharp one, which I kept in my belt, was for game, '*Marlu, kanyala,*' I said and mimed cutting meat. I swear the old man nearly had a heart attack. '*Wiya wiya, mulapa wiya.* Tsc tsc tsc tsc.' He shook his head in horror. He then grabbed me by the hand and proceeded to tell me that I must never under any circumstances cut the meat of a kangaroo, or skin it, or take its tail. He repeated this over and over and I swore I

180

would never do such a thing. And again that night, he made me promise that I would never break the law in this way. I reassured him. In any case it was extremely unlikely that I would shoot a kangaroo for myself. There was far too much meat for one person and a dog and I hated shooting these lovely animals. I shot at the many herds we passed to please Eddie, but missed every time. Rabbits I had no such qualms about. They had been introduced, along with flies, by Europeans, and were now in plague proportions destroying whole tracts of land. Although I thought rabbit the least edible of all the bush foods, Diggity and I ate it often. As far as I knew, there were no stringent rules applied to the hunting of rabbit, since it is an animal that did not come from the dream-time.

Unfortunately, it came time for us to cut back on to the road. We passed maybe one or two cars a day, and these mostly Aboriginal people visiting family and relations in the two settlements. It was nice to see the flip side of the coin. If ever a car of whites passed, Eddie surreptitiously and suspiciously stood beside the gun, just in case. If it was blacks, it was all laughter and talk and sharing up food or tobacco or pituri. We could usually tell if it was an Aboriginal car coming, because they invariably sounded like sick washing-machines. The process of selling broken-down second-hand cars to Aborigines at exorbitant prices in Alice Springs is a lucrative business. Luckily Aboriginal people are great bush-mechanics and can usually keep them going on bits of string and wire. There was one story at Docker River, of a group of young men who bought a car in Alice, four hundred miles away, and half way home the body of the car literally fell to pieces. They simply got out (all ten of them), took off their belts, tied it all together and drove happily home.

Having Eddie with me was magic in terms of being accepted by Aboriginal people. Everyone knew Eddie, everyone loved him. And because he was there, and because I had camels, they loved me too. We stopped one day at a small camp by a bore – where there were maybe twenty people. We sat down together outside a humpy and talked for hours, drinking weak, cool super-sweet billy tea and chewing damper. Because I was the guest, I was given the tin mug to drink out of instead of sipping it straight from the billy like the others. The mug had been used for mixing flour and water so great clumps of the stuff floated around on top. It didn't matter. By now my attitude to food had changed utterly. Food had become something you put in your mouth to give you energy to walk, that's all. I could eat anything, and did. Washing had become an unnecessary procedure by then too, I was putrid and rank and I loved it. Even Eddie, who was no sparkling example of cleanliness, suggested I should wash my face and hands one day. He was finickity about Diggity too, and refused ever to let her drink from his mug.

Neither of us liked being on the road after our time in the wild country, because we had to deal once again with that strange breed of animal, the tourist. It was very hot one afternoon, stinkingly hot, and the flies were in zillions. I had the three p.m. grumps, Eddie was humming to himself. A column of red dust hit the horizon and swirled towards us, hurtling along at tourist speed. We swerved off into the spinifex, pincushions for feet were better than idiots at this hour of the day. But they saw us, of course, a whole convoy of them, daring the great aloneness together like they were in some B-grade Western. They all piled out with their cameras. I was irritated, I just wanted to get to camp and have a cuppa and be left in peace. They were so boorish, so insensitive, these people. They plied me with questions as usual and commented rudely on my appearance, as if I were a sideshow for their amusement. And perhaps I did look a little eccentric at that stage. I had had one ear pierced in Alice Springs the year before. It had taken months to work up the courage to participate in this barbaric custom, but once the hole was made, I wasn't about to let it close over again. I had lost my stud, so put through a large safety pin. I was filthy and my hair stuck out from my hat in sun-bleached greasy tangles and I looked like a Ralph Steadman drawing. Then they noticed Eddie. One of the men grabbed him by the arm, pushed him into position and said, 'Hey, Jacky-Jacky, come and stand alonga camel, boy.'

I was stunned into silence, I couldn't believe he had said that. How dare anyone be so thick as to call someone of Eddie's calibre 'boy' or 'Jacky-Jacky'. I furiously pushed past this fool, and Eddie and I walked together away from them. His face betrayed no emotion but he agreed when I suggested that there'd be no more photos and that they could all rot in hell before we'd talk to them. The last of the convoy arrived a few minutes later. I reverted to my old trick of covering my face with my hat and shouting, 'No photographs.' Eddie echoed me. But as I went past I heard them all clicking away. 'Bloody swine,' I shouted. I was boiling, hissing with anger. Suddenly, all five foot four inches of Eddie turned around and strutted back to them. They continued clicking. He stood about three inches from one of the women's faces and put on a truly extraordinary show. He turned himself into a perfect parody of a ravingly dangerous idiot boong, waved his stick in the air and trilled Pitjantjara at them and demanded three dollars and cackled insanely and hopped up and down and had them all confused and terrified out of their paltry wits. They'd probably been told in Perth that the blacks were murderous savages. They backed off, handing him what money they had in their pockets and fled. He walked demurely over to me and then we cracked up. We slapped each other and we held our sides and we laughed and laughed the helpless, hysterical tear-flooded laughter of children. We rolled and staggered with laughter. We were paralysed with it.

The thing that impressed me most was that Eddie should have been bitter and he was not. He had used the incident for his own entertainment and mine. Whether he also used it for my edification I do not know. But I thought about this old man then. And his people. Thought about how they'd been slaughtered, almost wiped out, forced to live on settlements that were more like concentration camps, then poked, prodded, measured and taped, had photos of their sacred business printed in colour in heavy academic anthropological texts, had their sacred secret objects stolen and taken to museums, had their potency and integrity drained from them at every opportunity, had been reviled and misunderstood by almost every white in the country, and then finally left to rot with their cheap booze and our diseases and their deaths, and I looked at this marvellous old half-blind codger laughing his socks off as if he had never experienced any of it, never been the butt of a cruel ignorant bigoted contempt, never had a worry in his life, and I thought, O..K. old man, if you can, me too.

We were almost at Warburton. I had not been using maps at all, they were superfluous with Eddie around. Hoping for an exact mileage, I asked some young Aboriginal people in a car how far away the settlement was.

'Hmmm, might be little bit long way, that Warburton. Maybe one sleep, two sleeps, but little bit long way for sure.'

'Oh, I see, thanks, little bit long way eh? Right. Of course.'

There seemed to be several categories of distance, divided up like this: little bit way, little bit long way, long way, and long long way, too far. This last was used for describing my distance to the sea. I would tell people I was going to the sea (*uru pulka*, big lake) which none of them had ever seen, and they would invariably raise their eyebrows, shake their heads slowly, and say, 'Long, long, loooooong way, too many sleeps, too far that uru pulka eh? Tsc tsc tsc tsc.' And they would shake their heads again and wish me luck, or chuckle and hold my arm and look at me, astonished.

While I was tying Goliath to a tree on a sandhill above our camp one evening, and while Eddie was busily engaged

184

in building a wilcha, two young men hooned up on bikes. They spotted me and came up to sit with me on the sandhill. After two weeks with Eddie I was a different person. I had been conversing with him in mime and Pitjantjara and had entered a different world – a parallel universe. I was finding swapping realities from Aboriginal to European quite difficult. It required a different set of concepts and a different variety of small talk. I could feel my brain's rusty old gears changing, but I was managing O.K. and they were pleasant enough people. Just as I was settling into semi-normal conversation, Eddie charged over the hill, rifle in hand, a belligerent and deeply suspicious look on his face. He sat down on my left, facing the young men, gun in lap and demanded in Pitjantjara to know who they were and if they could be trusted. There followed the most ridiculous scene. I tried to reassure everybody (the men looked decidedly uncomfortable) that everything was quite all right and nobody was about to shoot anybody. Only the different languages got hopelessly tangled and confused so that I'd address the bikers in dialect and then turn to tell Eddie in English, 'They're all right, honestly, I'm just going to make them a cup of tea,' which I then hastily translated into Pitjantjara. He replied, simply and adamantly, '*Wiya.*'

You don't have to speak a foreign language to understand a negative, especially from a very stern-looking gentleman with a rifle in his arms. The men sidled like crabs down the hill and roared off into the dusk.

This desocializing process – the sloughing off, like a snake skin, of the useless preoccupations and standards of the society I had left, and the growing of new ones that were more tuned to my present environment – was beginning to show. I was glad the men didn't stay, it would have been a strain, trying to make sense to them, trying to remember the niceties of conversation, the triviality of those almost forgotten patterns of interaction with my own kind, who were like animals circling each other – unsure, on guard. I liked, still like, the person who emerged from that process far better than the one who existed before it – or since it. In my own eyes, I was becoming sane, normal, healthy, yet to anyone else's I must have appeared if not certifiably mad then at least irretrievably weird, eccentric, sun-struck and bush-happy.

We camped later than usual the next night. I unsaddled the camels and my heart skipped about five beats, then thumped around in my chest like a kangaroo, making up for lost time. Where was my gun? MY GUN? 'EDDIE, HAVE YOU GOT MY GUN?' No gun. I had become so dependent on that rifle. In my mind's eye I pictured being sat on by a host of giant bull camels. Eddie said he would wait while I rode back to look for it. For some unaccountable reason, I had slung the scabbard over Zeleika's saddle, which was not designed for it, and the rifle had slipped out. I resaddled Bub and headed back down the track into the delicate blue and pink glow along the eastern horizon. I rode maybe five miles, wondering when Bub would throw me to the ground and break my neck; he was shying at rocks, birds and trees, in fact anything the imbecile could use as an excuse. I have often wondered about Bubby's neuron capacity.

A Toyota drove up, at which of course Bub leapt six feet sideways. The car contained a geologist who had not only my Savage .222 over-under rifle, but several Mars bars and a soft drink as well. Wonderful. And through delicious squishy disgusting mouthfuls of chocolate I argued with this man for half an hour about mining uranium, out there in the middle of nothingness, with a large moon bulging over the horizon.

Bubby wanted to bolt back to camp. I let him pace. 'O.K. you little sap, if you're so full of energy, you can carry half Zelly's pack tomorrow.' He was by far the most unreliable of the three adult camels. Perhaps because I had trained him badly, perhaps because he was still young and silly, or perhaps because it was in his genetic make-up to be brainless. He had almost sent Eddie flying one day. He started to pig-root for no apparent reason and although I was leading him, he was difficult to bring back under control. Eddie clung on through it all like a monkey. I couldn't help laughing. He did not lose one iota of dignity.

People often asked me why I didn't ride more during the trip. Three reasons. One was Bub. It is unwise, when you are three hundred miles from the nearest person, to be thrown off a camel, break your leg, and watch your beasts tearing off into the dusty distance. I would have much preferred to ride either of the other two but their saddles were not designed for it. The second reason, and the most foolish, was that I thought my camels were carrying more than enough weight as it was, without adding an extra nine stone. The third was that although feet can get very painful, bums can suffer even more.

I rode triumphant into camp. By this stage, I had told Eddie about the rifle that would be waiting for him in Warburton. Our conversations at night always ended up centred around this rifle. Was I really giving him a rifle, would it be exactly like this one, was I sure it was for him and not somebody else? Over and over he would repeat these questions, then break into a cackle when I had reassured him that it was true. Every night it was the same. I also tried to tell him about Rick and *Geographic*, but what's the Pitjantjara word for American magazine? I was worried about seeing Richard in Warburton. I knew Eddie would not understand why a thousand and one photographs were really necessary. Knew he would not like it. I didn't want to jeopardize my relationship with my new friend. On the other hand, I was looking forward to seeing Rick again. And Warburton was close.

Eddie was uncharacteristically voluble that night. He talked about the country we had been through, the story places, the things that had happened to us. Over and over the funny incidents were repeated, all the things that had gone right or wrong were discussed. Then the inevitable talk of the rifle and Rick and so on. Then silence. I was about to go to bed, when the old man sat me down beside him again, and produced a small water-worn pebble. He folded my hand over it, and went into a long monologue, only parts of which I understood. It was to protect me against perishing, or so I thought. I put it away in a safe place. Then he gave me a small chunk of ironstone. I had no idea what that was for and he said little about it. Then we went to sleep.

The next night was our last together on the track. Eddie insisted that he would find a reliable old man in Warburton to continue on with me to Carnegie station. He said that it must be an old man, an elder, a *wati pulka* (literally 'big man'), someone with a grey beard – not any young fellow. Definitely not. I was ambivalent about this. I loved being with Eddie but the next section after Warburton would be through completely wild desert, and I wanted to do that on my own – test out this new-found confidence. Four hundred miles of spinifex wastes known as the Gibson Desert, without a particle of water that I knew of. And how would that old man get back to Warburton? Eddie was O.K., Glendle was coming to pick him up. But even without that, there were enough relations travelling back and forth for him to get a lift with them. But Carnegie was a cattle station, and Warburton was the last Aboriginal outpost in that country. I decided against it. Eddie, although not pleased over this decision, accepted it.

Richard arrived in our camp at about three a.m. How he managed to find us is beyond me. He is one of those enviable people upon whom good luck falls like snow. He always managed to find me, usually through a series of unbelievable chances. His whole life runs like that. The coincidences that constantly follow him defeat statistics. He had been driving for two days, hadn't slept and was brim-full of zippy energy and enthusiasm. Every time he came out, he was the same. The culture shock he must have experienced, after just finishing some high-pressure cover story for *Time*, then plonking himself down in this silent desert, would have totally befuddled anyone else. It usually lasted a day. He had brought mail and Eddie's rifle. We began chattering and laughing together, but it was plain that Eddie wanted to get back to sleep, and didn't quite know what was going on. We decided to leave the opening of presents until morning.

We all woke early. It was like Christmas morning. Eddie was ecstatic over his new rifle. I feverishly read messages from friends. Rick took photos. I had primed Eddie enough for him to expect the odd photograph. But this? Rick was sitting, kneeling, squatting, lying down, click click click click click. Eddie looked at me and scratched his head. 'Who is he, what does he want, why all these photos?'

I tried to explain, but what could I say. 'O.K., Rick, that's enough.' Rick pulled out another camera. 'Look, I've got the perfect solution.' It was an S.X. 79, an instant polaroid. He took a photo of Eddie and handed it to him.

I was furious. 'Oh, I see, sort of like beads for the natives. Look, Rick, he doesn't like being photographed, so quit it.'

It was unfair. I knew that Rick had not meant it that way and was hurt. 'The only reason I brought it', he said, 'is because photographers are always promising to send photos and they never do. Besides, it's an exchange – a sharing of the image immediately.' But I knew Eddie would see it as a cheap trick. And he did. He didn't like Rick, didn't like being photographed, and certainly didn't like being handed this useless bit of paper with his face on it, as a bribe. Tension.

Rick drove a couple of miles up the track and Eddie and I packed up in silence. He asked me again why this was happening and I tried again to explain. Hopeless. What I had feared might happen was happening, and out of control.

We walked up the road together. There was Rick's car with Rick standing on top, a long lens poking out of his eyeball. I decided to let Eddie handle the situation. As we approached the car, he lifted his hand, and said in English, 'No photograph,' then in Pitjantjara, 'It makes me feel sick.' I laughed. Rick captured that one moment and then desisted. When we had that photo developed much later on, there was a woman smiling at an old Aboriginal man, whose hand was raised in a cheery salute. So much for the discerning eye of the camera. That one slide speaks volumes. Or rather lies volumes. Whenever I look at it now, it sums up all the images of the journey. Brilliant images, exciting, excellent, but little to do with reality. While I love the photos Rick took, they are essentially of his trip, not my own. I don't think dear Richard has ever understood this.

Later in Warburton, Glendle asked Eddie what he would do with the polaroid of himself. 'Oh probably burn it,' he said nonchalantly. We cracked up.

But all this is unfair to Richard. He was good-natured and tried hard not to intrude. He never pushed or imposed as most would have done. And if he didn't quite grasp why photos were a no-no, that was understandable. He had never spent time with Aboriginal people, and if he felt left out and frustrated at times, he handled it well. The difficult situation resolved itself much more easily than I had expected.

Warburton was a hole. After the magnificence of the country, and the charm of the tiny settlements I had passed through, it came as an unpleasant shock. Every tree for miles had been knocked down for firewood. Cattle had eaten out the country around the water-hole and dust rose in suffocating billowing clouds. The flies carpeted every square inch of skin, even though it was mid-winter. And in the middle of this desolation, surrounded by the lean-tos and shanty town humpies of the Aboriginal people, was a hill where the whites' buildings clustered together, fortified (presumably against Aboriginal aggression) by high cyclone fences and barbed wire. But the children were there, bursting with life as usual, and, unlike the older people, loved having their pictures taken. Rick handed out polaroids by the dozen.

Despite the pervading gloom of the place, a party atmosphere persisted for the whole time I was there. Glendle arrived, there was Warburton's school teacher, and Rick. Eddie took me down to camp constantly to introduce me

to his friends and relations, and we would sit in the dust, letting time waft gently by, talking for hours about the trip
and where I was going and what a good time we had had
and camels, camels, camels. One old man asked me if I had
slept with Eddie. I was momentarily taken aback, then realized
that he meant it literally. Sleeping next to someone in the
same wilcha connoted friendship, togetherness. They were
so sensible these people.

When it was time for Eddie to leave me, he looked sideways at me for a moment, held my arm, smiled and shook
his head. He wrapped his rifle in a shirt, put it in the back
of the truck then changed his mind and put it in the front,
then changed it again, and laid it carefully in the back. He
waved out the window and then he and Glendle and
Glendle's friend *wala karnka* ('fast crow') were swallowed up
in the dust.

I spent a week in Warburton, floating with happiness. I
could not remember ever associating that emotion with
myself before. So much of the trip had been wrong and
empty and small, and so much of my life previous to it had
been boring and predictable, that now when happiness
welled up inside me it was as if I were flying through warm
blue air. And a kind of aura of happiness was being generated.
It rubbed off on people. It built up and got shared around.
Yet nothing of the past five months had been anything like
I had imagined. None of it had gone according to plan, none
of it had lived up to my expectations. There'd been no point
at which I could say, 'Yes, this is what I did it for,' or 'Yes,
this is what I wanted for myself.' In fact, most of it had been
simply tedious and tiring.

But strange things do happen when you trudge twenty miles
a day, day after day, month after month. Things you only
become totally conscious of in retrospect. For one thing I had
remembered in minute and Technicolor detail everything
that had ever happened in my past and all the people who
belonged there. I had remembered every word of conversa-

tions I had had or overheard way, way back in my childhood and in this way I had been able to review these events with a kind of emotional detachment as if they had happened to somebody else. I was rediscovering and getting to know people who were long since dead and forgotten. I had dredged up things that I had no idea existed. People, faces, names, places, feelings, bits of knowledge, all waiting for inspection. It was a giant cleansing of all the garbage and muck that had accumulated in my brain, a gentle catharsis. And because of that, I suppose, I could now see much more clearly into my present relationships with people and with myself. And I was happy, there is simply no other word for it.

Richard described this as magic. I laughed at him for it, teased him for using such suspect language. But he was deeply affected. I look back on that time now with a kind of yearning disbelief. We were actually beginning to talk in terms of magic. Fate. We both of us secretly believed in an external power that one could tap if one were in tune with events. Oh dear.

23–5 *Top*, the Gunbarrel Highway stretched for 300 miles across the desolate Gibson Desert. *Left*, witchetty grubs (maku) supplemented my diet. *Right*, Diggity, who had been with me for four years, died after aking poison bait laid for dingoes.

26   Surprised on the way to Wiluna by a group of press reporters who
had hired an Aboriginal tracker to find me.

10

I LEFT Warburton somewhere around July. I had approximately one month to go before I could expect to see another human being. Despite the fact that this leg would be the first real test of my survival skills, despite the fact that if I was going to die anywhere it would most likely be along this lonely treacherous stretch of void, I looked forward to it with new-found calm, a lack of fear, a solid reliance on myself.

The Gunbarrel Highway (Australians have such a strange sense of humour) was two parallel ruts that sometimes disappeared, but generally ran dead straight and due west through a most inhospitable waterless patch of nothing for hundreds of miles. It had originally been built as a survey line, and could now expect an average of six four-wheel-drive vehicles a year.

I put on a new pair of sandals. I had tried every type of footwear, but these were incomparably the best. Boots were too heavy and hot, running shoes were comfortable for about an hour in the morning, before the sweat and sand formed ridges under the balls of the feet. Although loose sandals did not protect my feet from stakes and prickles and spinifex spines, they only required a day or two of agony and blisters to be broken in. Besides, by this stage I was so fit, I was virtually immune to cold and pain. My threshold had reached absurd heights. I had always been jealously in awe of people (particularly men) who could hurt themselves, and pretend they didn't feel it. Now I was the same. I would cut or scrape a great wedge of flesh out and just murmur 'oops' and promptly forget about it. I was usually too preoccupied with what I was doing to be able to afford to dwell on it.

Rick had decided to drive across the Gunbarrel in front of me and leave the car in Wiluna, our next meeting place. I asked him to drop a couple of drums of water for me on the way. I would need every drop of that water. The country would be dry and hot, with, presumably, little feed for the camels. Although Aboriginal people could have directed me to the rockholes, there was nothing marked on the maps. But, and I felt stupid feeling this way, I didn't want to see Rick's fresh tyre tracks all the way. I was more concerned for his safety than I was for my own. If that car broke down ... I made sure he had enough water for himself, so that if that did occur, I could meet him along the track and take him with me. Glendle had also insisted that he drop two drums of water for me half way along the track. He had to drive a total of 800 wretched miles over spinifex and sand to do this – such is the quality of friends.

I set off in my new sandals and after a few hours I decided to cut across country rather than follow the track. There was nothing but sandhills and spinifex and interminable space. I was perhaps treading now on country where no one had ever walked before, there was so much room – pure, virgin desert, not even cattle to mar it and nowhere in that vastness even an atom of anything human. The sandhills here were not the parallel waves that I had been through before, but jumbled, crashing together like chop against the wind, or breakers against a rip-tide. They had not been burnt so were different in character from the ones I had experienced. Not as clean, or as deceptively lush with green. The drab, inedible spinifex covered them and kept them stationary.

Throughout the trip I had been gaining an awareness and an understanding of the earth as I learnt how to depend upon it. The openness and emptiness which had at first threatened me were now a comfort which allowed my sense of freedom and joyful aimlessness to grow. This sense of space works deep in the Australian collective consciousness. It is frightening and most of the people huddle around the eastern seaboard where life is easy and space a graspable concept, but it produces a sense of potential and possibility nevertheless that may not exist now in any European country. It will not be long, however, before the land is conquered, fenced up and beaten into submission. But here, here it was free, unspoilt and seemingly indestructible.

And as I walked through that country, I was becoming involved with it in a most intense and yet not fully conscious way. The motions and patterns and connections of things became apparent on a gut level. I didn't just see the animal tracks, I knew them. I didn't just see the bird, I knew it in relationship to its actions and effects. My environment began to teach me about itself without my full awareness of the process. It became an animate being of which I was a part. The only way I can describe how the process occurred is to give an example: I would see a beetle's tracks in the sand. What once would have been merely a pretty visual design with few associations attached, now became a sign which produced in me instantaneous associations – the type of beetle, which direction it was going in and why, when it made the tracks, who its predators were. Having been taught some rudimentary knowledge of the pattern of things at the beginning of the trip, I now had enough to provide a structure in which I could learn to learn. A new plant would appear and I would recognize it immediately because I could perceive its association with other plants and animals in the overall pattern, its place. I would recognize and know the plant without naming it or studying it away from its environment. What was once a thing that merely existed became something that everything else acted upon and had a relationship with and vice versa. In picking up a rock I could no longer simply say, 'This is a rock,' I could now say, 'This is part of a net,' or closer, 'This, which everything acts upon, acts.' When this way of thinking became ordinary for me, I too became lost in the net and the boundaries of myself stretched out for ever. In the beginning I had known at some level that this could happen. It had frightened me then. I had seen it as a chaotic principle and I fought it tooth and nail. I had given myself the structures of habit and routine with which to fortify myself and these were very necessary at the time. Because if you are fragmented and uncertain it is terrifying to find the boundaries of yourself melt. Survival in a desert, then requires that you lose this fragmentation, and fast. It is not a mystical experience, or rather, it is dangerous to attach these sorts of words to it. They are too hackneyed and prone to misinterpretation. It is something that happens that's all. Cause and effect. In different places, survival requires different things, based on the environment. Capacity for survival may be the ability to be changed by environment.

Changing to this view of reality had been a long hard struggle against the old conditioning. Not that it was a conscious battle, rather it was being forced on me and I could either accept it or reject it. In rejecting it I had almost gone over the edge. The person inside whom I had previously relied on for survival had, out here and in a different circumstance, become the enemy. This internal warring had almost sent me around the bend. The intellectual and critical faculties did everything they could think of to keep the boundaries there. They dredged up memory. They became obsessed with time and measurement. But they were having to take second place, because they simply were no longer necessary. The subconscious mind became much more active and important. And this in the form of dreams, feelings. A growing awareness of the character of a particular place, whether it was a good place to be with a calming influence, or whether it gave me the creeps. And this all linked up with Aboriginal reality, their vision of the world as being something they could never be separate from, which showed in their language. In Pitjantjara and, I suspect, all other Aboriginal languages, there is no word for 'exist'. Everything in the universe is in constant interaction with everything else. You can not say, this is a rock. You can only say, there sits, leans, stands, falls over, lies down, a rock.

The self did not seem to be an entity living somewhere inside the skull, but a reaction between mind and stimulus. And when the stimulus was non-social, the self had a hard time defining its essence and realizing its dimensions. The self in a desert becomes more and more like the desert. It has to, to survive. It becomes limitless, with its roots more in the subconscious than the conscious – it gets stripped of non-meaningful habits and becomes more concerned with realities related to survival. But as is its nature, it desperately wants to assimilate and make sense of the information it receives, which in a desert is almost always going to be translated into the language of mysticism.

What I'm trying to say is, when you walk on, sleep on, stand on, defecate on, wallow in, get covered in, and eat the dirt around you, and when there is no one to remind you what society's rules are, and nothing to keep you linked to that society, you had better be prepared for some startling changes. And just as Aborigines seem to be in perfect rapport with themselves and their country, so the embryonic beginnings of that rapport were happening to me. I loved it.

And my fear had a different quality now too. It was direct and useful. It did not incapacitate me or interfere with my competence. It was the natural, healthy fear one needs for survival.

Although I talked constantly to myself, or Diggity or the country around me, I was not lonely – on the contrary, had I suddenly stumbled across another human being, I would have either hidden, or treated it as if it were just another bush or rock or lizard.

The sandhills proved tough going. Crawl up, slide down for ever. The camels were carrying full capacity now, and they worked like demons. They never gave up, never complained, even when one would stumble over a giant clump of spinifex and pull on the nose-line of the one behind. Such stoic animals. The spinifex, that ubiquitous desert grass, was enough to make you want to burn every clump you saw. These clumps were usually about six feet across, and four feet high, with just the narrowest of gaps between them. They made walking difficult, tiring and painful. A clump is all spikes, and the tiny filaments on the ends of the spikes stick in flesh and itch and burn. I would be leaving sandhill country behind me soon, and heading into the endless flat, hot, homogeneous spinifex wastes, relieved only occasionally by a shallow gully containing mulga and, if lucky, some other titbits for the camels. I wondered how the desert would treat them.

After mile upon countless mile, after the monotonous drag of those endless dunes, I decided that the energy required to traverse this country outweighed the pleasantness of being away from anything human. I had lost my compass, and without panic back-tracked until I found it. A stupid mistake however. Even sticking to a compass course was difficult in that country. There would suddenly rise up, in my way, a dense thicket of impenetrable bushy mulga, which, if I tried to go straight through it, caught and ripped at the pack and at me until I had to give up. This would require circling sometimes a mile out of my way. Or a hill, covered in sharp shattered laterite, would have to be circumvented. I decided to cut back on to the track. I did not know how visible the track would be, or if I would choose to cross it at some stony patch where Rick's tyre marks would not be visible. I walked thirty miles that day, hoping to find it before nightfall. It nearly killed me. My hip felt as if I had dislocated it and walking was excruciatingly painful. The limping drained away even more of my energy than the sun, which burned and seared into my face and dried and cracked my lips. The track, as it turned out, was easy to spot, and I set up camp as soon as I saw it.

At dawn I could see the Gunbarrel stretch away into the distance as far as the eye could see. And on either side of it, the endless rolling spinifex plains, all delicate fronds of gold and pink which would change as the sun rose to dull grey-green horror. The seed heads made the stuff look alluring, even fragile as it bent and rippled with the cold morning breeze. How deceptive this country was. And the extremes in temperature were something to be felt to be believed. From those pale icy below-zero dawnings, to boiling mid-day, to the settling longed-for cool of evening and back to the crystal cold of night. I wore only trousers, light shirt and sheepskin coat which I usually took off while I was loading up. (Loading only took half an hour now.) I learnt to shiver myself warm. The other thing I learnt was not to drink during the day. I would have four or five mugs of tea in the morning, maybe a short drink (half a cup) at midday, and then nothing until I camped at night, when I would quaff down eight or nine cups of liquid. It is a strange thing that, when the sun and the dry air suck gallons of sweat out of you during the day, the more you drink the more thirsty you become.

Because of the sameness of the plains, any different geographical feature was absurdly welcome. I would fall into raptures over some pitiful little gully, which could only be seen as attractive if you compared it with the country around it. One day I camped in a dust-bowl under a few straggly shadeless trees, which did more to my aesthetic senses than the Taj Mahal could do. Here would be some feed for the animals and a place where they could roll in the dirt to their hearts' content. They were unsaddled by mid-afternoon and immediately began to play. I had been watching and laughing at them for a while and suddenly, spontaneously, threw off all my clothes and joined them in a romp. We rolled and we kicked and we sent the dust flying over each other. Diggity went apoplectic with delight. I was covered with thick caked orange dust and my hair was matted. It was the most honest hour of unselfconscious fun I had ever had. Most of us, I am sure, have forgotten how to play. We've made up games instead. And competition is the force which holds these games together. The desire to win, to beat someone else, has supplanted play – the doing of something just for itself.

When I left the next morning I took out my clock, wound it, set the alarm for four o'clock and left it ticking on the stump of a tree near our dust bath. A fitting and appropriate end for that insidious little instrument, I thought, and that was that preoccupation taken care of. I executed, in celebration, clumsy little steps like a soft-shoe dancer with lead in his feet. I probably looked like a senile old derelict in fact, with my over-large sandals, filthy baggy trousers, my torn shirt, my calloused hands and feet and my dirt-smeared face. I liked myself this way, it was such a relief to be free of disguises and prettiness and attractiveness. Above all that horrible, false, debilitating attractiveness that women hide behind. I pulled my hat down over my ears so that they stuck out beneath it. 'I must remember this when I get back. I must not fall into that trap again.' I must let people see me as I am. Like this? Yes, why not like this. But then I realized that the rules pertaining to one set of circumstances do not necessarily pertain to another. Back there, this would just be another disguise. Back there, there was no nakedness, no one could afford it. Everyone had their social personae well fortified until they got so drunk and stupid that their nakedness was ugly. Now why was this? Why did people circle one another, consumed with either fear or envy, when all that they were fearing or envying was illusion? Why did they build psychological fortresses and barriers around themselves that would take a Ph.D. in safe-cracking to get through, which even they could not penetrate from the inside? And once again I compared European society with Aboriginal. The one so archetypally paranoid, grasping, destructive, the other so sane. I didn't want ever to leave this desert. I knew that I would forget.

I was nearly half way along the Gunbarrel. I couldn't

know when it was because by then I had realized that in the desert time refused to structure itself. It preferred instead to flow in curlicues, vortices and tunnels, and besides it didn't matter. I was about five miles away from some hills. Hot. It was hot. I hadn't seen anything but gibbers and spinifex for days. Oh how I wanted to be by those hills. I could see trees on them and near them. TREES. And suddenly, what should I see floating like spectres towards me out of the heat shimmer – not one, not two, not even three, but *four* wild bull camels, all blowing froth and looking for trouble and cows.

Right. Don't panic, D. Hold back that cold sweat that's trickling down the yellow streak on your spine, and clogging up your eyebrows. Just obtain cover (will a clump of spinifex do?) and shoot to kill.

Right. But the difficult thing is, I like camels. I don't like to hurt camels. I'm a pal to all camels. I fired a warning shot first, hoping to hell they'd run away in abject terror. One of the wild camels said, 'What was dat, a mosquito?' and kept coming. Arrogant swine. O.K. I'll have to shoot one. When the others smell blood they'll leave. I walked up close, knelt down and aimed for the head. But when I pulled the trigger, nothing happened. Nothing. Zip. Gun jammed. Gun no good. Oh dear, I said as I felt the yellow streak leap off my back and run yelling 'Help, help,' all the way back to War-burton. Oh dear, oh dear, I said as the camels came closer. I bashed the gun on the ground and shouted at it and tried to fix it with my knife, all to no avail.

I spied the burnt-out stump of a corkwood to tie Bub to, then, as an added precaution, lashed his nose-line to his leg, knowing that if he got a real fright he would snap it like a piece of cotton, uproot the stump and head for home. I had no time to think about Diggity or Goliath because the new camels were now a mere ten feet away and they was BIG. Dookie and Zel were getting up and down like yoyos and decidedly touchy. I threw a rock at one of the bulls. He burbled and disgorged his mouth bladder (a hideously repulsive pink, purple and green balloon, covered in slobber and smelling indescribably foul, that female camels perversely find attractive), shook his head at me and we played merry-go-rounds. I threw another rock and threatened him with my iron digging stick. He backed off and looked at me as if I was an idiot. It took half an afternoon of this cat and mouse game and many other crafty anti-camel manoeuvres to get rid of those animals. Much to my relief, they eventually got bored with terrorizing me and stalked off into the glue-like mirage-riddled horizon. None of them had actually attacked – well, I'd be dead if they had – and I thought I had been unnecessarily careful in shooting all the other bulls so far. Then I remembered Dookie's turn and slapped myself on the wrist.

It was a very long afternoon. One of the longest I've ever experienced. But I got through it O.K. No damage except a few minor alterations to the brain circuitry, and the ruining of my gun and knife of course. My wits got me through where the gun didn't.

The principal difference between an adventurer and a suicide is that the adventurer leaves himself a margin of escape (the narrower the margin, the greater the adventure). A margin whose width and breadth may be determined by unknown factors, but whose successful navigation is determined by the measure of the adventurer's nerve and wits. It is always exhilarating to live by one's nerves or towards the summit of one's wits.

Tom Robbins, *Even Cowgirls Get the Blues*

Yes, exactly.

I pulled into camp that night under the protection of two lovely hills, and I sat down to write letters. They were happy, positive and calm. I kept thinking that I should be quaking with fear. That I should be writing for reassurance, that I should be writing to people because I needed them there to protect me. I kept thinking that I should be wanting to be back there with them where it was safe, and instead I found myself telling them that I wouldn't swap places with them for anything in the world, that safety was a myth and security a sneaky little devil. I have included one of the letters here, written over a period of days, because letters were the closest thing I kept to a diary. They describe what was happening much more clearly than I could now remember from my poky London flat.

Dear Steve,

Sitting by my lovely fire 150 miles from anyone or anything, billy's singing tea shanties, camels returning from nightly munch a-jingling, Diggity farting silently but lethally beside me on the swag. I have found myself a magic place, fringed by delicate mulga laces, bottomed by soft red sand and protected by two red and yellow mesas. A little spot of heaven on the lonely desert trail, where I'm staying for a few days to fortify my 'wā'. This morning before dawn (grey silk sky and Venus) I saw one crow carving up wind currents above the hills. Went hunting with the sun and saw one kanyala and missed. Thank heavens. But we are meat hungry. Came back and cooked a golden crusty damper and then had a wash – the first water, sudsy or otherwise to touch my fetid skin in weeks. Hooooeeeee. I'm surprised I didn't find a cluster of mushrooms growing under there somewhere.

I just rushed off for a minute, raving at the camels who were once again raiding the food bags. Cheeky and impertinent beasts. How I love them though.

Now the cold is welling up from the ground and swirling about my be-socked and be-sandalled feet. Cuds are being chewed in rhythm and the bloodwood and sandalwood fire is jujitsuing with the cold. Oh zing zing zing go my heartstrings, it's good to be alive. And words just can't tell you what it's like. Words are the memory twitching after the reality of the dance ...

A few days later. Well, a few days ago in your time that is. In my time, I could just as well say I wrote that tomorrow or a thousand years ago. Time ain't the same out here you know. Maybe I've gone through a black hole. But let's not get involved in time concepts – I could really lose the thread doing that.

Today was a wham-bammer of a day – still is in fact. Although now as I stare out at the glinting gibbers and dead trees ... but let me begin at the beginning.

Today began like most others except there were clouds in the sky. Two in fact, just pinkly peeping over the northern horizon. Rain, I think, was the first thing I thought as the first light slithered under my eyelids and blankets. The clouds evaporated in seconds though, and the next thing I thought was, 'I can't hear any camel bells.' You're right, mountain-man, the camels had evaporated also. Well, two had anyway, and the other one, I was soon to discover, didn't evaporate because he couldn't walk.

A very wise friend in Alice once said to me, 'When things go wrong on the track, rather than panic, boil the billy, sit down and think clearly.'

So I boiled the billy and I sat down and I went through the salient points with Diggity.

1 We are 100 miles from anything.
2 We have lost two camels.
3 We have one camel who has a hole in his foot so big you could curl up and go to sleep in it.
4 We have enough water for six days.
5 My busted hip is still intolerably painful.
6 This is a god-awful place to spend the rest of our lives, which according to my mathematical calculations will be about a week.

So, having tidied all that up, I panicked. Many hours later, I found my lost beasties and brought them back to the fold. They were chastened. That only left the problem of the cripple. Now, Dookie is normally a quiet, reserved, dependable kind of fella. But when he has a hole in his foot, he changes into a raging demon. Well, he struck, he kicked, he twisted, he snarled, he vomited, he rolled, he gawped and he gurgled, and finally I had to truss him up like a turkey to get at his foot, which sounds easy on paper but I swear I lost a gallon of sweat in that struggle. And remember how I was saying before (salient point 5 I think) about my poor old hip, the poor old hip that's dislocated in about 7 places, well, isn't it always the way, *that* was the hip Dookie got with his front leg. But, to cut a long grumble short, I got him down, I tied him up, and I gouged four sandhills and six boulders out of that hole in his foot, and I packed it with cotton wool and terramycin, and I covered it with a patch, and I kissed it all better and at last we got under way.

Sweet holy Jesus, mountain-man, there's a herd of camels coming into my camp RIGHT NOW. As I write. There's absolutely nothing I can do, so I'm writing to still my panic. Why oh why does this happen to me. Looks O.K., no bulls with this lot thank heavens. But I have my rifle loaded just in case. You know, the rifle that doesn't work. Well you never know, miracles can happen. Now, where was I. Got to write because I'm feeling desperate. O.K., left camp about midday and then I came to the most beautiful place I've ever seen – Mungilli claypan.

Let me try to describe it to you. You come down an incline and suddenly you're in another country. There is shade everywhere and the sand is soft salmon pink. Giant ghost gums glisten and sway and there are birds tweeting and warbling. On the right, like a tidal estuary that hasn't seen the sea in aeons, is the claypan. It's empty and flat and rimming it all round are low swells of dunes and trees and red-berried salt-bushes. Some of the trees have smooth pink trunks, like shot silk, which glow crimson in the evening sun, and their leaves are deep deep shining green. Now, I know most people would drive through that three miles of heaven and not even gasp, let alone pull out the prayer mat, but it sent ripples to the pit of my stomach. I wish I could explain it to you. What a piece of country – so moving, so subtly powerful. Didn't stop long though. Dookie's foot-hole was growing in my consciousness like a triffid in the tropics.

So now I am here, one ear cocked for the burbling of bull camels (where there are mums there are usually dads, unfortunately).

Funny thing about this trip you know. One day it has me flying through the clouds in ecstasy (although, having been to the clouds, I can honestly say they're a nice place to visit but I wouldn't want to live there, the cost of living's too high) and the next day ...

Now, as I stare out at the glinting gibbers and dead trees, if you want me to be perfectly truthful, mountain-man, and this is just between you and me, and I wouldn't want it getting around, I'm just a weensy bit tired of this adventure. In fact, to be quite honest, fantasies are beginning to worm their way between the spinifex clumps, skeletons and rocks – fantasies pertaining to where I'd like to be right now.

Somewhere where cool clover comes almost to your crutch, where there are no tidal waves, tai-funs, stray meteors, camels, nasty night noises, blaring, thrumming, cancer-producing sun, no heat shimmer and raw rocks, no spinifex, no flies, somewhere where there's lots of avocados, water, friendly people who bring cups of tea in the morning, pineapples, swaying palms, sea breezes, puffy little clouds and mirrored streamlets. A silk farm perhaps, where you can just sit and listen to the worms spinning money for you as you lazily build wind-chimes for select friends and when you get tired of that you can stroll down to your own huge bath in a little shoji house in your garden and eat frosty pink water-melon cut into exquisite shapes while a six-foot, slim slave slides ice-cubes down your back and ...

Sorry, sorry Stevie, I was getting carried away.

But you know what I mean.

Christ, right now I'd give anything for a friendly face. Even an unfriendly face. Even a human noise would be nice. Yes, even the resonating base blart of a human fart from behind that dead salt-bush over there would do. I must be crazy, I'm sitting here wondering if I'll ever get out of this alive, wondering if I'll ever see Sydney neon and venom again, writing like crazy to people who only exist in the warped recesses of my memory, who could be all dead, and all I can do is laugh and crack pooh jokes. If I do depart this world out here, let it be known that I went out grinning will you, and loving it. LOVING IT.

Finishing a letter's harder than starting one. Full golden moon just bulged over the eastern tree-line. Worth it all for a moonrise? At this stage, yes. My skin's as dry as dog-biscuits, my left leg may have seen its day, my lips are cracked and blistered, I've run out of toilet paper and have to use spinifex, there's a skin-cancer trying to take over my nose (how do you keep your cool at *Geographic* cocktail parties when your nose drops off in a martini?) I'm slowly but efficiently going peculiar, I'm so scared of dying that the knocking of my knees wakes me up in the morning and has it all been worth it? Yes, mountain-man, definitely.

I can't sleep. There's tea coming out of my ears, eyeballs and hip-pockets, and I'm feeling so GOOD. I could howl at the moon up there (and Arcturus and Aldebaran and Spica and Antares etc.) and I really want to tell somebody. Steve, are you listening? I FEEL GREAT. Life's so joyous, so sad, so ephemeral, so crazy, so meaningless, so goddam funny. What's wrong with me that I feel this good? Have I gone bush-crazy? Am I moon-struck? Probably both and I don't care. This is paradise, and I wish I could give you some.

This writing of letters out in the middle of nowhere may seem a little peculiar, especially since it would be months before I could post them, and I would probably see my friends before I ever got a reply. But it helped in recording events and emotions at the time. My diary was a mish-mash of these letters, most of them never sent, and uninteresting sentences like, 'Is it July or August, anyway, lost camels this morning.' Then there would be a month with no entries whatsoever.

The jocularity of those letters reflected the pervading mood of that month along the Gunbarrel. It wasn't that I was becoming reckless, it wasn't that I had discarded fear, it was simply that I was learning to accept my fate, whatever it might turn out to be.

The incident with the lost camels was slightly more hair-raising than the letter lets on. They had been spooked by wild camels in the night and I had slept through the whole thing. The tracks told me what had happened in the morning. I had been letting them go at night either loosely hobbled, or not hobbled at all. Sallay would have shot me on the spot had he known this. But my reasoning went this way – we were in dry desert country and the camels were working hard – they had to range a fair distance from camp to find the feed they needed. Goliath was always tied up securely and I firmly believed Zeleika would never leave him. (She was to shock me out of my complacency a couple of months later.) And I believed I could now track them over anything.

This business of tracking is a combination of sixth sense, knowledge of the behaviour of camels, keen eyesight and practice. The place we camped that afternoon was gibber country and cement-hard claypan. You could drive a sledge-hammer into that stuff and it would hardly leave a dent. Finding the direction they had gone in therefore required circling away from camp until I found the tracks (which had become mixed up with a couple of other cameloid footprints) and trying to follow this general direction, by searching for the scuff marks, looking for freshly eaten fodder, and keeping an eye open for fresh dung. (I could tell my camels' dung from any others'.) It required a lot of circular and frustrating walking. As it turned out I found them not too many miles away, stirred up and nervous, heading back to camp. They came straight up to me, like errant children, begging forgiveness. Their friends had left. Rather than putting the fear of god into me, this incident reinforced my confidence in them, and I continued to leave them unhobbled at night. Stupid perhaps, but the camels did gain a little weight that month.

As if walking twenty miles a day wasn't enough, I often went out hunting or just exploring with Diggity after I had unsaddled the camels of an afternoon. On one such afternoon, I had got myself vaguely lost. Not completely lost, just a little bit, enough to make my stomach tilt, rather than turn. I could, of course, back-track, but this always took time and it was getting dark. In the past, whenever I wanted Diggity to guide me home, I simply said to her, 'Go home, girl,' which she thought was a kind of punishment. She would flatten those crazy ears to her head, roll her amber brown eyes at me, tuck her tail between her legs and glance over her shoulder, every part of her saying, 'Why are you doing this to me. What did I do wrong?' But that evening, she made a major breakthrough.

She immediately grasped the situation; you could see a light bulb flash above her head. She barked at me, ran forward a few yards, turned back, barked, ran up and licked my hand, and then scampered forward again and so on. I pretended I didn't understand. She was beside herself with worry. She repeated these actions and I began to follow her. She was ecstatic, overjoyed. She had understood something and she was proud of it. When we made it back to camp, I hugged her and made a great fuss of her and I swear that animal laughed. And that look of pride, that unmistakable pleasure in having comprehended something, perceived the reason and necessity for it, made her wild, hysterical with delight. When she was pleased over something or someone, her tail did not go back and forward, it whipped round and round in a complete circle and her body contorted into S-bends like a snake.

I am quite sure Diggity was more than dog, or rather other than dog. In fact, I have often thought her father was a vet perhaps. She combined all the best qualities of dog and human and was a great listener. She was by now a black glossy ball of health and muscle. She must have done a hundred miles a day with her constant scampering and bounding after lizards in the spinifex. The trip, of necessity, had brought me much closer to all the animals, but my relationship with Diggity was something special. There are very few humans with whom I could associate the word love as easily as I did with that wonderful little dog. It is very hard to describe this interdependence without sounding neurotic. But I loved her, doted on her, could have eaten her with my overwhelming affection. And she never, not ever, not once, retracted her devotion no matter how churlish, mean or angry I became. Why dogs chose humans in the first place I will never understand.

O.K., you fusty old Freudians, you laudable Laingians, my psyche is up for grabs. I have admitted a weak point. Dogs.

Animal lovers, especially female ones, are often accused of being neurotic and unable to relate successfully to other human beings. How many times had friends noted my relationship to Diggity, and, with that baleful look usually associated with psychiatrists, said, 'You've never thought of having a child, have you?' It's an accusation that brings an explosive response every time because it seems to me that the good lord in his infinite wisdom gave us three things to make life bearable – hope, jokes and dogs, but the greatest of these was dogs.

I was by now quite happy about camping by or on the track. The thought of anyone driving down it had long since faded into the impossible. But I had not taken into account madmen and fruit-cakes. I was awakened from my slumber

one night by the roar of an engine. I struggled out of deep
sleep with Diggity barking in fury, and a voice calling from
the dark, 'Hey, is that the camel lady, it's the overlander here.
Do I have permission to enter camp?'

'What the ...?'

An apparition appeared before me, with Dig biting at his
trouser legs. The 'overlander', as it turned out, was some nut
testing a Suzuki vehicle by driving it across the widest part
of Australia, over spinifex, sand and gibbers, just as fast as
he possibly could. He was breaking some kind of record. He
was also manic, and, presumably, out of his mind on speed.
His eyeballs hung out on his cheeks and he kept slapping his
upper arms, commenting on the cold, and hinting that he
wouldn't mind camping here. I most certainly didn't want
him camping anywhere near here, and neither did Dig. I
made this quite plain without being out and out rude. He
sat and raved at me for half an hour, with Dig quietly growling at the foot of my bed, and me pointedly yawning and
saying very little except, 'Hmm, oh really, that's nice, yawn,
hmm, you don't say,' and so on. He then informed me that
he had been following my tracks for miles, which, considering he was coming from the opposite direction, was no mean
feat. He eventually left. I scratched my head for a while, and
shook it just to make sure I hadn't been hallucinating, and
went back to sleep. I forgot about it. Had I known what he
was going to do when he got back to civilization, I would
have wrung his fat neck then and there.

We were getting close to Carnegie. On the one hand, I
didn't want to be anywhere but in this desert and on my own;
on the other, I was running very low on food, my last meal
before I got there being dog-biscuits liberally laced with cus-
tard powder, sugar, milk and water. And I was nervous about
seeing people again. By now I was utterly deprogrammed.
I walked along naked usually, clothes being not only putrid
but unnecessary. My skin had been baked a deep terra-cotta
brown and was the constituency of harness leather. The sun

211

no longer penetrated it. I retained my hat, because my nose had peeled so often I thought it might disappear altogether. I might be left with just a bare lump of sizzling cartilage sticking out there. And I honestly could not remember, or put into context, etiquette. Did it matter, I would think to myself, if all the buttons had gone from my shirt and trousers? Would anybody notice or care? And what about menstrual blood? From my position, it didn't matter a damn whether it followed the natural laws of gravity and ran down my leg, the way it was meant to do, but would others feel the same way? Would it make them confused and unhappy? But why on earth would it? I wouldn't cover a cut in embarrassment would I? I was in an agony of confusion, because I just DIDN'T KNOW. I'm amazed at how quickly and absolutely this sense of the importance of social custom fell away from me. And the awareness of its absurdity has never really left me. I have slowly regained a sense of the niceties, but I think, I hope, that I will always see the obsession with social graces and female modesty for the perverted crippling insanity it really is.

It is extraordinary that the two most commonly asked questions about the trip (after 'Why did you do it?') are . . . one, What did you do when you ran out of toilet paper? and two (and this is always whispered over in the corner by women who giggle a lot), What did you do when you ran out of Meds? What on earth do they think I did? Ran to the nearest chemist shop to barter? Well, for all those who remain morbidly curious over body functions, when I ran out of toilet paper, I used smooth rocks, grass and, when lucky, a kindly desert plant known as pussy-cat tails. When I ran out of Meds, I didn't care.

In fact, to this day, I think one of the major breakthroughs I made on that trip was learning the gentle art of farting. I had never farted before. Well, maybe once or twice, but then only pathetic little pfffttts. God knows what happened to all that air. Must have seeped through the pores of my skin at night I suppose. Ah, but now, now I could blart with the best of them – good solid base thrums which spooked the camels and scared flocks of spinifex pigeons into the air. Diggity and I had competitions: she always won for poisonousness, I for sonorousness.

I arrived at Carnegie to find it abandoned and more desolate and depressing than I can describe. Suddenly, dramatically, as soon as I hit the boundary fence, the country was ruined. Broken. Eaten out by cattle. Destroyed. I had been so in tune with the marvellous untouched country I had been through that I felt this change like a slap. How could they do this? How could they overstock their country and, with that great Australian get-rich-quick drive, lay it bare. There was nothing, not a thing, for my camels to eat. I thought I had come through the worst part, only to find the true desert, man's desert, beginning. I shouldn't be too hard on the graziers. They were suffering a four-year drought and many of their cattle had died. But there is good management and bad management, and in my opinion anyone who overstocked his country deserved everything he got. Some species of plants have disappeared from cattle country for ever, simply because of this greedy bad management. Inedible, poisonous plants (like the turpentine bush) had taken over. I had seen only very few of this species before, but now it was everywhere. It was the only green thing left alive, and it was doing very nicely thank you. Even the mulga, the only thing that would keep my camels going, was brown and dry.

Then, out of the blue, two very friendly young men arrived. They had driven out there to pick up an old jeep they had seen on the Carnegie dump. They had not known the place was abandoned either. Apparently it had happened only recently. They were so nice. One of them made a leather boot for Dookie's foot and then they offered me great quantities of food. I handed them money which they at first refused to take. When I told them that I would use it for toilet paper

213

or lighting fires if they didn't, they acquiesced. And then I started raging at them about the demise of the country. I commented on the difference, which was to me like chalk and cheese, between the country on that side of the fence, and this side. They hadn't noticed. I was astounded. Couldn't they see? No. One needs to have one's eyes peeled, and one needs to feel part of the earth before it is possible to notice the difference. And six months before, I probably would not have been able to see it either.

I had not expected this turn of events. I had thought the going from here on would be like a holiday. I had planned to head straight through cattle country to Wiluna. I changed my mind and studied my maps. I decided to go due north to Glenayle station, then meet up with the Canning stock route, which I thought would be free of cattle and better still, people. I had heard dreadful stories about this stock route. It had been abandoned years ago because too many cattle and camels had perished along it. It went straight through one of the worst deserts in Australia. There would be wells along it, but since these had not been kept up, most of them would be useless. However, I was only going to attempt the easiest and most southerly part and someone had told me it was glorious country. I headed off for Glenayle.

By now we all badly needed a rest. Although the country inside Glenayle was slightly better (I deduced from that, that whoever ran the place was more in tune with the land and would probably be the salt of the earth), the camels were still having a hard time getting enough to fill their bellies. My worry over them was absurd really, camels will survive where nothing else will, but Zeleika in particular was a bag of bones. Her hump had degenerated into a pitiful tuft of hair capping a set of extruding ribs. I shared out her baggage among the others, but this was not the problem. She was stupid over Goliath. He was rolling in fat and spoilt beyond redemption. The more frail she became, the more my relationship to this little parasite deteriorated. There was nothing

I could do to cut down his suckling. I tried to design an udder bag but he always managed to bury his nose through it. And she would come to feed him great quantities of milk at night, no matter how close I tied him to a tree. When we stopped at midday, I always sat the camels down under some shade for an hour's rest. They deserved it, welcomed it, and would sit gazing off into the distance chewing their cuds, engrossed in deep camel speculation about the meaning of life. But I had a job keeping Goliath away from his mother. He would sneak up when I wasn't looking, nudge and push at her, demanding that she feed him. When she refused, he would grab her nose-line in his mouth and tug it. She'd bellow and leap to her feet and like lightning the little creep would dive straight at her udder. He may have been a brat but he wasn't stupid. The other nasty habit he developed was charging up beside the camels at full gallop and letting out a sideways kick at me. I put a stop to this finally by holding a large mulga waddie close to my body, then breaking it full force over his leg as he grazed perilously past – a short sharp shock that stopped him in his tracks and set him to plotting for revenge. While I grudgingly admired Zeleika's self-sacrifice, I thought she was a bit door-mattish with her first-born.

Even the wild animals were dying off. They continued to live on station country where water, in the form of bore, windmill, tank and trough, was plentiful, but cattle had eaten what little feed there was left. I seldom camped by these bores at night. They were always dust-bowls strewn with desiccated animal carcasses twisted into hideous attitudes of pain, hardly places to lift the spirit. I usually tried to rest by them at midday, so the animals could drink and I could have a wash, then continue on for ten miles or so and camp where the feed was a little better. This was not always possible, and one night, before reaching Glenayle, I set up camp half a mile from one of them.

I had never chastised Diggity for chasing kangaroos, since I was certain she could never catch one. But she woke me up that night, tearing after some poor skeletal old boomer heading out from a drink. Before I had gathered my wits to call her back, she had disappeared into the black. I went back to sleep. She returned to my swag some time later, licking me awake and whimpering, urging me to get up and follow her. 'Jesus, Dig, you didn't catch it, did you?' Whimper whimper scratch lick. I loaded the rifle and followed her. She led me straight to her prize. He was a huge grey male and at death's door. I think what happened was that he was simply too weak to withstand the chase. Diggity had not touched him, wouldn't have known how to I suspect, and the poor old thing had suffered a stroke. He was lying on his side, panting softly. I knocked him on the head. The next morning, I went past the carcass and bent down with my knife to take the haunch and tail. And then I froze. What had Eddie told me about cutting meat? 'But that doesn't apply to you, you're white.' 'Are you sure it doesn't? How do you know?' There was no way I could carry the whole kangaroo, he was much too heavy, but to leave such delicious meat just rotting there seemed crazy. After five minutes of indecision, I put the knife away and continued on.

When the beliefs of one culture are translated into the language of another culture, the word 'superstition' often crops up. Perhaps it was superstition that made me leave that kangaroo intact, or perhaps it was rather that I had seen too much to be quite sure any more where truth and bogus met. Because I wasn't sure, I didn't think I was in any position to take chances.

I was right about the people at Glenayle. They were not only the salt of the earth, they were charming, kind, generous, and pretended not to notice my eccentricities, chatting amiably while I belched, scratched, gulped tea and ate home-made scones like a ravenous pig. I pulled up to their front gate in mid-afternoon. On the other side was a grey-haired, genteel woman in a crisp pressed summer dress watering her flower garden and all she said, without even

216

a raising of the eyebrows, was, 'Oh hello, dear, how nice to see you, won't you come in for a cup of tea?'

Eileen, Henry and their son Lou asked me to stay for a week. I was delighted. Not only were they pleasant company, but they fed me up and looked after me with true outback hospitality. This generosity and openness is part of the bush code of ethics and I'm sure it is universal. It goes hand in hand with a belief in honesty, hard work, simplicity and love of the land. My camels all needed to pick up a little before we attempted the Canning, and Henry gave me the horse paddock to let them roam in. This horse paddock was a couple of square miles of dead rocks, grey inedible spinifex and dust. But there was a little mulga left alive, a few dull green bloodwoods, and another bright green acacia that presumably did not require any water at all. Either that or its roots went down for hundreds of feet. It would be my camels' mainstay for the next month.

The more I got to know these people, the more impressed I was by their stoic, irrepressible good humour. They had every reason to be wringing their hands, weeping and bemoaning their fate. Cattle were dropping dead everywhere, horses were bags of bone and air that were now trying to eat spinifex, and there was not a cloud in sight. Glenayle was the furthest station out into the desert, and perhaps it was this very remoteness that made the Wards such a united family. That, and the fact that Henry was an excellent bushman, loved the country, and none of them would have swapped places with a city dweller for all the rain in the world. They took me out mustering while I was there – trying to scrape together a few steers before they died. The money they got for this meat would only just cover the cost of freight, if at all. We would camp at night, eat beef, laugh, and sing along to Slim Dusty, yodelling away about the wonderfulness of mothers.

For those who don't know, Slim Dusty is Australia's greatest contemporary country-western bard. Although most of my friends gag when I play him, I put that down to the fact that they have never been to the Mount Isa rodeo. It is not until you have been to such an outback function, and been woken at four a.m. to the sound of Slim over the loudspeakers stirring the participants from a booze-clogged dream to get them cracking on the important things in life like bronk-riding, steer-roping, and drinking; heard him twang and croon all day for a solid week, ventured down the local pub known as the snakepit to drink with your cobber ocker stone-the-crows fair-crack-of-the-whip-mate mates, and danced to the tinny twang of the steel guitar of some cowboy and his tatty tinselly cow-girl back-up team playing the Urandangi Dandy; then, wonder of wonders, been part of a hopelessly inebriated audience on the last night of the rodeo when Slim appears in the flesh complete with flash hat and purple silk shirt and surprisingly good musicians, and you've sung along with tears in your eyes and in your beer to 'a tall dark man in the saddle' – that you can really understand the full emotive force of this Aussie bush poet.

On my last day there, I went out to track up my camels. If they hadn't gained weight they did seem slightly rounder at the corners and Zeleika looked a little less like Sad Sack. All in all, they were in as fine a fettle as I could hope for. Bub was the first one to come up as usual, snuffling around for hand-outs. I gave him his share and was not watching the others. Dookie, who has always had a jealous streak, who has always considered himself the boss of the outfit, me included, took my whole head between his jaws, which fitted around it like a crash helmet. He slobbered in my hair for a second, then spun on his hind legs and bounded and bucked away, looking extremely pleased with himself. He could have squashed my cranium like a grape had he wanted to. I did not normally allow such transgressions amongst my animals, because how was I to know when they might one day decide amongst themselves that they didn't like being dragged half way across a continent any more, and mutiny. But what could I say, with Dookie looking at me so coquettishly, trying to see whether I got the joke or not.

Henry went through the maps with me, showing me where to join up with the Canning at well ten, telling me which tracks were there and which were not, and where to turn south. He also told me which wells were usable along the road. Road? I was surprised at this. I had expected a faint or invisible track. I had thought I would have to rely on my compass. Mining was one of the causes of this tracking up of the wild places. Roads would appear from nowhere and disappear to nowhere.

In a way, I was disappointed. The Canning was to be the last stretch of non-station country I was to see, and I thought sadly as I saddled up that the heart of the journey was coming to a close. I calculated that it would take me three weeks to reach Wiluna, the first town since Alice Springs.

The first two days were dreadful. The earth was scorched and bare, ugly grey dust covered everything and I got sick twice, the only illness I suffered on the whole trip. I had taken a freezing bore bath in the evening, and walked along naked to dry off. I woke up that night with a severe case of cystitis. Pills for that – thank the lord I brought them. But it was a sleepless night. A day or two later I found myself suffering acute stomach cramps, doubtless from some bad water I had drunk. It came on me with a sudden uncontrollable rush, and as I struggled out of my trousers, muttering ugh ugh disgusting ugh, I was overcome with – embarrassment. The desocializing process had only gone so far. I burnt the trousers, and wasted a gallon of water trying to get clean.

But after that, the country started to pick up. Whatever rains had occurred in the last four years had swept through this more northerly desert country, bypassing the cattle stations to the south. While it was anything but bountiful, there was at least a meagre picking for the beasts. What would have made me turn my nose up earlier in the trip,

219

now appeared lush to my eyes. It was a magnificent landscape in a fossilized primordial sort of way. A twisted freakish wasteland of sandstone break-aways, silent, and seemingly aloof from the rest of the earth's evolution. God's country it may have been but it was extremely hard on the camels. The stony escarpments strained them and hurt their feet. They were carrying almost a full load of water, and I knew I would have to rest them as soon as I could find suitable water and feed.

From a study of the maps, well six looked promising. I was hot and frustrated, because I kept expecting the creek-bed marked on the map to be just a little way on. It wasn't. The hill to my right was never-ending. I shouted at Diggity and laid a kick at her when she spooked the camels. I was seething with bad temper, poor little Dig had no idea what she had done wrong and walked along disconsolate with her tail between her legs. She had accepted a lot of punishment lately, or what she considered punishment. The Wards had given me a leather muzzle to put on her to protect her from strychnine baits, which were dropped way out in the desert from light aircraft to exterminate the Australian native dog, the dingo. But she had hated it. She had whined and scratched at it and looked such a picture of misery and heart-break that I eventually took it off. She was not in the habit of picking at dead carcasses and I kept her well-fed enough so that she wouldn't be tempted.

I reached the end of the hill at last, and walked down a rim of high rolling sand-dunes. As I came over the crest I saw an infinitely extended bowl of pastel blue haze with writhing hills and crescents floating and shimmering in it and fire-coloured dunes lapping at their feet and off in the distance some magical, violet mountains. Have you ever heard mountains roar and beckon? These did, like giant lions. A sound meant only for the ears of madmen and deaf mutes. I was paralysed by that sight. Nothing as wildly beautiful as that had I ever seen, even in my dream landscapes.

Here was the confluence of several major types of country. The rolling plains and plateaux covered in spinifex and blue distant mists, the vibrantly coloured sand-dunes, the deep red striated sandstone hills, and through it all, that serpentine stretch of creek-bed, all green and hard, glittering white. We skipped down that last dune and made for the well. The camels could see the feed and were straining to get there. The well itself was difficult to see and overgrown with acacia. It was fifteen feet down and smelled like rotten swamp. But it was wet and would get us by for the necessary few days. It tasted foul – like muddy soup, but with enough coffee I could get it down. Above it was an ancient whip bucket which I had Buckley's and none* of being able to use. Even hauling up five gallons in my own tin drum almost caused me a triple hernia.

That evening the camels played in the white dust, raising balloons of cloud that the fat, red setting sun caught, burst and turned to gold. I lay on a foot-thick mattress of fallen leaves which scattered golden jangles of firelight in a thousand directions. Night calls and leaf sighs floated down to me on the breeze and around me was a cathedral of black and silver giant ghost-gums, the thin sliver of platinum moon cradled in their branches. The heart of the world had been found. I drifted into sleep in that palace and allowed the mountains to fade along the rim of my mind. The heart of the world, paradise.

I decided to stay in that place as long as the water held out. Rick and responsibilities were so far away from me now, so remote, I didn't give them a moment's consideration. I planned to enter the sandhills and ride out to those distant mountains. But first the camels must rest. There was feed here to burn. Salt-bush, camel thorn, mulga, everything their little hearts could desire. Diggity and I explored. We found a cave in Pine Ridge which had Aboriginal paintings plastered all over it. Then we climbed up a narrow, treacherous rocky

* no chance.

gap, the wind howling and whistling down at us. We pulled ourselves up to the flat top, where freakish rock strata ran in great buttresses and giant steps. The trees up there were gnarled into crippled shapes by the roar of the wind. Along the distant horizon I could see a sandstorm being whipped up into a cloud of red, straight out of *Beau Geste*. Further west, we discovered ancient desert palms, called black-boys. Rough black stumps shooting out fountains of green needles at the top, all huddled together by themselves, like an alien race left behind on a forgotten planet. There was a haunting hallucinatory quality about this place. I felt swelled by it, high as a kite. I was filled with an emotion I had not felt before – joy.

Those days were like a crystallization of all that had been good in the trip. It was as close to perfection as I could ever hope to come. I reviewed what I had learnt. I had discovered capabilities and strengths that I would not have imagined possible in those distant dream-like days before the trip. I had rediscovered people in my past and come to terms with my feelings towards them. I had learnt what love was. That love wanted the best possible for those you cared for even if that excluded yourself. That before, I had wanted to possess people without loving them, and now I could love them and wish them the best without needing them. I had understood freedom and security. The need to rattle the foundations of habit. That to be free one needs constant and unrelenting vigilance over one's weaknesses. A vigilance which requires a moral energy most of us are incapable of manufacturing. We relax back into the moulds of habit. They are secure, they bind us and keep us contained at the expense of freedom. To break the moulds, to be heedless of the seductions of security is an impossible struggle, but one of the few that count. To be free is to learn, to test yourself constantly, to gamble. It is not safe. I had learnt to use my fears as stepping stones rather than stumbling blocks, and best of all I had learnt to laugh. I felt invincible, untouchable, I had extended myself, and I believed I could now sit back, there was nothing else the desert could teach me. And I wanted to remember all this. Wanted to remember this place and what it meant to me, and how I had arrived there. Wanted to fix it so firmly in my head that I would never, ever forget.

In the past, my bouts of gloom and despair had led, like widdershins,* to the same place. And it seemed that at that place was a signpost saying, 'Here it is,' here is the thing you must push through, leap free of, before you can learn any more. It was as if the self brought me constantly to this place – took every opportunity to show it to me. It was as if there was a button there which I could push if I only had the courage. If I could only just remember. Ah, but we always forget. Or are too lazy. Or too frightened. Or too certain we have all the time in the world. And so back up the ravines to the comfortable places (the sane ones?) where we don't have to think too much. Where life is, after all, just 'getting by' and where we survive, half asleep.

And I thought I had done it. I believed I had generated a magic for myself that had nothing to do with coincidence, believed I was part of a strange and powerful sequence of events called fate and I was beyond the need for anything or anyone. And that night I received the most profound and cruel lesson of all. That death is sudden and final and comes from nowhere. It had waited for my moment of supreme complacency and then it had struck. Late that night, Diggity took a poison bait.

We were running low on dog food, and I was too lazy, too high to want to go and shoot her some game. So I rationed her. She woke me up sneaking sheepishly back into the swag. 'What's up, Dig, where've you been, little woofing?' She licked my face profusely, snuffled her way under the covers, and snuggled as usual into my belly. I cuddled her. Suddenly she slunk out again and began to vomit. My body went cold. 'Oh no, no it can't be, please, Jesus, not this.'

* water-worn gulleys.

223

She came back to me and licked my face again. 'It's O.K., Dig, you're just a little bit sick. Don't worry, little one, you come and snuggle in here and get warm and you'll be O.K. in the morning.' Within minutes she was out again. This couldn't be happening. She was my little dog and she couldn't be poisoned. That was impossible, couldn't happen to her. I got up to check what she had brought up. I remember trembling uncontrollably and droning to her, 'It's all right, Dig, everything's all right, don't worry,' over and over. She had eaten some dead animal but it didn't smell rotten, so I repeated to myself that she couldn't be poisoned. I forced myself to believe it yet I knew it wasn't true. My head raced through what you do for strychnine poisoning. You have to swing them around your head to make them get rid of it all, but even if you do it immediately there's virtually no chance of survival. 'Well, I won't do that anyway, because you're not poisoned, you're not poisoned. You're my Dig and it can't happen to you.' Diggity started wandering around retching violently and coming back to me for reassurance. She knew. Suddenly she ran away to some black acacia bushes and turned to face me. She barked and howled at me and I knew she must be hallucinating, knew she was dying. Her two mirror eyes burnt an image into my brain that will not fade. She came over to me and put her head between my legs. I picked her up and swung her round my head. Round and round and round. She kicked and struggled. I tried to pretend it was a game. I let her down and she went crashing through the undergrowth barking like a mad dog. I raced for the gun, I loaded it and went back. She was on her side convulsing. I blew her brains out. I knelt frozen like that for a long time then I staggered back to the swag and got in. My body shook with uncontrollable spasms. I vomited. Sweat soaked into the pillow and blankets. I thought I was dying too. I thought that when she licked me, I had swallowed some strychnine. 'Is this what it feels like to die? Am I dying? No, no, it's just shock, stop it, you must

224

27–9   *Top*, coming into Cunyu station, where the camels were hidden from enquiring newsmen. *Left*, Rick drove me to Peter Muir's homestead on the outskirts of Wiluna until the fuss had died down. *Right*, Peter Muir.

30–1 *Top*, near the end of the journey Zeleika contracted an infection and had to be injected with massive doses of antibiotic. *Below*, eight months after setting out, the camels had their first sight of the ocean before going into a well-earned retirement on Woodleigh station.

go to sleep.' I've never been able before or since to do what I did then. I shut my brain off and willed it into immediate unconsciousness.

I woke well before dawn. The sick, steely, pre-dawn light was enough to find the things I needed. I caught the camels and gave them some water. I packed my belongings and loaded up and forced myself to drink some water. I felt nothing. Then suddenly it was time to leave that place and I didn't know what to do. I had a profound desire to bury the dog. I told myself it was ridiculous. It was natural and correct for the body to decay on the surface of the ground. But there was an overwhelming need in me to ritualize, to make real and tangible what had happened. I walked back to Diggity's body, stared at it, and tried to make all of myself face what was there. I didn't bury her. But I said goodbye to a creature I had loved unconditionally, without question. I said my goodbyes and my thank-yous and I wept for the first time and covered the body with a handful of fallen leaves. I walked out into the morning and felt nothing. I was numb, empty. All I knew was I mustn't stop walking.

Part Four

On the Far Side

11

I MUST have walked thirty or more miles that day. I was afraid to stop. Afraid that the feeling of loss, guilt and loneliness would swamp me. I eventually pulled into a wash-away and built a bonfire. I had hoped that I would be so exhausted that I would fall asleep without having to think. I was in a strange state. I had been expecting a lack of control over my emotions, but instead I was cool, rational, hard-edged, accepting. I decided to finish the trip in Wiluna, not because I was wanting to run away from it, but because I felt that the trip had ended itself; had reached some psycho-logical conclusion, had simply become complete, like the last page of a novel. I dreamt that night, and most following nights for months, that Diggity was all right. In my dreams I would relive the sequence of events, only it always turned out that she survived, and that she forgave me. She was often human in these dreams, and talked to me. They were disturb-ingly vivid. I woke to the reality of loneliness, and was sur-prised at the strength which enabled me to accept it.

It may seem strange that the mere death of a dog could have such a profound effect on someone, but it must be remembered that, because of my isolation, Diggity had become a cherished friend rather than simply a pet. I'm sure, had the incident occurred back in the city, surrounded by my own kind, the effect would not have been anywhere near as great. But out there, and in that changed and stretched state of mind, it was as traumatic as the death of a human, because to a large extent she had become just that, she had taken the place of people.

Henry Ward had shown me on my map where to turn south. From the mark I had made on that map, it seemed a good few miles past a certain bore. I had obviously made a mistake – I was still travelling due west across monotonous flats, watching what I considered must be the pass in the hills dwindling away behind me. I camped that night on a small sandhill that looked like an island left behind by the tide. This was peculiar, oppressive country. It was dead flat, covered in white gypsum dust dotted with clumps of a salty succulent at intervals of twelve feet. And out of this vast expanse would rise the occasional still wave of sand, covered in taller trees and scrub. It had an abandoned quality and it gave me the creeps.

I decided to use my hated radio set that night to call Henry and check up on the direction. I wasn't so much panicked as uneasy. I wanted to talk to someone. Everything was so still and there was no Diggity to play with or talk to or hold. It took me half an hour to set the wretched thing up – a long bit of wire draped over a tree, and another along the ground. It didn't work. I had carried this monster for fifteen hundred miles, loaded and unloaded it hundreds of times, and the only occasion I needed it, it wouldn't work. It had probably been broken all along.

I was woken that night by the most chilling, hair-lifting sound I had ever heard. A soft, high-pitched keening that got louder and louder. I had never been afraid in the dark, and if I heard a sound I couldn't place, it didn't disturb me too much. Besides, Dig had always been there to protect and comfort me. But this? Ripples ran up and down my back. I got up and wandered around camp. Everything was perfectly still, but the noise was now a continuous unmodulated wail. I was beginning to recognize the first tell-tale signs of panic – this noise had to have a rational explanation. Either that, or I was going mad again, or some spirit was out to drive me that way. And then I felt the first stirrings of breeze. Of course, the noise I was hearing was the wind whistling through the top tips of the trees I was under. There had not been a breath of turbulence on the ground, but now the pre-dawn wind, that solid unflagging front of cool air, was chilling me to the bone and making the coals of the fire glow red. I crawled back into my swag shivering, and tried to get back to sleep. I would have given anything just then, to be able to hold that familiar warm dog flesh – the need was like a physical ache. Without her, I was suddenly susceptible to all those swamping, irrational feelings of vulnerability and dread.

Most of the rest of that week or ten days was a timeless blur. The ground travelled under my feet unnoticed until some piece of country shocked me out of my mental machinations. I kept getting the odd sensation that I was in fact perfectly stationary, and that I was pushing the world around under my feet.

I came across an almost dried-up, green putrescent water-hole, filled with rotting carcasses of cattle, horses and kangaroos. Around this water-hole were stretches of stone walls, high up on the banks. I suspected that they were Aboriginal hunting blinds, perhaps thousands of years old. The hunters would have waited patiently behind these walls, upwind of the animals coming down to drink, then leapt out with their spears. They would have kept the hole clean in former years. Now, with none of them left to maintain and take care of this potentially beautiful watering place, even my camels turned their noses up at it. It was a horrible sewer and it smelt of death and decay. I made sure the camels had enough to drink from my drums that night before letting them go, just in case. Luckily, it was too cold for them to want to wallow in it.

At about this time I entered and spent a day exploring what was probably the most impressive surreal piece of landscaping I had seen on the whole journey. A vast depression had sunk away from the broken plateau. Rimming it all around the horizon were cliffs of every imaginable hue. Some of these faces were as smooth and glossy as fine porcelain. Some were pure dazzling white, some pink, green, mauve, brown, red and so on. The depression was covered in samphire, which I then thought was 'sand-fire'. It was such a perfect name. When this plant dried out, it changed into myriads of colours – rainbow colours, reflecting the glow and iridescence of the cliffs. And dotted throughout this lost world were weirdly sculptured mounds of rock and pebbles. A martian landscape seen through multi-coloured glasses. I picked up and kept one small rock – pale pink sandstone studded with glitter, one side rippled into tiny sharp ridges.

But even this exploratory walk felt empty. I had to force myself to do it. Everything I did now was like that – unspontaneous, forced. I had even given up cooking for myself at night. I would scrabble around in the bags for something to eat, forcing myself to nibble even though I wasn't hungry

The other topographic freaks that stopped me in my tracks were the claypans. Mile after mile these perfectly flat brown hard-baked Euclidean surfaces ran, without a blade of grass on them, without a tree or an animal or a clump of spinifex – nothing but towering, thin, crooked, brown pillars of whirling dust being sucked up into a burning, almost white sky. Looking at these claypans was like gazing at a calm ocean, only you could walk on this stuff. Right next to one huge pan was a dwarf replica, about a hundred yards across A bush ballroom. An outback amphitheatre. I tied up the camels for their midday break and in that searing, clean bright, dry heat, I took off my clothes and danced. I danced until I could dance no more – I danced out everything Diggity, the trip, Rick, the article, the whole lot. I shouted and howled and wept and I leapt and contorted my body until it refused to respond any more. I crawled back to the camels, covered in grime and sweat, shaking with fatigue dust in my ears and nose and mouth, and slept for about an hour. When I woke, I felt healed, and weightless, and prepared for anything.

I was well and truly back in station country now. The tracks here were well used. I had a bath and a swim at the next bore, washed my hair and clothes and hung them on the saddle to dry. It takes about five minutes out there. And I promised myself as I walked along that I would eat properly that night – I was too light-headed, too close to the edge to continue on the way I was doing, and I needed to bring myself down.

I spotted a vehicle coming, belting along with a train of red dust behind it stretching to the horizon. I thought it must be station people out to do their check on the bores. I hastily put on my clothes and tried to twist my mind into shape for a short and simple chat with some bush folk. They were usually people of few words, but I was actually frightened of that car.

It wasn't bush folk. It was the jackals, hyenas, parasites and pariahs of the popular press. By the time I saw the long-lens camera trained at me, it was too late to hide, or get out the gun and blast it at them, or even realize that I was crazy enough to do such a thing. Out they spilled.

'We'll give you a thousand dollars for the story.'

'Go away. Leave me alone. I'm not interested.'

My heart was pumping like a cornered rabbit's.

'Well, for Christ's sake, might as well come and have a cold beer anyway.'

They had the human psyche so well tapped that they could bribe me with one beer where they couldn't buy me for a thousand bucks. I accepted the bribe as much to find out what was happening back in the world, and why they were here, as anything else. They sneaked in a few questions, some I answered perfunctorily, others I refused to comment on.

'Where's your dog?'

I didn't know how to sidestep these people – had once again forgotten the rules of the game. It was either blow their brains out and run or shrink into an acquiescent quivering blob, fighting hard to stay in control.

'She's dead, but please don't print that as it would make a few old people back home very distressed.'

233

'Yeah, O.K. we won't.'

'Is that a promise – your word?'

'Sure, sure.'

But they did print it of course. They flew back to Perth with a scoop, made up a story, and the myth of the romantic, mysterious camel lady was launched.

That night I camped well off the road in a dense thicket. This was something I had not expected at all. Those light planes I had seen buzzing around all day and vaguely felt curious about were for me. What on earth had got into those people back there? I had noticed a kind of hysteria in the reporters when they talked of the press reports so far. 'World-wide,' they had said. I couldn't believe that. And they'd scuttled off home playing their part in the great ugly farce called 'the public has a right to know'. I decided to wait there for a couple of days. If the press were really after me it would be better to hide out until it all blew over.

It was the overlander who had really set me up. When he arrived back in civilization, longing for any limelight he could stand under, he told a story of this marvellous woman he had 'spent a night with' in the desert. The quote ran something like, 'It was romantic. Her bare shoulders protruded from the sleeping bag, bells were tinkling on the pack, and I talked with her for many hours in the moonlight. I didn't ask her why she was doing it, she didn't ask me why I was doing it. We understood.' Not a bad description of a sun-crazed loony in a sweat-soaked, camel-bespattered, grimy swag, who had been innocently pushing up zeds from the pit at the time. The worm. Maybe he thought he was doing me a favour.

I ran into the bushes when the first cars arrived, television cameras and all. These jerks had hired a black tracker. But my fighting spirit was coming back to me now. They were so stupid, so heavy, these people – they didn't belong here and I had the edge on them there at least. I giggled to myself and whispered silent Indian war whoops from behind my camouflage. I circled right round through the thicket so that I was only twenty feet from them. The place where I had camped was sandy, so a blind fool could have tracked me. My footprints stood out like neon signposts, like Mac truck tracks on a sandhill.

'All right, fella, where is she?' One of them, the fat one with sweat staining his red T-shirt and a scowling heat-struck look over his matching face, addressed the black tracker.

'Gee, boss, that camel lady might be real smart one, she might be cover up them tracks. I can't see where she gone.' And he shook his head and rubbed his chin in thoughtful puzzlement.

Yippee and whoop whoop. I could have leapt out and kissed him for that. He knew exactly where I was and he was on my side. The fat one cursed and grudgingly handed over the ten dollars' wages. The Aborigine smiled and put it in his pocket, and they took off – 150 miles of dirt track back to Wiluna.

I went back to my camp, stoked up the fire and felt raw. Invaded. As if my skin had been pulled off. I felt vulnerable and my stomach had knotted into a tight cold ball of tension. What in god's name was happening here? People had done trips like this before, how come I was copping the attention? I still had no idea of the extent of the furore. I thought of covering my tracks but that wouldn't fool any Aboriginal – eventually one of them would find me. I thought of scaring them all off with a few shotgun pellets but dropped that immediately – it would just be another story.

And then I saw Rick's car charging past at the speed of light with several other cars chasing him. 'Oh my god, what is going on?' Rick came back in five minutes, turned in on my tracks and drove up to me. He only just had time to give me a vague outline before they all piled out. Some were from the London press, some were from television, some were from the Australian papers. I hissed and snarled and ground my teeth at them. I stomped into the bushes and ordered them point-blank from behind a tree to put their cameras down. Rick told me later that I looked and behaved like a mad woman. Exactly what they had expected. I had washed my hair in a salty bore, so it stuck out of my head in a frizzed, bleached electric halo. I was frazzled and burnt black by the sun and I hadn't been sleeping much in the last week or so, so that my eyes were piggy little slits, with brown sag beneath them. I was also out of my tree. I had not recovered from the loss of Diggity and couldn't handle this invasion of what looked to me then like inter-galactic war-lords. I was so adamant and so crazy that they shuffled their feet with embarrassment and did as they were told. I came back. And then, like a fool, I partially relented. Curiosity killed the cat. When I look back I marvel at myself. At what makes me instantly apologetic to people I have stood up to when they have been prepared to walk all over me. I still allowed no photos so one of them photographed my campfire. 'Can't go back with nothing, I'd get fired.'

One man even apologized after he had defended television as a medium, even mildly castigating me for not sharing myself with the public. He said, 'It's funny how truth always seems to get in the way.'

Others rationalized my dislike for publicity by saying, and later printing, that I was committed to a magazine, that I had done the trip for the magazine and therefore couldn't talk to anyone else about it. Why couldn't they understand that some of us just don't want to be famous – that anonymity cannot be bought for any price, once you have lost it? Richard played protector. I was glad of it, I felt too weak and confused to be able to do it for myself. Besides, he spoke their language. They left eventually, and Rick and I were free to talk. He told me of his own ordeal. Of reading in some obscure overseas newspaper of how the camel lady was lost, and how he had not slept for four days trying to reach me before the wave of reporters did, and wondering if I were dead. He had been leapt upon by reporters in Wiluna and had tried, unsuccessfully, to shake them off. He showed me some of the papers he had picked up. Pictures of me smiling into the camera.

'How the hell did they get hold of these?' I was stunned.

'Tourists have been selling them to the papers.'

'Jeeeeeesus.'

Some of the reports were at least entertaining. They said things like, 'Miss Davidson lived on berries and bananas[?] and said she would kill her camels for meat if she was starving,' or, 'Miss Davidson was met by a lone and mysterious Aboriginal man one night who travelled with her for a time, then disappeared, as silently as he had come,' or (this from an American bush-walker's magazine), 'No points this week to Robyn Davidson the camel lady, for wilfully destroying the Australian native[?] camel. Perhaps she thought she was on a big game hunt.' Idiots.

And enemies had suddenly switched sides. All those people back in Alice Springs who wouldn't have spat on me if I were burning in those frugal, anonymous days, were suddenly on the publicity bandwagon. 'Sure,' they said, 'I knew her, I taught her everything she knows about camels.'

And it was only then that I realized what I had let myself in for, and only then I realized how bloody thick I had been not to have predicted it. It would seem that the combination of elements – woman, desert, camels, aloneness – hit some soft spot in this era's passionless, heartless, aching psyche. It fired the imaginations of people who see themselves as alienated, powerless, unable to do anything about a world gone mad. And wouldn't it be my luck to pick just this combination. The reaction was totally unexpected and it was very, very weird. I was now public property. I was now a kind of symbol. I was now an object of ridicule for small-minded sexists, and I was a crazy, irresponsible adventurer (though not as crazy as I would have been had I failed). But worse than all that, I was now a mythical being who had done something courageous and outside the possibilities that ordinary people could hope for. And that was the antithesis of what I wanted to share. That anyone could do anything. If I could bumble my way across a desert, than anyone could do anything. And that was true especially for women, who have used cowardice for so long to protect themselves that it has become a habit.

The world is a dangerous place for little girls. Besides, little girls are more fragile, more delicate, more brittle than little boys. 'Watch out, be careful, watch.' 'Don't climb trees, don't dirty your dress, don't accept lifts from strange men. Listen but don't learn, you won't need it.' And so the snail's antennae grow, watching for this, looking for that, the underneath of things. The threat. And so she wastes so much of her energy, seeking to break those circuits, to push up the millions of tiny thumbs that have tried to quelch energy and creativity and strength and self-confidence; that have so effectively caused her to build fences against possibility, daring; that have so effectively kept her imprisoned inside her notions of self-worthlessness.

And now a myth was being created where I would appear different, exceptional. Because society needed it to be so. Because if people started living out their fantasies, and refusing to accept the fruitless boredom that is offered them as normality, they would become hard to control. And that term 'camel LADY'. Had I been a man, I'd be lucky to get a mention in the *Wiluna Times*, let alone international press coverage. Neither could I imagine them coining the phrase 'camel gentleman'. 'Camel lady' had that nice patronizing belittling ring to it. Labelling, pigeon-holing – what a splendid trick it is.

Rick had met a man in town – Peter Muir. An ex-dogger, brilliant tracker, and who turned out to be one of the finest, multi-talented bushmen I have ever met – a dying breed. He came out to visit us with his wife Dolly and their children. It was nice to see some calm pleasant quiet people. We talked about the country I had just been through. Peter knew it probably better than anyone. He had spent his life oscillating between white and Aboriginal cultures and had combined the best elements of both. He told us what was happening in Wiluna. The town was being invaded by reporters offering money to anyone who could find me – a kind of siege; the police were receiving international calls all through the night, and were, understandably, ready to wring my neck; and the flying doctor radio was clogged with calls, to the point where real emergencies were not getting through. I was really angry now – deep down seething angry. Oddly enough, all the people in town (there were approximately twenty whites in Wiluna and a large group of blacks living in humpies on the outskirts) were on my side. As soon as they heard that I didn't want the publicity they went out of their way to protect me from it. The town clammed up.

Peter and Dolly offered me their second house, several miles out of Wiluna, to hide in. The people at Cunyu invited me to let my camels stay in their horse paddock, and continued to play dumb as to my whereabouts.

'Camel lady? Sorry, mate, no idea.'

I drove into Wiluna with Rick and then he told me that he had arranged for Jenny and Toly to come out and see me. Dear Rick. They were just what I needed.

After stocking up our hideaway with luxuries, we drove to Meekatharra, a slightly larger town a hundred miles west, to pick up Jen and Toly from the airport. I couldn't speak when I first saw them, but I held on to them tight. Then we went into town for a coffee and a spilling of our various ripping yarns. Seeing them and touching them was like a dose of tonic. They understood. They stroked my ruffled feathers and forced me to laugh at the insanity of it all. I began to feel less like a hunted criminal and more like a normal human being. As I have said before, friendship in certain sub-sections within Australia amounts almost to religion. This closeness and sharing is not describable to any other cultural group to whom friendship means dinner parties where one discusses wittily work and career, or gatherings of 'interesting' people who are all suspicious, wary, and terrified of not being interesting after all.

And there was mail. Acres of it. There were letters from friends, loved ones, and hundreds of anonymous people too, whose general message was, 'You have done something I would have liked to do, but never had the courage to try.' They were almost apologetic, and their letters puzzled me and frustrated me the most, because I kept wanting to shake them and tell them that courage had much less to do with it than sheer good luck and staying power. Some were messages from young men who on page three gave detailed descriptions of themselves (usually the tall blond handsome variety), then said they knew a great jungle in Peru and was I interested in exploring it with them? There were letters from old pensioners and young children, and a surprisingly large proportion from people in mental hospitals. These were at once the most interesting and the most difficult to follow. Lots of diagrams and arrows and strange cryptic messages which a week before I'm sure I would have understood perfectly. There was a telegram from an old friend which read, 'They say the sands of the Ryo-an are even more infinite ...' I liked that.

We laughed and joked and shed a few tears that day, and went to play pool in the local pub, where a woman (the local runner for the A.B.C.) noticed Rick's cameras and asked him if he knew where the camel lady was. He answered that he'd heard she was going to be in Meekatharra in about a week's time, and from there was travelling south, but could she please not print that as he knew the camel lady was extremely upset over the publicity. She tsc tsced, and said yes, wasn't it awful, poor thing etc., and immediately skulked home to type out a piece which put everyone off the scent and had us rolling in the aisles. Rick had said all that with a perfectly straight innocent face, and begged her in the name of common decency to do the right thing, knowing full well that she would not. I was beginning to appreciate just how bright and talented Richie was, in the gentle art of manipulation. We then loaded up the Toyota with yet more foodstuffs and sped back to our hole in the wall in Wiluna.

We all camped together in one room with a roaring fire – we sat in there swaddled in blankets, we toasted marshmallows, and talked and talked and talked; and we drank real coffee and Baileys and we cooked spinach pies and other culinary delights and we went out to visit the camels at Cunyu; and because I had gone into such raptures over the country I had been through and because I felt in a sense that I had missed *really* seeing it, being in such a state over the dog, we decided to drive back a-ways along the Canning.

The first part was O.K., the station roads were quite good, but once we got further out into the desert, we cut back down to five m.p.h. And just as I was eulogizing about the wilderness, the untamed pure quality, the magic and aloneness and freedom of this country, we turned a corner to see a helicopter perched on a creek-bank. Uranium prospectors. Was nothing sacred?

We spent two or three days of bliss on the Canning, then returned to Wiluna, where a gymkhana was being held. Almost every station person for a radius of hundreds of miles attended. There aren't too many social events in the back of beyond, so even when there's a drought on, everyone makes a concerted effort to go. This old ghost town with its empty buildings, once sumptuous with the flush of gold, now covered in graffiti and broken glass, normally housed the police, the publican, the post-master and the store-keeper. It was now a bush metropolis – a shadowy reminiscence of its former bustling self. A dance was arranged for that evening, to which my friends and I were cordially invited. When we arrived, however, we were met at the fallen-down hall by a bouncer in a suit. He didn't know who we were and said we couldn't come in because we weren't wearing ties.

This was a polite way of keeping Aborigines out. Groups of blacks hung around outside the doors.

This was a difficult situation for me. While Jen and Toly were indignant at this treatment of the blacks, I was caught between two versions of the truth. I liked station people and knew that they do not consider themselves racist. When they look at the sordid camps around town, they see only the violence and dirt and the incomprehensible lack of protestant work ethic. While they usually have a patronizing respect for the older Aboriginal people, they are unable to see beyond the immediate and beyond their own values, to understand why the demise occurred and what their part in it is, either traditionally or at present. Wiluna had a wealth of social problems and was a good example of what destruction of culture can produce.

We left Wiluna a day later. My last night with Jen and Toly on the track finally convinced them that camels are virtually human. Mine had a habit of hanging around camp, looking for hand-outs, or waiting until I wasn't watching so they could sneak their long-lipped faces into the food bags. As we ate dinner that night, we were entertained by Dookie, who kept trying to get at the large tin of honey he knew was hidden in a pack-bag just near where I was sitting. I told him to piss off. There followed a game of, 'See how far you can push Rob without getting a clout.' He inched forward ever so nonchalantly. Had he been human the parallel behaviour would have been hands behind back, eyes gazing up at the sky, and whistling. We pretended to keep eating but we were all watching him out of the corner of our eyes. He made a dive for the bag, I flicked him on the lips and he retreated about six inches. We continued eating. And then, to Toly's uncontrollable hysteria, Dookie pretended to eat a completely dead bush, his eyes rolling so he could keep his beady stare on the honey, and when he thought he had fooled us sufficiently with his innocence and diversionary tactic, he dived for the bag and tried to take off with it. 'All right,

Rob, I take it all back, you don't anthropomorphize at all.'

I had learnt the hard way to pack the food up tight at night after an incident with Bub along the Gunbarrel. I had opened a tin of cherries (the ultimate in luxury out there) and to eke the pleasure out, had left half in the tin beside my swag, for breakfast. I woke up in the morning with Bub's head in my lap, suspicious cherry stains all over his lips. Curing this bumming in them was impossible. Besides I kind of liked it, it made me laugh, and I reinforced it constantly by giving them whatever I could spare. They were indiscriminate over what I gave them. I could pick a piece of mulga, exactly what they were eating anyway, and they would all fight over it, just because it came from my hand.

Those next couple of weeks with Rick were easy and pleasant. The strange thing about being with a person in a desert is that you either end up the bitterest of enemies or the closest of friends. It had been touch and go in the beginning. Now, without the pressure of my feeling he had robbed me of something, or rather, with my acceptance of things turning out the way they did, plus the fact that Rick was a changed person, the friendship was firmly cemented. It had a rock-hard basis called shared experience, or the tolerance developed from seeing someone at their best and at their worst, and stripped of all social value – the bare bones of another human being. He had learnt a great deal from the trip; sometimes I think he got far more out of it than I did. We had shared something miraculous which had fundamentally changed us both. We knew each other very well I think. Besides, he had now moved out from behind his camera and become part of the trip.

The feed situation for the camels during that time was worse than I had expected. It didn't matter too much with Rick around. He was marvellous. He must have driven a thousand extra miles, relaying bales of oats or lucerne to me from Meekatharra.

He had been extremely upset over the death of the dog. I don't think he had ever had a pet and this was the closest relationship to an animal he'd experienced. They had been nauseatingly in love with one another. I had never seen Diggity take to a person like that before. A couple of weeks out from Wiluna, Rick returned to camp late one night, after having driven a few hundred wretched miles of mercy run to pick up feed – he was extremely tired and he was not feeling well. He woke me up from a particularly disturbing dream in which Diggity was circling camp, whining, but would not come when I called her. Rick was quite out of it with exhaustion, and when he came over to me he said, 'Hey, what's Diggity doing over there – I nearly ran over her when I came into camp.' He had forgotten. I don't know how to explain that one – won't even try to, but it was not the only incident of its kind that happened in those weeks.

By now we were taking turns in leading the camels. Or rather, I grudgingly and nervously allowed Rick to lead them sometimes. He managed very well except that Dookie hated him with a jealously burning passion. Oh how I snickered. If Rick tried to do anything at all with him, Dookie would roll his eyes, lift his head, swell out his neck and mock-burble threateningly the way he dimly remembered bulls do. It amounted to, 'You're not my boss and if you touch me I'll snap you in half like a twig, you pip-squeak.' I knew Dookie would not really hurt Rick – well, I was 99 per cent sure – but Rick much preferred leaving the handling of Dookie to me. It really was funny. I'd stand near Rick and ask him to try to put the nose-line on him, and Dook would go into his act and then put his head down to me and snuffle and nibble and go all gooey with love, just to show this upstart interloper where his affections lay.

I can't say enough good things about camels. And they did eventually win over the honey. Rick and I had driven back to a station to send a message to *Geographic* and when we returned the whole camp was upturned and there were

244

copious amounts of honey spread over everything – pack, sleeping bags, camels' lips, camel eyelashes, camel rumps, everything. They knew exactly what they had done and took off as soon as they saw me.

The station people I met all through that area were incredibly kind. Once again you wouldn't know by their faces that the drought was ruining them. They fed us and the camels until we rolled along like little puddings. And they told me that there would doubtless be a welcoming committee in Carnarvon, the town I planned to reach on the coast. Oops. Revision of plans. I had met some people on the road months before, one of the few groups I immediately liked. They owned a sheep station a couple of hundred miles south of Carnarvon and close to the sea and they had asked me to drop in on them. I decided to do exactly that. And if they were prepared to take the camels, that would be one of my major problems solved.

12

I HAD less than a couple of hundred miles to go when the
final disaster occurred. With Rick around I had been lulled
into a false sense of security. Surely nothing could go wrong
now, we had been through so much and come so far and
the rest was going to be a piece of cake. We were travelling
through the stations along the Gascoyne River, the feed
seemed to be picking up a little, Rick was there, all seemed
well. Then Zeleika began to bleed internally.

I couldn't tell whether the blood was coming from the
vagina or the urethra. I made a tentative diagnosis of urinary
tract infection and dosed her up with forty of my pills a day.
These I concealed in an orange. I also injected her with huge
doses of terramycin and hoped for the best. She had fed
Goliath all the way and was now nothing but skin and bone.
Rick drove to the next station, Dalgety Downs, to see
if he could get some hand-feed and medicines. Zeleika was
refusing to eat – I thought she was certainly going to
die.

The people at Dalgety sent Rick back laden with supplies
and driving a cattle truck to load Zelly on so she could be
taken to the station in comfort, where she could rest properly
and be hand-fed. Station hospitality.

The stubborn old cow refused to have anything to do with
that truck. We tried everything. We shovelled a ramp for
her – nothing. We ran ropes behind her, bribed her, cajoled
her, and beat her, she would not set foot on that thing for
love nor money. I decided to saddle up and walk to Dalgety,
letting Zelly go free so she could follow us. And it was then
she totally surprised me. Goliath or no Goliath, she was heading back for Alice Springs. Twice I tried it, and twice she

made a bee-line due east, for home. I tied her on behind and walked slowly to Dalgety.

We camped that first evening by a water-hole, and heard the roar of a light aircraft overhead. It circled over us a few times, dipped its wings, then, much to our amazement, landed on the corrugated dirt track. Rick drove up to see who the brave maniac pilot was. He returned ten minutes later with a ten-gallon-hatted, riding-booted and bespurred man sitting on the front of the vehicle. He leapt off and crunched my knuckles warmly and introduced himself. He said he'd heard I had a sick camel so he thought he'd just drop by to see if I needed anything. He owned a station we had been through earlier, but had been away at the time. I took him over to the camels, while he busily told me his father had owned camels back in the old days, so he knew a thing or two about them. 'Yeah, she's pretty crook, the old girl,' I said, slipping easily into outback jargon. 'Like a crow on jam tins really. Yeah, nothing but crow-bait, poor old cow.' Zeleika, who looked now like an Auschwitz survivor, was standing with the other two healthy bullocks. The man calmly walked up to Dookie, looked at him thoughtfully, shook his head slowly and sadly and said, 'Yeah, by crikey, you've got yourself a sick camel there all right. Poor old blighter. Tsc tsc tsc. Dunno what you can do for her though.' Richard and I tried gallantly to control our sputtering and smirking, while the man continued to tell us about camels. Richard drove him back to the plane, he took off in a cloud of bull-dust, dipped his wings and flew home. We still laugh over that.

A day later, we clanged into Dalgety. Margot and David Steadman fell in love with the camels at first sight and spoilt them outrageously. After a week there, Zeleika had improved to the extent where I thought she would easily make it to the coast. I believed a swim would do the old girl a power of good. I had kept Goliath away from her with the aid of cattle yards and this had sped her along the road

247

to recovery. The calf did not stop screaming and wailing and cursing me for one second, even though I gave him bucket after bucket of milk and molasses. Little pig. It was traumatic for Zeleika too – she kept trying to press her udder through the railing for him to suckle. Another week of pampering and she looked better than she had for the whole trip. She even managed a buck or two in the early morning light.

I decided to take them all to Woodleigh station, where Jan and David Thomson were eagerly awaiting our arrival. The property was a mere fifty miles from the ocean, and a blessed one hundred miles from Carnarvon, the welcoming committee and the press. I was still nervous about reporters, so just to make sure they wouldn't hunt me down, we decided to send a fake telegram over the Steadmans' two-way, from me to Rick, saying, 'Zeleika still ill, will be in Carnarvon mid-November' – a dirty trick but a good one as I discovered later on. I wanted to travel this last short distance by myself and Rick and I arranged to meet at Woodleigh in a few weeks' time.

The weather was turning now. There is no real spring or autumn in the desert. The weather is either cold, hot, very hot, or bloody hot. It was getting into the bloody hot. While the stations around Dalgety consisted of good fertile country, the ones I hit further south were quite different. Undulating red ridges of sand covered in stunted khaki-coloured scrubby trees called wanyu – a kind of mulga that was meant to be reasonable camel fodder, but which mine refused to touch. They had never seen it before. Within days they lost all the condition they had built up at Dalgety. I tried to convince them it was delicious but they didn't believe me. Didn't trust me. And there was virtually nothing but wanyu. By the time I reached Callytharra, the last station before Woodleigh, I was again worried about them.

George and Lorna came to my rescue this time. I pulled into their homestead – a tiny corrugated iron shack with a lot of charm, but set in a boiling hot dust-bowl surrounded by bits of dying and dead machinery and tamed feral goats. These two people astonished me. They had nothing. No electricity, no money, and the drought had hit them badly. They were extraordinary people. They shared with me everything they had. One old bottle of beer that Lorna had kept under her bed for god knows how long, for horse colic, was brought out for the occasion. She gave me expensive feed for the camels and she looked after me like a long-lost daughter. They were perfect examples of what are known in Australia as 'real battlers'. Lorna, a woman of about fifty or sixty (it was hard to tell), was still breaking in horses bareback. George kept all his station bores and machinery going with bits of wire and kicks. And somehow they clung on, remained kind, generous, warm and uncomplaining with absolutely nothing. The night after I left them, they drove out in their old jalopy to bring me yet more camel feed, and a warm bottle of lemonade. The car had broken down on the way but George could fix anything and they arrived in camp late at night. Of all the outback people I met on the trip, I think George and Lorna personified battling bush spirit the best.

I was only a couple of days from Woodleigh now, and of course everything started to disintegrate. The pack suddenly developed holes and rips, saddles began rubbing camel backs overnight, and my last pair of trusty sandals broke. I had to tie them on with string, which hurt and cut into my feet, because I could not go barefooted any longer. You could have fried an egg on that sand. And the country was all the same, the bores were salty and warm and I just wanted to get to Woodleigh and sit in some shade and drink cups of tea. I had taken my clothes off because of the heat when I stumbled across the homestead. It was marked wrongly on the map and I came upon it ten miles too soon. I hastily dressed and clanged up to the house.

It's hard to say who Jan and David were more pleased to see – me or the camels. I knew my beasts could enjoy a happy and pampered retirement here – to this day, my friends at Woodleigh are the only people I can really discuss camel behaviour with ad nauseam and know that they will understand. They dote on them as much as I do and are virtual slaves to their every whim. Dookie, Bub, Zelly and Goliath had landed on their feet. This was their new home, and they immediately took over.

Rick arrived a few days later, all speedy and bouncy and uncontrollable from his dealings with the world outside. He had been hanging out of helicopters in Borneo this time. He told me that when he went to have the car fixed in Carnarvon the day before, the garage mechanic said, 'Hey, have you heard what's happened to your girlfriend? Her camel's sick and she'll be here in mid-November.'

Jan and David offered to truck the camels to a spot just half a dozen miles from the ocean. That was fine with me – I was no purist. Besides it was hot. I tied the camels down this time, leaving Goliath to squeeze in last. He leapt in without any trouble. He wasn't about to see his milk supply carted off.

I was dropped off with the camels. Jan and David promised to come and pick us up in a week. I saddled up and rode those last miles, filled with apprehension. I didn't want this trip to end. I wanted to head back to Alice, or the Canning, or anywhere. I liked doing this. I enjoyed it. I was even reasonably good at it. I had visions of myself spending the rest of my life as a tinker, wandering around the desert with a herd of dromedaries behind me. And I loved my camels. The thought of leaving them was unbearable. And I didn't want Rick waiting for me at the ocean either. I wanted to be alone for that bit. I asked him not to take photos at least. He got that petulant thwarted look. Oh well, I smiled and thought wryly to myself, as it was in the beginning so shall it be in the end. It wasn't all that important. Poetic justice really.

And now I could see the afternoon sun glinting on the

Indian Ocean behind the last dune. The camels could smell it and were jumpy as hell. And here I was at the end of my trip, with everything just as fuzzy and unreal as the beginning. It was easier for me to see myself in Rick's lens, riding down to the beach in that clichéd sunset, just as it was easier for me to stand with my friends and wave goodbye to the loopy woman with the camels, the itching smell of the dust around us, and in our eyes the fear that we had left so much unsaid. There was an unpronounceable joy and an aching sadness to it. It had all happened too suddenly. I didn't believe this was the end at all. There must be some mistake. Someone had just robbed me of a couple of months in there somewhere. There was not so much an anticlimactic quality about the arrival at the ocean, as the overwhelming feeling that I had somehow misplaced the penultimate scene.

And I rode down that stunningly, gloriously fantastic pleistocene coastline with the fat sun bulging on to a flat horizon and all I could muster was a sense of it all having finished too abruptly, so that I couldn't get tabs on the fact that it was over, that it would probably be years before I'd see my beloved camels and desert again. And there was no time to prepare myself for the series of shock-waves. I went numb.

The camels were thunderstruck at the sight of that ocean. They had never seen so much water. Globs of foam raced up the beach and tickled their feet so that they jumped along on all fours – Bub nearly sent me flying. They would stop, turn to stare at it, leap sideways, look at one another with their noses all pointed and ridiculous, then stare at it again, then leap forward again. They all huddled together in a jittery confusion of ropes. Goliath went straight in for a swim. He had not yet learnt what caution was.

I spent one delirious week on that beach. As chance had it, I had finished my trip on a stretch of coastline that was unique in all the world. It rimmed the inner arm of an inlet, known as Hamelin Pool. A seagrass sill blocked the entrance to the ocean, so that the water inside this vast, relatively shallow

pool was hyper-saline, a happy chance for the stromato-
lites, primitive life forms that had lived there for 500 million years. These strange primeval rocks rose up out of the
water's edge like a bunch of petrified Lon Chaneys. The
beach itself was made up of tiny coquina shells, each as perfect
and delicate as a baby's fingernail. A hundred yards back from
this loose shell was compacted shell, leached with lime until
it formed a solid block that went down forty feet or more,
which the locals cut up with pit saws to build their homes.
This was covered with gnarled stunted trees and succulents,
all excellent camel fodder, and behind all that were the gypsum flats and red sand swells of the desert. I fished for yellow-
tail and swam in the clearest turquoise waters I've ever seen;
I took the camels (all except Zeleika who stubbornly refused
even to paddle) for swims; I crunched my way over the beach
that was so white it was blinding and gazed at little green
and red glass-like plants, and I relaxed in the firelight under
bloodshot skies. The camels were still dazed by the water –
still insisted that it was drinkable, even after pulling faces and
spitting it out time and time again. Often they would come
down to the beach at sunset to stand and stare.

And once again, and for the last time, I soared. I had pared
my possessions down to almost nothing – a survival kit, that's
all. I had a filthy old sarong for hot weather and a jumper
and woolly socks for cold weather and I had something to
sleep on and something to eat and drink out of and that was
all I needed. I felt free and untrammelled and light and I
wanted to stay that way. If I could only just hold on to it.
I didn't want to get caught up in the madness out there.

Poor fool, I really believed all that crap. I was forgetting
that what's true in one place is not necessarily true in another.
If you walk down Fifth Avenue smelling of camel shit and
talking to yourself you get avoided like the plague. Even
your best American buddies will not want to know you. The
last poor fragile shreds of my romantic naïvety were about
to get shrivelled permanently by New York City, where I

252

would be in four days' time, shell-shocked, intimidated by the canyons of glass and cement, finding my new adventuress's identity kit ill-fitting and uncomfortable, answering inane questions which made me feel like I should be running a pet shop, defending myself against people who said things like, 'Well, honey, what's next, skateboards across the Andes?' and dreaming of a different kind of desert.

On my last morning, before dawn, while I was cooking breakfast, Rick stirred in his sleep, sat up on an elbow, fixed me with an accusing stare and said, 'How the hell did you get those camels here?'

'What?'

'You killed their parents, didn't you?'

He sneered and gloated knowingly for a second then dropped back into unconsciousness, remembering nothing of it later. There was some kind of rudimentary truth hidden in that dream somewhere.

Jan and David arrived with the truck and I loaded my now plump and cheeky beasties on it and took them back to their retirement home. They had many square miles to roam in, people to love and spoil them, and nothing to do but spend their dotage facing Mecca and contemplating the growth of their humps. I spent hours saying goodbye to them. Tearing myself away from them caused actual physical pain, and I kept going back to sink my forehead into their woolly shoulders and tell them how wonderful and clever and faithful and true they were and how I would miss them. Rick then drove me to Carnarvon, one hundred miles north where I would pick up the plane that would wing me back to Brisbane, then to New York. I remember nothing of that car ride, except trying to hide the embarrassingly huge amounts of salt water that cascaded out of my eyeballs.

In Carnarvon, a town about the size of Alice Springs, I suffered the first wave of culture shock that was to rock me in the months ahead, and from which I think I have never fully recovered. Where was the brave Boadicea of the beaches? 'Bring on New York,' she had said. 'Bring on *Geographic*, I'm invincible.' But now, she had slunk away to her shell under the onslaught of all those freakish-looking people, and cars and telegraph poles and questions and champagne and rich food. I was taken to dinner by the local magistrate and his wife who opened a magnum bottle of bubbly. Half way through the meal I collapsed and crawled outside to throw up over an innocent fire truck, with Rick holding my forehead saying, 'There there, it will all be all right,' and me saying, between gasps, 'No, no it's not, it's awful, I want to go back.'

As I look back on the trip now, as I try to sort out fact from fiction, try to remember how I felt at that particular time, or during that particular incident, try to relive those memories that have been buried so deep, and distorted so ruthlessly, there is one clear fact that emerges from the quagmire. The trip was easy. It was no more dangerous than crossing the street, or driving to the beach, or eating peanuts. The two important things that I did learn were that you are as powerful and strong as you allow yourself to be, and that the most difficult part of any endeavour is taking the first step, making the first decision. And I knew even then that I would forget them time and time again and would have to go back and repeat those words that had become meaningless and try to remember. I knew even then that, instead of remembering the truth of it, I would lapse into a useless nostalgia. Camel trips, as I suspected all along, and as I was about to have confirmed, do not begin or end, they merely change form.

Select Bibliography

Books mentioned in the text:

Adler, Renata, *Speedboat* (Random House, New York 1976; Hamish Hamilton, London 1977, and Picador, London 1978)

Gilbert, Kevin, *Because a White Man'll Never Do It* ... (Angus and Robertson, Sydney 1973)

Robbins, Tom, *Even Cowgirls Get the Blues* (Houghton Mifflin, Boston, Mass. 1976)

Books providing background information:

Barker, H. M., *Camels and the Outback* (Angus and Robertson, London 1964)

Carnegie, Hon. David Wynford, *Spinifex and Sand. A narrative of five years' pioneering and exploration in Western Australia* (C.A. Pearson, London 1898)

Farwell, George, *Land of Mirage: The story of men, cattle and camels on the Birdsville Track* (Cassell, London 1950; Seal Books, Adelaide 1975)

Giles, Ernest, *Geographic Travels in Central Australia from 1872 to 1874* (Melbourne 1875)

Giles, Ernest, *Australia Twice Traversed ... Being a narrative compiled from the journals of five exploring expeditions ... from 1872 to 1876* (Sampson Low and Co., London 1889)

Meggitt, Mervyn John, *Desert People. A study of the Walbiri aborigines of Central Australia* (Angus and Robertson, Sydney 1962)

Reiter, Rayna R. (ed.), *Toward an Anthropology of Women* (Monthly Review Press 1975)

Roberts, Janine, *From Massacres to Mining: The colonization o Aboriginal Australia* (CIMRA and War on Want, London 1978)